AppSensor Guide

Application-Specific Real Time Attack Detection & Response

Version 2.0

Lead Author

Colin Watson

Co-Authors

Dennis Groves   John Melton

Other Contributors, Editors and Reviewers

Josh Amishav-Zlatin   Ryan Barnett   Michael Coates   Craig Munson   Jay Reynolds

Version 1 Author

Michael Coates

The AppSensor Guide is primarily written for those with software architecture responsibilities, but can also be read by other developers and those with an interest in secure software. Implementation requires a collaborative effort by development, operational and information security disciplines.

Version 2.0 published 2nd May 2014

© 2008-2014 OWASP Foundation

This document is licensed under the Creative Commons Attribution-ShareAlike 3.0 license

Tables of Contents

OWASP AppSensor Project Founder
Michael Coates

OWASP AppSensor Project Leaders
Dennis Groves   John Melton   Colin Watson

Full A-Z of Project Contributors

All OWASP projects rely on the voluntary efforts of people in the software development and information security sectors. They have contributed their time and energy to make suggestions, provide feedback, give advice, write, review and edit documentation, give encouragement, make introductions, produce demonstration code, promote the concept, and provide OWASP support. They participated via the project's mailing lists, by developing code, by updating the wiki, by undertaking research studies, and through contributions during the AppSensor working session at the OWASP Summit 2011 in Portugal and the AppSensor Summit at AppSec USA 2011. Without all their efforts, the project would not have progressed to this point, and this guide would not have been completed.

Josh Amishav-Zlatin	Erlend Oftedal	Craig Munson
Ryan Barnett	Sean Fay	Giri Nambari
Simon Bennetts	Dennis Groves	Jay Reynolds
Joe Bernik	Randy Janida	Chris Schmidt
Rex Booth	Chetan Karande	Sahil Shah
Luke Briner	Eoin Keary	Eric Sheridan
Rauf Butt	Alex Lauerman	John Steven
Fabio Cerullo	Junior Lazuardi	Alex Thissen
Marc Chisinevski	Jason Li	Don Thomas
Robert Chojnacki	Manuel López Arredondo	Christopher Tidball
Michael Coates	Bob Maier	Kevin W Wall
Dinis Cruz	Jim Manico	Colin Watson
August Detlefsen	Sherif Mansour Farag	Mehmet Yilmaz
Ryan Dewhurst	John Melton	

Cover

Light Installation by David Press
Kinetica Art Fair 2012, Ambika P3 Gallery, London, photograph Colin Watson

OWASP Summer of Code 2008

The AppSensor Project[1] was initially supported by the OWASP Summer of Code 2008, leading to the publication of the book AppSensor v1.1[2].

Google Summer of Code 2012

Additional development work on SOAP web services was kindly supported by the Google Summer of Code 2012.

Other Acknowledgements

The project has also benefitted greatly from the generous contribution of time and effort by many volunteers in the OWASP community including those listed above, and contributors to the OWASP ESAPI project, members of the former OWASP Global Projects Committee, and support from the OWASP Project Reboot initiative. The second version of the guide was conceived during the AppSensor Summit held during AppSec USA 2011 in Minneapolis.

Contents

Preamble 1
   Introduction 2
   How To Use This Guide 10

Part I : AppSensor Overview 1
   Chapter 1 : Application-Specific Attack Detection & Response 2
   Chapter 2 : Protection Measures 8
   Chapter 3 : The AppSensor Approach 16
   Chapter 4 : Conceptual Elements 20

Part II : Illustrative Case Studies 29
   Chapter 5 : Case Study of a Rapidly Deployed Web Application 30
   Chapter 6 : Case Study of a Magazine's Mobile App 31
   Chapter 7 : Case Study of a Smart Grid Consumer Meter 33
   Chapter 8 : Case Study of a Financial Market Trading System 34
   Chapter 9 : Case Study of a B2C Ecommerce Website 35
   Chapter 10 : Case Study of B2B Web Services 37
   Chapter 11 : Case Study of a Document Management System 38
   Chapter 12 : Case Study of a Credit Union's Online Banking 39

Part III : Making It Happen 41
   Chapter 13 : Introduction 42
   Chapter 14 : Design and Implementation 47
   Chapter 15 : Verification, Deployment and Operation 54
   Chapter 16 : Advanced Detection Points 60
   Chapter 17 : Advanced Thresholds and Responses 69
   Chapter 18 : AppSensor and Application Event Logging 79
   Chapter 19 : AppSensor and PCI DSS for Ecommerce Merchants 83

Part IV : Demonstration Implementations 85
   Chapter 20 : Web Services (AppSensor WS) 86
   Chapter 21 : Fully Integrated (AppSensor Core) 89
   Chapter 22 : Light Touch Retrofit 92
   Chapter 23 : Ensnare for Ruby 95
   Chapter 24 : Invocation of AppSensor Code Using Jni4Net 98
   Chapter 25 : Using an External Log Management System 100
   Chapter 26 : Leveraging a Web Application Firewall 103

Part V : Model Dashboards 107
   Chapter 27 : Security Event Management Tools 108
   Chapter 28 : Application-Specific Dashboards 112
   Chapter 29 : Application Vulnerability Tracking 117

Part VI : Reference Materials 121
   Glossary 122
   Detection Points 125
   Responses 152
   Data Signaling Exchange Formats 161
   Awareness and Training Resources 168
   Feedback and Testimonials 171
   References 172

Tables of Contents

List of Figures

Figure 1	The Spectrum of Acceptable Application Usage Illustrating How Malicious Attacks are Very Different to Normal Application Use	4
Figure 2	Pseudo Code Illustrating the Addition of AppSensor Detection Point Logic Within Existing Input Validation Code	23
Figure 3	Pseudo Code Illustrating the Addition of Completely New AppSensor Detection Point Logic	23
Figure 4	Schematic Arrangement of AppSensor Conceptual Elements	27
Figure 5	An Imaginary AppSensor Dashboard Under Normal Operational Conditions i.e. Blank	57
Figure 6	The Imaginary AppSensor Dashboard When A User Is Identified as an Attacker	57
Figure 7	The Imaginary AppSensor Dashboard Demonstrating AppSensor Cross-System Integration	57
Figure 8	The Spectrum of Application Acceptable Usage Illustrating How Normal Use Requires Input Validation to Cater for a Range of User-Provided Input	64
Figure 9	The Spectrum of Application Acceptable Usage Showing How Some Unacceptable Data Input Are Much More Likely to Indicate a Malicious User	65
Figure 10	The Spectrum of Application Acceptable Usage Showing How Application-Specific Knowledge Increases the Ability to Differentiate Between Normal and Malicious Input	66
Figure 11	Schematic Arrangement of the AppSensor WS Reference Implementation	87
Figure 12	Schematic Arrangement of the AppSensor Core Reference Implementation	89
Figure 13	Schematic Arrangement of Example Light Touch Retrofit to Existing Code	92
Figure 14	Schematic Arrangement of the Ensnare Implementation	95
Figure 15	Schematic Arrangement of Example AppSensor Code Invocation Using Jni4Net	98
Figure 16	Schematic Arrangement of Example External Log Management System	100
Figure 17	Example Use of Common Event Format for Event Signaling	102
Figure 18	Schematic Arrangement of Example Leveraging a Web Application Firewall	103
Figure 19	Example AppSensor Event Data Using Delimited Name-Value Pairs	108
Figure 20	AppSensor Data Feed Addition to Splunk	109
Figure 21	AppSensor Event Summary in Splunk	109
Figure 22	AppSensor Event Detail in Splunk	110
Figure 23	AppSensor Event in the AuditConsole Dashboard	111
Figure 24	An Example AppSensor Dashboard for an Ecommerce Website	112

Figure 25	An Example Detection Point Indicators on Website Functionality Map	113
Figure 26	Illumination of Detection Point Indicators	113
Figure 27	System Trend Detection Points	114
Figure 28	Highlighting of Changes to System Trend Detection Points	114
Figure 29	Detection Points Event Log Display	114
Figure 30	Response Event Log Display	115
Figure 31	Ensnare Violations Listing	115
Figure 32	Ensnare Metrics page	116
Figure 33	ThreadFix Dashboard Showing Mock Up of CWE vs Attack Chart Overlay	118
Figure 34	Detailed View of Chart Overlay Mockup	118
Figure 35	Mockup Illustrating How URL Paths Could be Used To Match Vulnerabilities Identified Through Security Scanning Correlate with Where Attacks are Occurring	119
Figure 36	Diagram Showing the Assignment of Detection Points to All the Categorizations	129
Figure 37	Diagram Showing the Related AppSensor Detection Points	130
Figure 38	Example Detection Point Definition Overview Sheet for an Instance of IE2	149
Figure 39	Example Detection Point Definition Overview Sheet for an Instance of ACE3	150
Figure 40	Part of Example Detection Point Schedule for IE2	151
Figure 41	Example Detection Point Schedule for AE3	151
Figure 42	Example Threshold Schedule No1	158
Figure 43	Example Threshold Schedule No2	158
Figure 44	Example Threshold Schedule No3	159
Figure 45	Basic AppSensor Event Format for JSON Data	162
Figure 46	Important HTTP Headers and Example JSON Event Data	162
Figure 47	Extended AppSensor Event Format for JSON Data Showing Optional and Custom Fields	163
Figure 48	AppSensor Event Format Data Value Definitions	164
Figure 49	Basic AppSensor Event Data Using CEF	166
Figure 50	Basic Additional CEF Field Values in the Context of AppSensor	166
Figure 51	Example CEF AppSensor Event Data Using CEF Predefined Keys	167

List of Tables

Table 1	Pros and Cons of the Most Commonly Implemented Responses	25
Table 2	List of Conceptual Elements in the AppSensor Pattern	26
Table 3	Properties for the Case Study of a Minimal AppSensor Implementation for a Small Rapidly-Built Web Application that Already has a Strong Input Validation Module	30
Table 4	Properties for the Case Study of a Magazine's Mobile App to Identify Authentication Attacks, Account-Sharing and Blatant XSS Attempts	31
Table 5	Properties for the Case Study of a Smart Grid Consumer Meter for the Detection of Attempted and Actual Tampering.	33
Table 6	Properties for the Case Study of a Financial Market Trading System for the Detection of Collusion Between Traders.	34
Table 7	Properties for the Case Study of a B2C Ecommerce Website	35
Table 8	Properties for the Case Study of B2B Web Services	37
Table 9	Properties for the Case Study of a Document Management System	38
Table 10	Properties for the Case Study of a Credit Union's Online Banking	39
Table 11	AppSensor Aspects Mapped to Open SAMM Activities	44
Table 12	AppSensor Aspects Mapped to BSIMM Activities	45
Table 13	AppSensor Aspects Mapped to BITS Software Assurance Framework Areas	46
Table 14	AppSensor Aspects Mapped to MS SDL Processes	46
Table 15	Example Thresholds and Responses for Individual Per User Detection Points	74
Table 16	Example Multiple Thresholds and Responses for the Overall Number of Events Per User in a Single Fixed Time Period	75
Table 17	Example Response Thresholds for the Overall Number of Events Per User For a Range of Time Periods	76
Table 18	Example Response Thresholds for a System Trend Detection Point Monitoring the Usage Rate of an Application's "Add a Friend" Feature	77
Table 19	Typical Event Logging Properties for Web Applications	80
Table 20	Possible Detection Points if the Only Event Source are Web Server Logs	81
Table 21	List of Detection Point Categories Supported by AppSensor Core	90
Table 22	List of Response Categories Supported by AppSensor Core	90
Table 23	List of Detection Point Categories Implemented in this Example Light Touch Retrofit	93
Table 24	List of Response Categories Implemented in this Example Light Touch Retrofit	93

Table 25	List of Detection Point Categories Implemented in Ensnare	96
Table 26	List of Response Categories Implemented in Ensnare	96
Table 27	List of Response Categories Possibly Available to an External Log/Event Management System	101
Table 28	List of Detection Point Categories Implemented in ModSecurity Core Rule Set	104
Table 29	List of Response Categories Implemented in ModSecurity Core Rule Set	105
Table 30	Summary of AppSensor Detection Point Identifiers and Titles Grouped by Exception Category	125
Table 31	AppSensor Detection Points Categorized by Suspicious and Attack Events	127
Table 32	AppSensor Detection Points Categorized by Whether They are Discrete, Aggregating or Modifying	128
Table 33	Descriptions of Request Exception (RE) Detection Points	132
Table 34	Descriptions of Authentication Exception (AE) Detection Points	134
Table 35	Descriptions of Session Exception (SE) Detection Points	136
Table 36	Descriptions of Access Control Exception (ACE) Detection Points	138
Table 37	Descriptions of Input Exception (IE) Detection Points	139
Table 38	Descriptions of Encoding Exception (EE) Detection Points	141
Table 39	Descriptions of Command Injection Exception (CIE) Detection Points	142
Table 40	Descriptions of File Input/Output Exceptions (FIO) Detection Points	143
Table 41	Descriptions of Honey Trap (HT) Detection Points	144
Table 42	Descriptions of User Trend Exception (UT) Detection Points	145
Table 43	Descriptions of System Trend Exception (STE) Detection Points	146
Table 44	Descriptions of Reputation (RP) Detection Points	147
Table 45	Summary of AppSensor Response Identifiers and Titles, Grouped by the Effect on the User	152
Table 46	Assignment of AppSensor Responses to Categorizations	153
Table 47	Descriptions of AppSensor Responses Listed Alphabetically by Code	154
Table 48	Mapping of AppSensor Event Format (AEF) Terms to Common Event Format (CEF) Keys	166

Tables of Contents

Foreword

The security of our applications and services is of paramount importance. Internet connected applications play a role in every aspect of our lives and the operations of society. From financial and medical, through everyday personal and business interactions, to important infrastructure, applications process an immense amount of critical information every single day.

Despite the importance of these systems, we are yet to integrate advance defenses in many of these applications. The attackers are determined and backed by criminal organizations, activist groups, nation states, private enterprises and more. These attackers have the funding, tools and time to infiltrate critical applications. Everyday attacks are launched to inspect and probe applications searching for weaknesses and vulnerabilities. The sad reality is that nearly every application is completely blind to these attacks until it is too late.

Organizations may place false trust in antiquated defenses such as signature based detection of generic attacks or reactive log review; however, these approaches are trivially bypassed by attackers every day. We need more. We need a better approach. We need a defense that understands the custom nature of the application; how business logic works, how access control is enforced, and all of the unique aspects of the application. The defense we need must not only detect generic attack techniques, but also custom attacks targeting an application's specific design and architecture.

But advanced detection alone is not enough. The path forward requires a defensive system that can identify a malicious attacker before they find and exploit a vulnerability. This approach requires the ability to detect and contain an attacker while they are probing for vulnerabilities throughout the application. The response must be swift and fully automatic to eliminate the threat from the application. Reactive analysis by humans is too slow. By the time a human sees an attacker, the attacker will already be gone, along with the critical data they've compromised.

The future of application defense is a system that can understand custom attacks against an application, correlate them against a malicious attacker, and react in real-time to contain and eliminate the threat. This defense is OWASP AppSensor – an open source project created through the contributions of security experts with years of experience assessing, securing and breaking the security systems of applications for financial systems, government bodies, businesses and major organizations around the world.

Michael Coates
AppSensor Project Founder

Preamble

Introduction

AppSensor is the most important advancement in Application Security in the last decade. Now this is a very large claim, and the reasoning and justifications follow in the paragraphs below. These can be broken into roughly three key areas, philosophy, architecture, and statistics. Let me explore them briefly with you now.

- *Philosophy*: OWASP AppSensor presents a new methodology to security. Incidentally, that new methodology is actually not new at all; however it is the road that is very much "less traveled in the IT industry". This road is heavily traveled in industries where actuarial sciences are used to control risk, such as healthcare, pharmaceuticals, and aviation. Once exposed to the idea; you will have a not only have a new tool in your security tool chest, but one you will increasingly want to use and apply to your IT risk.
- *Architecture*: OWASP AppSensor is both a set of security patterns and practices. This guide will discuss in detail the practices. OWASP AppSensor started as a development practice. However, this set of practices can be decomposed into a methodology. After doing this it became apparent that OWASP AppSensor is actually a new security pattern. Further, this pattern can be used to evaluate and practice security in both the design as well as development of applications.
- *Statistics*: This is perhaps the most exciting part of OWASP AppSensor. OWASP AppSensor captures data for analysis that is currently discarded. Unfortunately, this discarded data contains incredible amounts of valuable information about the security of the application.

On those three pillars, OWASP AppSensor improves the effectiveness of your entire information security management program, and it is very exciting indeed.

Philosophy

To start the philosophy discussion, begin with a thought exercise. Imagine tomorrow we have a pistol duel. If we loose we will be shot and likely die, if we win our opponent takes the bullet instead and dies. Let's agree to analyze this event following the process which matches our information security management practices. We will do a risk analysis, then reduce the risks identified and then we will go have our duel. So the question is "What can we do to improve our chances of survival?"

Lets begin our risk analysis now. To begin with we need far more information if we want to survive.

It would be really important to know what the rules of our pistol duel are to start out with. Incidentally, there are two types of pistol duels. There are Victorian era and Western movie film genre pistol duels. And depending on which of these we are participating in greatly changes both our risks and the strategies we require to survive.

In a Victorian pistol duel, opponents stand back to back, take ten steps away from each other, turn and fire. The fairness of this kind of duel depends on neither party turning at the ninth step or earlier. So it is a game of trust, that depends on neither party cheating. However, cheating means we are not killed. And since our goal is to survive and our pistol duel is a Victorian duel; then we have our first risk reduction strategy. We simply turn after step one and shoot our opponent.

Increasing speed, or being faster is a key security metric. In fact it is the entire basis for time based security. Time based security states that our protection time must be greater than or equal to detection time plus response time. A great example of this principle in action was the final scene of the 1999 Hollywood movie The Matrix where Neo can dodge the bullets. He is able to detect and react before the bullets reach him; this causes him to be invincible for all practical purposes. We all know what the longer it to fix security bugs, the greater risk we are at, as attackers are able to attack us until we can patch. Similarly, the longer it takes for us to fix our own bugs the more vulnerable we are. This metric can be applied in many circumstances, and organizations are encouraged to try and apply it to things in their own environment and to start measuring security from this perspective.

Now the other kind of duel we may be having is a Western duel. A Western duel is the one in all the western cowboy films where the opponents meet at high noon. We no longer have to trust our opponent, instead we have place and time that decides when the duel begins. Punctuality is important otherwise someone you love will be killed in your place. Opponents face one another from twenty paces and draw pistols from holsters. It is difficult to cheat at the Western duel, but you should try anyway.

Additionally, it is a good idea to know whom our opponent is. Actually it is essential otherwise you have no ability to understand the threat you face and mitigate risks accordingly. For example, if we were put in a situation where the opponent was one of our loved ones or immediate family, many of us would loose on purpose. For the purpose of this exercise however imagine the opponent is a next door neighbor - a 6 foot 4 inch, 63 year old man. Because of this disadvantage, we use a Western duel to keep things fair.

Now we may be feeling a bit relieved to know that we are facing an old man, and one who has a fairly large surface area to aim for. In application security we very rarely consider who our opponent is, what they are motivated by and how many resources they have at their disposal to attack us. But it is critical. To further emphasize this point let us learn a bit more about the 63 year old neighbor. His name is Johnny Brusco, and he was the fastest quick draw in the United States until 1974 when he retired from quick draw competition. Suddenly, with a single new piece of information our assessment of the risk went from a risk of "mostly harmless" to "we are seriously, very dead".

Preamble

This scenario is not unlike the one we face with our web applications every day. Attackers significantly out number defenders. Additionally, attackers do not have tight budgets, deadlines and last minute changes to requirements to manage. Attackers only have to find a single vulnerability, defenders have to find and fix them all; something we know can not be done, so we rank them in order of importance by perceived risk. Indeed all is not hopeless, industry experience tells us risk treatment is the "best practice" today. And we can use the same principles here in our duel where we are seriously out gunned by our opponent.

Risk can be defined simply as the probability of the vulnerability times the threat. And the two most widely used strategies for managing risk are to reduce the probability of a threat and/or reduce the probability of a vulnerability. To reduce the probability of a threat we reduce the attack surface. This is a fancy way of saying we patch the vulnerabilities that are identified so there are "less places for attackers to attack". The other things we do is to hire penetration testers, and to do internal code reviews and testing of our own security. This is how we identify vulnerabilities. By finding our vulnerabilities before the bad guys we can fix them before they are exploited.

We can apply the same to our gunfight tomorrow. We can reduce our attack surface by not turning so our shoulders are "square" with our opponent which would expose our entire torso to bullets. But rather we can stand perpendicular to our opponent minimizing the surface area of our bodies subject to bullets. We can also reduce our vulnerabilities by hiring a gunslinger to teach us the art of gunslinging and practice. This is like penetration testing; the gunslinger will identify what we are doing wrong and help us to eliminate the bad habits thus reducing our vulnerabilities or bad habits that are likely to get us shot.

We can still improve our chances tomorrow however, by attempting to predict in advance where our opponent will shoot and move out of the way. This is similar to our risk prediction models where we rank the identified vulnerabilities according to perceived risks. When we do this we are making a prediction that on vulnerability is more likely than another to be exploited. So for example if the gunman is right handed he may well fire on his right side and so moving to the left will increase the probability that you will survive. Incidentally, there are actually three options you can move left, move right and stay in the middle. Which is your optimal strategy if you want to survive?

Now, as it happens the correct answer to this question is far more difficult that it initially seems. Indeed, it is a subject of research[3] in the field of "game theory". Now it just so happens that the correct answer can only be derived from playing hundreds if not thousands of games. In the case of a Western duel; this requires us to derive the answer from getting shot at hundreds if not thousands of times. Now that seems like certain death.

Imagine that you have a 50% chance of surviving. And let us represent that chance by a fair toss of a coin that lands heads up. If you survive the first toss - do you really want to toss the coin a second time? Hopefully it is obvious you do not, as you have only a 25% chance of living through the second toss. Although the odds of any given toss are 50%, you actually only have a 1 in 4 chance of heads coming up a second time in a row. Given that kind of odds, a tails is almost certainly going to come along and ruin your day eventually. Try it for yourself[4]. Perhaps you get "No heads 48%" - so would have died once out of every 2 duels. Therefore, you do not want to have a gun fired at you hundreds if not thousands of times if your goal is survival.

We will assume that we are able to practice those 100 duel shots using blanks before noon tomorrow and learn the correct answer, perhaps we hired a consultant who could teach us the answer or a seasoned gunslinger who knows his trade. In the case of our applications, this is not a penetration testing consultancy, but rather a subject matter expert in information security who is able to coach and mentor us with valuable strategic information that comes only from a lifetime of experiences in the field. We are now armed with knowledge about the "best strategy" for survival in our duel tomorrow.

So while pistol duels and application security are very different; the security problems in each domain share a common thread. So, lets recap the 7 best practices that we identified:

- Perform a Risk Analysis
- Use Time Based Security Metrics
- Know the Enemy
- Practice Risk Reduction
- Reduce Surface Area
- Use Risk Prediction
- Practice, Practice, Practice.

Now, while we can all agree on these best practices or security principles, there are many more. Incidentally, 193 such security principles are now publicly documented as the OWASP Security Principles project[5]. What is universally observed, is that organizations "at best" do "at most" a handful of such practices that they happen know about. And even the most seasoned security practitioners are unable to identify more than a dozen such principles. It seems this is why we are failing to secure those things that matter most to us.

It is possible to try to attempt to identify the "Pareto Efficient" security principle (or principles as it happens to be). Using the 80/20 principle, one day we may be able to identify the 20% of the security principles that give you 80% of the risk reduction. In this way, a definitive minimal roadmap of security best practices can be developed.

To date, at least one of the security principles is a Pareto Efficient one, and there will be others. Incidentally, this principle happens to be one that most people have never heard of, and consequently never practice. This is the principle of Impact Reduction sometimes known as Risk Optimization. Although, it is rarely practiced, it is a very effective method. The goal of this principle is to examine ways that you can reduce the impact of events when the occur.

Preamble

Returning to our pistol duel the most obvious way to implement the security principle of impact reduction is to wear a bullet proof vest. That is to say when we get hit by a bullet, it reduces the impact of the bullet when we get hit. Mind you, we still do not want to get hit and are going to do our best to avoid it. And if we get hit, it is still going to hurt like crazy, but we will very likely survive. A bullet proof vest is obviously going to do more to save our lives at high noon tomorrow than all of the other 7 practices combined.

If we get hit, our chances of survival are greatest if we have a bullet proof vest, but we would be equally foolish to rely on the bullet proof vest alone. Indeed we will still combine the bullet proof vest with the other 7 practices in order to maximize our chances of survival tomorrow. Naturally this begs the question how do we apply an impact reduction strategy to our web applications? What do we do?

This is exactly what the OWASP AppSensor is. This book, the OWASP AppSensor Guide, is entirely about what to do. And just to be clear, AppSensor is not a panacea anymore than a bullet proof vest. You do not want to be shot in general, but if you do get shot you want to be wearing a vest. And If you get shot while wearing a bullet proof vest, it is going to hurt; it may potentially break bones however, you will survive what would otherwise have been a fatality. Similarly, OWASP AppSensor will reduce the impact of a successful attack but it does not entirely eliminate risk of a successful attack.

We all know the devil is in the details; even a bullet proof vest is not a one size fits all solution. Vests are rated according to the ability to stop different masses and speeds of projectiles. And the true is this is also true of OWASP AppSensor as well.

Hopefully this has demonstrated sufficiently how important the philosophy and practice of impact reduction is, and it is so exciting. Risk Optimization is actually how risk is managed across a wide range of disciplines outside of IT and it has been found to be very effective, and when applied to IT projects it has been equally effective.

Architecture

Most software today is built according to Weinberg's Second Law which states that if builders built buildings the way programmers wrote programs, then the first woodpecker that came along would destroy civilization. Nowhere is this more true than in the discipline of software security, where the woodpeckers are the so called "hackers", and indeed there is no question in my mind that we are witnessing in the news daily evidence of the degradation of civilization as a result.

IT architects have long been highly concerned with the technical aspects of software, and very little focus in any at all has been placed on the human aspects. And as a result software is not only ugly, and confusing it is fragile and breaks easily, and particularly when placed under stress as hackers will do. Software is not so much designed, as organically evolved, and consequently form does not follow the function further increasing the complexity and fragility.

> *"Form follows function - that has been misunderstood. Form and function should be one, joined in a spiritual union."*
>
> *– Frank Lloyd Wright, Architect*

This statement drives directly to the heart of the security problem with software engineering as it is widely practiced today. We first build the software and then we secure it after it is built, deployed or shipped. Sometimes this is necessary, due to requirements changing or the need to secure legacy software. However, in ideal circumstances, rather than after the fact, security and the application "should be one, joined in spiritual union." Software security must exist before the software, it must be part of the plans, the budgets, the schedule, the architecture, the design, and the engineering process.

Many people are starting to do this. Microsoft has its SDL. BSIMM project defines a methodology for building security in to the software development process, and OWASP has the Open SAMM and AppSensor projects. None of these are mutually exclusive; in fact they have a great deal in common. AppSensor differs in a number of ways from the others however. The first has already been discussed – OWASP AppSensor is designed around the philosophy of Risk Optimization or impact reduction.

Impact reduction is exactly how exactly how rescue services and first responders work. Think about it; their entire existence is to minimize the impact of an event so that as few lives as possible are lost and restore services as quickly as possible. This is how your smoke detector operates, it does not try and predict where a fire is likely and when it will happen. Rather it detects and responds as quickly as possible to minimize the impact of the fire to the occupants. The fire department acts to reduce the impact of the fire to the property.

> *'Think simples' as my old master used to say - meaning reduce the whole of its parts into the simplest terms, getting back to first principles."*
>
> *– Frank Lloyd Wright, Architect*

Architecture is about design principles. In the case of traditional architecture they are line, color, shape, texture, space and form. In security architecture there are many principles, and as previously mentioned some are "Pareto Efficient". Where security architecture is concerned two are Separation of Duty, and Trust.

Separation of duty is perhaps the most important principle in security architecture. Inevitably applications are designed with security principles architects knew about, security folks included. However, as this demonstrated in our thought exercise, there are far more than just a "few" principles, most of which never make it into the design. For example, security design happens with perhaps a handful of principles:

Preamble

- Use Least Privilege
- Use Perimeter Security
- Practice Defence in Depth
- Practice Risk Reduction
- Reduce Surface Area
- Use Risk Prediction.

As a result, we regularly see designs without separation of privilege. Think about that – most web applications today have all their eggs in a single basket. The business logic, the identities, passwords, products, policy enforcement, security rules are all found in the same application database that makes up the typical website. It is little wonder then, that attacks on the database have been so completely devastating, since there is no separation of privilege.

The principles of trust can be examined in detail with data flow diagram tools. One way to understand AppSensor is to think of it as baking the above mentioned data flow diagrams (DFDs) into the application, and when it detects a violation of trust it raise an event, just like the smoke alarm. This event is then analyzed by an event analysis engine which then decides how to respond or not. This gives us two new and incredibly powerful and important features not found in other approaches.

Currently OWASP AppSensor is a reference implementation of a set of very specific and unique development practices. First we take some input from some place, we analyze it for validity according to rules that make sense, then we either raise events or continue normally. The event analysis engine decides to respond accordingly to the exceptions as required. This is an inter-process communications protocol for adaptation to events outside of the programs execution control. At first glance this does not seem so interesting, after all is this not what virus software does? It is not, because the virus checker is acting on behalf of the operating system. If you feed the right input into the virus checker it will crash. However, AppSensor is acting on behalf of the application, so it is defending itself and that is a critical difference.

AppSensor is actually a software security pattern for turning "fragile" software into "agile" software. And, while the OWASP AppSensor is currently demonstrated as a number of reference implementations and examples, it is not hard to identify this as an architecture pattern when you start to imagine how it can be scaled out just like any other software today. For example, in a service oriented architecture (SOA), the detection points are built into the application itself as normal, where as the analysis and response could be services that are consumable by secure web API, just like any other enterprise application built today. Perhaps it is XML, WSDL or more likely JSON. It does not actually matter because the security architecture pattern is the same.

In conclusion, we have demonstrated that OWASP AppSensor represents a significant security architecture pattern above and beyond the security protocol that the reference implementation demonstrates. In this guide we will look at half a dozen case studies and reference implementations. As you study them, pay special attention to what is common about each of them and synthesize a larger picture. There is far more to AppSensor than first appears.

Statistics

OWASP AppSensor captures so much data that that it becomes possible to apply big data analytics to security. And, more importantly, it opens up whole new possibilities of what you can do with it. OWASP AppSensor currently defines more than 50 detection points all with adaptive response. And this is just the tip of the iceberg. This is an area for AppSensor's future development and will be included in a subsequent version of this guide.

Conclusion

In conclusion, AppSensor is a powerful tool that can improve the effectiveness of your entire information security management program. However, while not a panacea, nor a quick fix for your security ills, OWASP AppSensor is a strategic investment in this program.

> *"I very frequently get the question: 'What's going to change in the next 10 years?' And that is a very interesting question; it's a very common one. I almost never get the question: 'What's not going to change in the next 10 years?' And I submit to you that that second question is actually the more important of the two -- because you can build a business strategy around the things that are stable in time. ... [I]n our retail business, we know that customers want low prices, and I know that's going to be true 10 years from now. They want fast delivery; they want vast selection. It's impossible to imagine a future 10 years from now where a customer comes up and says, 'Jeff I love Amazon; I just wish the prices were a little higher,' [or] 'I love Amazon; I just wish you'd deliver a little more slowly.' Impossible. And so the effort we put into those things, spinning those things up, we know the energy we put into it today will still be paying off dividends for our customers 10 years from now. When you have something that you know is true, even over the long term, you can afford to put a lot of energy into it."*
>
> *– Jeff Bezos, Founder Amazon*

Security is going to be important to your business 10 years from now, just like it was 13 years ago when OWASP was founded. Your investment in OWASP AppSensor will be paying dividends 10 years from now, and that is a sound investment over the long term.

Dennis Groves, MSc
Co-Founder OWASP

How To Use This Guide

The AppSensor Guide is divided into six parts.

Part I : AppSensor Overview

This first part provides a high-level overview including justification, comparison with other techniques, benefits, preliminary requirements and a summary of the conceptual elements.

Part II : Illustrative Case Studies

Inspirational summaries of how AppSensor can be used for a range of different software application architectures and business risk.

Part III : Making It Happen

This describes a detailed technology-agnostic process for planning, implementing and operating application-specific attack detection and response.

Part IV : Demonstration Implementations

In this part, OWASP and other practical examples of how the concept can be deployed, including some standalone components that could be utilized within an organization's own deployments, or to act as inspiration.

Part V : Model Dashboards

This part introduces the necessary concepts for visualizing AppSensor data, and presents example application-specific dashboards.

Part VI : Reference Materials

The final Reference Materials part contains a glossary, detailed listings of detection point types and response types, and the suggested logging and signaling formats. A list of AppSensor awareness and training resources is included, and a full list of other resources cited through the guide for further subject matter reading.

This part also includes details how to provide feedback or become involved with the project.

Part I : AppSensor Overview

The OWASP AppSensor Project defines the concept of real-time attack-aware detection and response services for software applications providing guidance and example code. Part I gives a high-level overview of the concept. It also details why it is different to traditional defensive techniques. This is then followed by a description of the general approach towards implementing AppSensor within application software projects.

Part I : AppSensor Overview

Chapter 1 : Application-Specific Attack Detection & Response

Purpose

Organizations are concerned about protecting their applications, the application users, and related data. The concept of AppSensor is to reduce the risks to these assets by detecting malicious activity within an application. AppSensor is designed to detect activities such as malicious users probing or attacking the application, and to stop them before they can identify and exploit any vulnerability.

This objective is possible because many software vulnerabilities can only be discovered as a result of trial and error by an attacker. Adding the AppSensor framework to an application gives that application the ability to respond to attack attempts by intervening early (oftentimes almost immediately), and blocking those attempts. This approach, if successfully implemented, would make it economically infeasible to attack that application.

Dynamic defense

In the same way that users are benefitting from responsive design in user interfaces and bandwidth utilization, with concepts like progressive enhancement, mobile first and graceful degradation, applications themselves should, and can, alter their behavior and posture in a pre-defined manner when under attack to defend themselves, their data and their users.

The application advantage

Detection is undertaken at the application layer where, unlike infrastructure protection devices, the software application itself has access to the complete context of an interaction and enhanced information about the user. The application knows what is a high-value issue and what is noise. Input data are already decrypted and canonicalized within the application and therefore application-specific attack detection is less susceptible to advanced evasion techniques. When appropriate detection points are selected, a very high degree of confidence in attack identification can be achieved..

Benefits to organizations and users

Application-specific attack detection and response is a comprehensive adaptive approach that can be applied to applications throughout the enterprise. It reduces the risk of unknown vulnerabilities being exploited. The benefits can include:

- Intelligence into whether your applications are under attack, how, and from where
- Certainty due to an extremely high degree of confidence in attack identification
- Fast and fluid responses, using application and user specific contexts
- Protection for software vulnerabilities that you are unaware of
- Defends against future unknown attack methods

- Early detection of both unsuccessful and successful attempts to exploit vulnerabilities
- Insight into users' accidental and malicious misuse
- Information enrichment for conventional network-based intrusion and attack detection systems.

The approach helps to defend organizations (e.g. increased system security, enhanced data protection, insight into attacks, identification of attempted espionage) and its application users (e.g. privacy protection, malware infection prevention).

It greatly increases the visibility of suspicious events and actual attacks. This can provide additional information assurance benefits:

- Lowered information security risk for data and information systems
- Improved compliance
- Reduced impact of attacks leading to increased system survivability.

In turn, these can provide improved service levels and resilience, and competitive advantage.

Architects and developers, who have the most knowledge about the intent of an application and its inner workings, can use the techniques described in this guide to build more robust applications that can defend themselves, by adapting the failure response to minimize the impact of the attack, and provide valuable insight into application usage for other systems and processes.

AppSensor attack-aware applications with real-time response

OWASP AppSensor Project defines a conceptual framework, methodology, guidance and example code to implement attack detection and automated responses. It is not a bolt-on tool or code library, but instead offers insight to an approach for organizations to specify or develop their own implementations – specific to their own business, applications, environments and risk profile – building upon existing standard security controls. AppSensor:

- Detects attackers, not vulnerabilities
- Is application-specific, not generic
- Does not use signatures, or try to predict anything
- Allows applications to adapt in real-time to an identified attacker
- Reduces the impact of an attack
- Provides security intelligence.

Part I : AppSensor Overview

This AppSensor Guide describes how to build detection capabilities into applications to identify unacceptable malicious attacks. The idea is similar to the approach taken for building fire protection. In the event of a fire (an attack), the smoke and/or heat sensors (detection points) signal the building's central control system which automatically warns the occupants to escape using a siren and lights, notifies fire fighters to attend, inactivates elevators, turns off air conditioning systems, primes the water sprinkler system, and closes fire doors and ventilation duct baffles. These actions (responses) reduce the spread of the smoke and fire to reduce the impact on people (users) and other assets (systems). The fire fighters respond in additional ways after they have received the alert and arrive on site. In the same way as building fire protection systems, applications should have self-protection built in.

Many application attacks are potentially obvious and not the result of "user error". They require the use of tools and/or bypass of the user interface controls. Application software usage behavior can be thought of as a continuum of unacceptable to acceptable behavior – AppSensor is only concerned with identifying and responding to clearly malicious events, beyond the range of normal user behavior:

Figure 1 THE SPECTRUM OF ACCEPTABLE APPLICATION USAGE ILLUSTRATING HOW MALICIOUS ATTACKS ARE VERY DIFFERENT TO NORMAL APPLICATION USE

Unacceptable — Acceptable

Malicious Attacks — Normal Application Use

Application-specific attack detection does not need to identify all invalid usage, to be able to determine an attack. There is no need for "infinite data" or "big data" in this approach. In the analogy of the bank, someone jumping over the counter is sufficient evidence; the bank does not need to wait until the robber starts using a thermal lance to drill through the safe door. Similarly in an application, receipt of modified data that the user cannot alter through normal usage should be enough to identify bad behavior and there is no need to wait for a SQL injection payload to be prepared, or tested or executed, regardless of whether there is a vulnerability or not.

The application has full knowledge about the business logic and the roles & permissions of users. Using this knowledge, AppSensor can make informed decisions about misuse, and identify and stop attackers with an extremely high degree of confidence. It also does this in real time.

Additionally, AppSensor can potentially make better use of information from other security devices to contribute to its pool of information for attack detection, increasing the value of those other systems.

Implementing AppSensor is like defining a whitelist for a subset of application functionality, and noting exceptions to this whitelist (for the functionality/entry points included). Only a sufficiently sized subset that covers the highest risks, or the most common things done by attackers is needed. AppSensor does not need to detect everything or know about every attack vector.

Once an attack has been identified, a predefined adaptive response can be undertaken in real-time. Responses can include anything possible in the application's code including logging users out, locking an account, hardening the application and sending alerts, signaling infrastructure devices to perform other actions, or sharing data with other systems or industry groups.

It has also been demonstrated[6,7] how AppSensor can be used to contain the effects of an application worm by detecting rapid escalation of functional usage, combined with an automated response that disables one part of the site, to allow the remainder of the application to continue to operate, and freeze the corruption of data. It has also been shown how a web application with access control detection points combined with an automated real time log out/lock out response seriously hinders automated vulnerability scanning software. So much in fact, that fuzzing data and entry URLs becomes almost impossible for any sort of reasonable timescales.

Technique adoption

The following use cases are most common:

- Identifying attacks (e.g. application or data enumeration, application denial of service, system penetration, fraud)
- Responding to attackers, including prevention
- Monitoring users (e.g. call center, penetration testing lab)
- Maintaining stability (e.g. application worm propagation prevention)
- Attack information sharing.

The Mozilla Foundation has established[8] an integrated application intrusion detection system across its enterprise-scale portfolio of web applications using AppSensor to identify application attackers.

Architects and developers realize they can deploy the AppSensor concept themselves. This is not just for a "big company" or using a "big budget" approach. The technique can be piloted, undertaken in stages, progressively extended and enhanced over time.

Part I : AppSensor Overview

Software assurance community

AppSensor was promoted to the US software assurance community in the Sept/Oct 2011 edition of CrossTalk (The Journal of Defense Software Engineering)[9] in a concise overview of the concept and method of implementation. The article is available to download[10] from the CrossTalk website.

AppSensor is a recommended component of resilient software, described on a page[11] in the Software Assurance (SwA) section of the US Department of Homeland Security's website. This discusses the need for defenses that are proactive, not reactive.

The BITS (Financial Services Roundtable) Software Assurance Framework[12] mentions software security intelligence as an emerging practice where "technology advancements include software and devices designed to monitor, and in some cases prevent, security threats within the production environment".

The Payment Card Industry Security Standards Council (PCI SSC) requires in-scope public facing web applications to address new threats and vulnerabilities on an ongoing basis (PCI DSS v3 requirement 6.6) with one option being "Installing an automated technical solution that detects and prevents web-based attacks...".

AppSensor-like functionality elsewhere

It cannot be claimed that the following are using AppSensor or ever heard of it, but the following information alludes to the adoption of production enterprise-scale AppSensor-like functionality.

In a discussion about distributed denial of service attacks against financial institutions[13], it was reported that "Some [financial institutions] also have implemented measures to turn off access to certain parts of their online sites, such as search functions, when DDoS activity is detected. These precautions, and others, have helped ensure sites are not completely taken offline by an attack, experts say.". This includes application layer responses – not just network layer responses.

A blog post "Monitoring of HTML and JavaScript entering an application by Etsy"[14] by a vulnerability researcher on how a vulnerability he had identified was fixed before he had been able to verify it, and the related link[15] to a presentation by Zane Lackey, Etsy's Engineering Manager for Application Security, about web application security at scale including the point about "instrument application to collect data points" and their instrumentation library[16,17] that runs on the Node.js platform and listens for statistics, from counters and timers.

The US Defense Department announced they are funding cyber security research that include "developing active defenses – technologies that detect attacks and probes as they occur, as opposed to defenses that employ only after-the-fact detection and notification"[18].

The principle of "cyber maneuver" in cyber security has been used to describe the defensive and offensive use of changing computing and information resources at machine speeds to achieve a position of advantage[19,20].

It was reported that Google Chrome's security team built in a detection trap to identify the exploit attack being used[21]. Furthermore, the Google Hack Honeypot (GHH)[22] is a website that mimics vulnerable behavior and monitors attacker reconnaissance once it has been installed and indexed by search engines. The information in the generated attack database can be used to "to gather statistics on would-be-attackers, report activities to appropriate authorities and temporarily or permanently deny access to resources".

Vendor implementations

OWASP is not affiliated with any company and does not endorse or recommend any commercial products or services. But there is a close fit in the following application-integrated (non network) products/services with some aspects of the AppSensor concept:

- Fortify Runtime[23] (formerly Fortify Real-Time Analyzer), supporting Java and .Net, includes dynamic injection of protection against malware and for logging and monitoring of application security activity and integrates with other HP Fortify Software 360 products
- Prevoty[24] highly-scalable software as a service that validates inputs, queries and tokens, with a range of SDKs for popular programming languages and frameworks such as C#, Java, Objective-C, PHP, Python and Ruby on Rails.

No review or assessment of these has been undertaken during the writing of this guide. Other commercial and open source products and services are expected in due course. This guide documents a number of free and open source demonstration and production implementations in *Part IV : Demonstration Implementations*.

Conclusion

AppSensor provides comprehensive visibility into attacks against applications, valuable intelligence, allowing real-time automated response. AppSensor is not a perimeter defense solution but assumes the application is operating in a hostile environment. AppSensor implementation should be a baseline for application defense and be part of "defense in depth" strategies.

Chapter 2 : Protection Measures

Intrusion detection and prevention fundamentals

AppSensor builds on the work of many researchers, but has taken the concepts of intrusion detection and prevention into the heart of application software. The most important work to date in the field of Intrusion Detection is Rebecca Bace's book titled Intrusion Detection[25]. Her NIST Special Publication on Intrusion Detection Systems[26] mentions application-based Intrusion Detection Systems (IDS). The subsequent SP 800-94 Guide to Intrusion Detection and Prevention Systems (IDPS)[27,28] mainly focuses on network-based, wireless, network behavior Analysis and Host-Based IDPS. These are all valuable sources of background information with many good referenced works, and are recommended reading to help understand the fundamental concepts, options, deployment and operational considerations, pros and cons.

Wile most research has been undertaken relating primarily to the network layer, AppSensor takes IDPS concepts to the application layer as ISO/IEC 7498-2[29] (twinned as ITU X.800[30]) predicted in 1989.

Detecting attacks on applications

AppSensor can be used to perform:

- Attack determination
- Real-time response
- Attack blocking.

It can help to protect software applications against:

- Skilled attackers probing looking for weaknesses
- Misuse of valid business functionality
- Propagation of application worms
- Data scraping and exfiltration
- Application-layer denial of service (DoS)
- As yet unknown attack methods and exploits.

AppSensor is not an application security magic bullet. AppSensor helps defend securely designed and developed applications. It is not a shortcut to deploy security controls. AppSensor will not do these for you. It depends on rigorous input validation practices at every point in the application. Using a Systems Security Engineering Capability Maturity Model[31] rating as an example, AppSensor provides a "Well Defined" (level 3) pattern for "Quantitative Control" (level 4) of application security. This constitutes a major organizational investment and it is not necessarily the right model or investment for every corporation.

If you have not specified, designed, developed, tested, deployed the application securely, you cannot benefit from AppSensor's capabilities. Attackers will be able to easily identify and exploit weaknesses. If you have an obviously insecure application, concentrate on solving that first. You must have existing authentication, session management, authorization, validation, error handling and encryption services available and implemented in a robust manner.

Localized security controls are not sufficient. Functions like authentication failure counts and lock-out, or limits on rate of file uploads are localized protection mechanisms. These themselves are not AppSensor equivalents, unless they are rigged together into an application-wide sensory network and centralized analytical engine. Similarly logging is necessary but not equivalent to its AppSensor counter part. AppSensor differs fundamentally from traditional alerting logging and alerting systems, and this aspect will be discussed in further detail subsequently. Logs may be a method of recording event and attack information and application security logging should exist for many other purposes[32], but can sometimes be used as part of an AppSensor implementation.

The issue of vulnerabilities

Most importantly, AppSensor does not detect software weaknesses or vulnerabilities. Instead it is used to detect users trying to find vulnerabilities.

AppSensor does not analyze an application's source code or examine the application in its runtime environment. AppSensor protects against attackers trying to find weaknesses. Organizations must already be undertaking information security activities throughout the software development life cycle (SDLC) to prevent vulnerabilities being deployed in production code, and be ensuring that supporting hardware and network infrastructure is secured.

Similarly AppSensor does not perform dynamic patching. There are promising integrations of web application firewalls with automated static analysis (source code review) and/or dynamic analysis (run time or penetration testing) to generate "virtual patches" for vulnerabilities discovered. These can be implemented in a web application firewall (WAF) while work is undertaken to remediate the source code if it is available. If there is a known weakness, solve it. AppSensor exists to help prevent attackers finding these, not stopping exploits that an organization is already aware of.

Comparison with other defensive mechanisms

In AppSensor, attack detection and prevention capabilities are added to an application instead of functioning at a lower or more generic level. By doing this, the organization gains

Part I : AppSensor Overview

the detection and response capabilities of other systems, coupled with detailed business specific data related to a specific application or set of applications.

AppSensor has been compared with more conventional alternatives using research and experimental techniques[33] by Pål Thomassen at the Norwegian University of Science and Technology in Tronheim. The thesis attempted to address four questions:

1. What is the current state of application-based intrusion detection and prevention systems?
2. How does OWASP AppSensor compare to other IDPS technologies?
3. In the given scenario, what are the benefits of using AppSensor compared with trying to stop the attacks in a IDPS or WAF?
4. How hard is it to built AppSensor into an application?

The paper primarily compares the use of Snort[34], ModSecurity[35] WAF using the OWASP ModSecurity Core Rule Set[36] and the reference AppSensor Core implementation - see *Chapter 21 : Fully Integrated (AppSensor Core)* - to protect a demonstration online banking web application in a lab environment subjected to attacks based on the OWASP Top Ten Most Critical Web Application Security Risks[37]. The conclusions to the four questions above includes the comment that "AppSensor shines in that in addition to detect the well known web application attacks it is also able to detect attack which exploits the internal workings of an application, such as failure in access controls mechanisms". The full paper and conclusions should be read to understand the context of this statement.

Comparison with infrastructure protection mechanisms

Three questions that can be used to identify if a mechanism is AppSensor-like are whether the system/service/solution/mechanism/device can:

1. Determine an attack where a user is stepping through a multi-step business process in the wrong order?
2. Understand the difference between a user who has access to a particular document today but not tomorrow, due to a change in user's role or a change in the information classification of the document?
3. Identify an attack that is an attempt to exceed an individual user-specific action threshold (e.g. payment transfer limit).

AppSensor can be used for all of these. Common non-AppSensor-like protective mechanisms that cannot do any of the above are described bovver the next few pages.

These are often cited as providing defense to applications, but they have no knowledge of custom application knowledge or insight into the context of user's actions. They do not provide application-specific protection, and if these are all an organization is replying on for application defense, the applications are dangerously exposed and the organization probably does not have insight as to whether the applications are really under attack. Some may be physical appliances, but they can also be software hosted locally or as a remote service.

Network firewall

Network firewalls control traffic source, destinations and ports. If an application needs say port 443 open to all internet users and no other ports open, a network firewall is the correct device. Similarly network firewalls might limit access to a particular application to only certain internal users. However, they have no insight into the application or the user context. A network firewall could be utilized to perform application-elected response such as blocking an individual IP address.

At this point it is also probably worth mentioning the use of HTTP over Transport Layer Security (TLS)/Secure Sockets Layer (SSL)[38] for web applications. The correct use of TLS/SSL provides confidentiality and assurance in the integrity of data sent between two points. It can also provide some degree of identity assurance. However, it does not protect web applications at all. Malicious payloads and activities can be undertaken just as well using TLS as not. And in many cases TLS will prevent the inspection of the data while in transit.

Application-aware firewall

Some network firewalls are rather confusingly called "application firewalls" or "application aware firewalls" or "next generation firewalls". These only allow or deny traffic for individual and groups of users to and from defined IP addresses, ports and URLs for many common applications (e.g. Facebook, Twitter). It sounds a like AppSensor, but looks like a network firewall with some extra social media aware configuration options.

Traffic/load balancer

Traffic/load balancers are used to distributed network and/or application traffic across a number of servers. Some of these can have the ability to inspect traffic at the application layer (e.g. an understanding of HTTP for example), but they are limited to knowledge gained from the data stream, and have no inherent understanding of the application. Some of these devices can have custom rules written and thus have some application firewall capabilities (e.g. like a basic Web Application Firewall - see below).

Anti DDoS system

Network firewalls, switches, routers, traffic/load balancers and intrusion protection systems often include some measures to protect against distributed denial of service (DDoS) attacks which intend to prevent legitimate access to the targeted system. However specialist systems (often as outsourced services) are also available that prevent these attacks reaching an organization's own network. These do not have knowledge of individual applications even if they are able to detect application protocol DDoS attacks.

Part I : AppSensor Overview

Web gateway

These devices scan incoming web traffic to an organizations' end-users who are browsing the web. They may incorporate data on blacklisted websites, signatures for malware present in web page content, email messages and files, and even perform live malware analysis. Web Gateways do not protect applications used by other people.

Intrusion Detection System (IDS) and Intrusion Prevention System (IPS)

As mentioned above (*Intrusion detection and prevention fundamentals*), typical IDS and IPS observe network traffic (NIDS) or activities on hosts (HIDS). They detect deviations from baseline behavior but have no knowledge of application behavior and thus have to use signature-based misuse detection or statistical based anomaly detection and are thus susceptible to a higher level of false positives. While policies, a continuously updated database of known attacks, and information sharing between users has improved performance, they have little understanding of application protocols and none of application logic, or even what entry points or user data is acceptable. Intrusion is not always the same as attack. And due to these factors IDS and IPS are more prone to false positives for attacks against applications.

Data Loss Prevention (DLP)

Data loss prevention is concerned with the detection and prevention of the loss, leakage or exfiltration of targeted data types. The exploit has already been performed and this useful technique is not an application protection.

Application firewall, filter or guard

These are usually protocol-specific application firewalls looking only at Layer 7 in the OSI[39] stack. They tend to be good at examining one particular data type (e.g. XML, PDFs) or protocol (e.g. SQL, HTTP) and can include some element of self-learning about "normal" traffic, but often include many blacklist signatures. Some may be self-learning, include web behavioral analysis and have some mitigating capabilities, but in the end they are a generic solution to generic attacks. They are not application-specific. See also Web Application Firewall below.

Web application firewall

Many applications are web-based and there are now a number of commercial and open source HTTP protocol application firewalls, built upon earlier HTTP filtering techniques. They are generally referred to as "web application firewalls (WAFs). WAFs understand HTTP traffic and can be an excellent way to screen web applications from generic attacks and can be used for virtual patching. Some WAFs have application traffic self-learning capabilities, and others support custom attack and application logic rule building including support for scripting languages. WAFs also have capabilities to drop connections, or interact with network firewalls to block IP addresses. However, WAFs are sometimes left operating in detection-only mode due to concerns about false positives leading to denial of service to normal users.

Certain types of AppSensor-like functionality can be built into a WAF, and some of these might be much more efficiently undertaken by a WAF for both detection (e.g. HTTP protocol misuse detection, generic blacklist input validation, web application denial of service identification) and response (e.g. HTTP logging, proxying requests, IP address blocking). However, a WAF still does not have insight into the full capabilities of each application such as user session and access controls. The demonstration implementation in *Chapter 26 : Leveraging a Web Application Firewall* discusses some of these many possibilities further.

Use of AppSensor with infrastructure protection mechanisms

The above mechanisms may often be deployed as well as AppSensor. If such devices block, change or mask application traffic or data, it is important to consider how these might affect the ability of the application to detect an attack.

Often the mechanisms can provide inputs to AppSensor (as external "reputational" detection points). This is certainly almost always true for web application firewalls in front of web server farms, database monitoring/firewalls in front of database servers, and for other similar application firewalls, filters and guards.

Application protection mechanisms

Applications must have their own in-built security controls such as services for authentication, session management, authorization, input validation, output validation, output encoding, and cryptography. They may also have discrete functionality that behaves very similarly to "attack response" such as:

- Counting multiple failed authentication attempts to lock a user account
- Detecting the use of the TRACE HTTP method to block requests
- Checking the IP address during a session and terminating the session if the IP address changes
- Displaying a message to the user about invalid input
- Logging unexpected requests
- Investigating suspicious incidents at a later date.

These alone are not sufficient to be considered AppSensor. These are typically be implemented as isolated processes and some may be undertaken reactively to events or performed largely in a manual way. AppSensor centralizes and formalizes this approach.

AppSensor is about implementing measures proactively to add instrumentation and controls directly into an application in advance so that all these events (and more) are centrally analyzed, using all the knowledge about the business logic and the roles & permissions of users, responding and adapting behavior in real time.

The event and attack information can be displayed using custom application-specific dashboards. Since attack events are hopefully rare, especially within the authenticated part of an application, operators can quickly identify and assess the attack and the responses being taken automatically by AppSensor.

These are discussed further in *Part III : Making It Happen - Chapter 15 : Verification, Deployment and Operation.*

AppSensor defining characteristics

AppSensor does not act as a security silver bullet for all the reasons above and more. AppSensor is another technique, with some unique benefits, that contributes to an overall software security assurance program. It also relies on other infrastructure defenses, but those are platform and architecturally specific.

So what properties would a system have to say it is AppSensor-like? The fundamental requirements are the ability to perform four tasks:

- Detection of a selection of suspicious and malicious events
- Use of this knowledge centrally to identify attacks
- Selection of a predefined response
- Execution of the response.

These tasks are fairly generic and can therefore be applied in many different ways to suit the systems architecture and an organization's policies, development practices and cultural preferences. AppSensor can often be completely contained within the application itself, but that is not the only way.

AppSensor improves system survivability in spite of malicious actions through all three survivability quality sub-factors[40]:

- Detection/recognition of attacks as they occur
- Prevention through changes to security posture
- Reaction/recovery through responses to attacks.

Applications of greater complexity are unlikely to have all these components built into the application's code itself. For example:

- Applications deployed across clustered servers

- Distributed applications
- Applications where a significant part of the business logic is external to the application (e.g. a mobile app that communicates with a central server)
- Detection point sensors deployed in related applications (e.g. databases, file integrity monitoring systems, anti-virus systems) and infrastructure components (e.g. web application firewalls, network firewalls).

If there is no capability to modify the source code or build AppSensor in from the start of a development, AppSensor concepts may all have to be externalized such as in a web application firewall (WAF) or logging system that communicates to a network firewall.

Different implementation models are discussed further in Parts II and IV.

Chapter 3 : The AppSensor Approach

Stop! Develop and operate secure applications first

Do not progress any further until this important information is understood. It has already been stated that AppSensor does not detect software weaknesses or vulnerabilities, and instead it is used to detect users trying to find vulnerabilities.

If in any doubt, make sure security considerations are already integrated into software acquisition and development practices using the techniques described in the Open Software Assurance Maturity Model[41] (Open SAMM), other software assurance models and frameworks. Consider the guidance listed by DACS/IATAC[42], ENISA[43] and OWASP[44], such as from BITS[45], CMU[46,47,48], CERT[49], ISO/IEC 27034[50], NIST[51], SAFECode[52], and the DoHS/SwA Forum[53,54], and publicly available information about actual assurance programs (e.g. Microsoft SDL[55], Oracle SSA[56] and the ongoing BSIMM[57] study and related work[58] such as vBSIMM[59] for software vendors from FSISAC). Practices should commonly include, but are not limited to:

- Creation and maintenance of coding and development standards
- Role-specific application security training
- Source code control and protection
- Security requirements
- Architectural and design reviews
- Source code review
- Security testing
- Infrastructure hardening
- Secure application deployment
- Backup and recovery processes
- Vulnerability assessment and penetration testing
- Patch management program
- Incident response plan.

OWASP's Application Security Guide for Chief Information Security Officers (CISOs)[60] discusses application security from governance, compliance and risk perspectives, the parallel CISO Survey and Report[61] provides tactical intelligence about security risks and best practices.

The objective must be to identify and treat vulnerabilities before software is released into production environments, and to ensure those environments are secure and continue to be maintained in that manner.

Other preliminary requirements

If an application has known vulnerabilities, fix those first. Do not attempt to use AppSensor to prevent the exploitation of vulnerabilities already known about – a single specially crafted payload, maybe perfected elsewhere, could be sent to the application to exploit it regardless of whether AppSensor is used or not.

Similarly, ensure the supporting network and application's host infrastructure (e.g. servers, workstations devices, other hardware as appropriate) are hardened, administrative access requires strong authentication, appropriately authorized ingress and egress network firewall rules exist, and that all system components have relevant security patches tested, deployed and verified.

Before embarking on the adoption of AppSensor, organizations must decide what needs to be protected and with how much effort. This can normally be linked with the outputs from an existing risk assessment processes. Identification and risk assessment will provide insight into the applications, but most importantly allows organizations to rank them based on their own business-relevant criteria. The criteria may be from the organization's viewpoint, but it is sometimes necessary to take into account the value of the data and system from other perspectives such as its users, other parties and society.

The application risk assessment should also identify common dependencies such as shared components, identical data access, common hosting or inter-related back-end systems which may mean all applications need to be considered at the greatest risk classification. An understanding of the dependencies and inter-relationships is necessary to ensure AppSensor detection points are selected and applied appropriately, and in the most efficient manner. Although it is usual to treat each application as a single item, in some cases, it may be possible to partition an application into sections, with different risk ratings, and this could be used to allocate AppSensor detection points in a more targeted manner.

One possibility to consider is whether the application can be partitioned into public areas, authentication, private areas for authenticated users and perhaps back-office functionality such as a web-based content management system or other website administration functionality. AppSensor defends against an attacker who might be able to find a vulnerability; for an unknown vulnerability, organizations do not know the likelihood or impact, but should know the exposure. Derive the impact from the risk assessment for the whole application.

Architecture

Conceptually, AppSensor can be considered to comprise of two modules, a detection unit and a response unit. The detection unit is responsible for identifying malicious behavior based upon defined policies. Detection points can be integrated into presentation, business and data layers of the application. The detection unit reports activity to the response unit.

Part I : AppSensor Overview

The response unit will take an action against the user. The action taken will depend upon whether the event is a suspicious situation or is obviously an attack.

AppSensor should be integrated into an application such that a specific exception will be thrown whenever the application detects a suspicious or attack event. AppSensor's detection unit should be aware of the exception thrown, and catalog the event together with relevant details. The response unit will take action against the user responsible using techniques such as a user warning, account lockout, application administrator warning, etc. Consequently AppSensor must have appropriate rights and hooks within the application to perform such response actions.

Although this guide discusses AppSensor on its own, as if it is something separate to the application, the concept is often highly integrated within an application's source code. Other architectures are certainly possible, may have certain benefits, and are discussed in *Part IV : Demonstration Implementations*. When reading "AppSensor", consider it to mean "those parts of the application and related systems that perform attack detection and response functionality", regardless of how/where it is performed.

The process

AppSensor can be applied to existing application code, or built into the requirements for new projects, whether developed in-house or out-sourced. The planning stages are probably the most time-consuming aspect of implementing AppSensor.

The implementation must ensure that high confidence in attack identification is not compromised by adding inappropriate detection points, or designing them in a way that leads to additional events being detected that are not attacks. The method presented also tries to build in consideration of business operations and usability, so that not only is the high degree of confidence in attack identification maintained, but processes are not unduly disrupted and the users are not subjected to difficulties through simple human error. In other words, building in a degree of human fault tolerance.

Although AppSensor works best within the authenticated portion of an application, it is also possible to apply the principles to other areas. In the latter, the range of "normal behavior" may be wider, the identity and location of users may be harder to pinpoint and some detection points may no longer be necessary. But the same benefits are possible.

AppSensor's individual detection point ideas are not necessarily novel, but extend common security principles. Some similar ideas may already exist in an application, but these will typically be implemented as isolated processes and some may be undertaken reactively to events or performed largely in a manual way. Some examples of these include:

- Counting multiple failed authentication attempts to lock a user account
- Detecting use of invalid HTTP methods to block requests

- Checking the IP address during a session and terminating the session if the IP address changes
- Logging unexpected requests
- Investigating suspicious events at a later date.

AppSensor focuses and formalizes this approach. AppSensor is about implementing adaptive measures to add instrumentation and controls directly into an application in advance so that all these events (and more) are centrally analyzed and responded to. It is necessary to build applications securely in the first place, and understand the risks the application faces. If an application has centralized and standardized modules for input and output validation, authorization and security event logging, these can provide a head start which can be extended to included AppSensor-like capabilities.

In general, the four stages necessary to adopt AppSensor are planning, implementation, deployment and operation. These should be incorporated into existing software acquisition and development practices, and are not meant to map to any particular software development life cycle.

Roles

The types of personnel involved in these stages for in in-house development process are dependent on each organization's structure and culture. However, successful implementation requires a mix of skills and it is usually requires a collaborative effort between Development, Information Security and Operational teams.

- Business owners will need to determine and approve the level of resources to commit for each application and also the rules of engagement for responding to attack events
- Designers, architects, information security staff and lead developers will have to consider how the agreed approach can be implemented by development, network and operational teams
- Developers and testers will need to undertake verification activities to ensure the AppSensor design has been implemented and tuned correctly, so that it does not affect normal usage and does not have any adverse side-effects
- Operation security, development leads and others as required will monitor AppSensor activity and respond to relevant alerts.

Where development is outsourced, there will be additional involvement from procurement and legal roles during the planning stage in particular, and the implementation stage will largely relate to the outsourced development provider.

Part III : Making It Happen describes the process of adopting AppSensor in greater detail. But in the next chapter further detail is provided on the necessary components.

Chapter 4 : Conceptual Elements

Introduction

The primary elements that need to be considered when adopting AppSensor are detection points, possible response actions available when an attack is identified, and the thresholds at which these occur. These are considered briefly here to provide background to the subsequent more detailed discussions of the methodology in *Part III : Making It Happen*.

Approach

The commonly cited process model for IDPS comprises information sources, analysis and response. Analysis approaches are usually either misuse detection or anomaly detection:

- Misuse detection identifies specific malicious activity (single or multiple events) by comparison with predefined attack patterns (also known as signature-based detection)
- Anomaly detection identifies unusual activity that is outside normal legitimate bounds.

AppSensor does not fit cleanly into either of these since it does not attempt to define numerous attack patterns (misuse detection) but instead primarily focuses only on blatantly malicious events but can also include predefined extreme trend aberration limits. This actually provides a unique benefit in that previously unknown attacks can also be detected, that is unavailable in any other defensive mechanism regardless of cost.

The approach pursued in this book and the demonstration code examples relate to defining application-specific events with related thresholds for attack detection and response. Statistical models also have strengths and weaknesses; as does machine learning, but these are not considered here.

Detection

It is necessary to understand what constitutes an attack, and how threats go about identifying, and probing targets, developing exploits and executing the exploit to achieve the desired result (e.g. data extraction, code/data addition, modification or deletion, denial of service). Although reports on application vulnerability prevalence from static (source code) and dynamic testing, and information from actual breaches of confidentiality are useful, there are other projects[22,62,63,64,65,66,67] providing tools and invaluable data about how attackers perform reconnaissance before the creation and deployment of an exploit.

The Common Attack Pattern Enumeration and Classification (CAPEC)[68], a dictionary of common approaches used to attack software, can be used to identify attack patterns. The results[69] from the 2011 ModSecurity SQL Injection Challenge[70] revealed that although it only took a matter of hours for attackers to find an exploit (evasion of a WAF using a negative security model to protect a known vulnerable web application), the number of requests submitted in this time was in the hundreds.

Suspicious or an attack?

When detecting malicious activity, the application must distinguish between two possible scenarios. Firstly, the some detected activities might equally have been caused by an unintentional user mistake, or by a crafty attacker snooping around or seeking to mask their other attacks. Since the detected activity could result in an undesirable system response, it is important not to disregard this type of activity altogether. This type of event will be referred to as "Suspicious" because it might be an attack. Examples of suspicious events are:

- Data is submitted for a username that includes the two characters '; at the end – this could simply be the result of the user accidentally hitting these tow keys on their keyboard when attempting to press enter, or it could be an attempt to discover a SQL injection vulnerability on the log in page.
- A web form is submitted from the middle of a multi-step check-out process without the previous steps being completed – the user might have bookmarked a web page and gone back to that, or it could be a forced browsing attempt to bypass business logic and perhaps obtain goods without payment.

Secondly, the event could be clearly an intentional malicious activity. These types of actions will never occur as the result of a user's mistake, are not permitted normal operations, and are therefore highly likely to be an attack against the application. This type of event will be referred to as an "Attack". Examples of attack events are:

- Data is submitted for a parameter's containing *0 OR 1=1--'* in the value which is normally an integer – This is clearly a SQL injection attack regardless of whether it is successful or not, and would never occur as the result of some sort of user error.
- Hundreds of files are uploaded for a user's avatar image in their profile – an individual user will never do this and it indicates some form of automated attack.

It is important to accurately classify detected events as suspicious or attacks so that the responsive action is not unjustly performed against a non-malicious user. Another way to think about these two categorizations is to ask the following questions:

- Is it impossible for the event to occur as the result of a typographic error, or a copy & paste mistake, or an inadvertent key press by the user?
- Does the user have to leave the normal flow of the application to perform the activity?

- Are additional software tools or special knowledge needed to perform the identified activity?

If the answer to at least two of these is "yes", it is almost certainly an attack event.

User identification (attribution)

The AppSensor technique in general works best where the user can be identified, such as within the authenticated part of an application, or where the "user" is a defined external application, service or other systems. However, system trend type detection points (see later), do not track individual users at all – they track groups of users – and are therefore always candidates for use regardless of knowledge about an individual attacker's identity.

But even in the case of a highly distributed attack, AppSensor could be used to identify if an attack is under way and will provide insight into the attack, making it a useful operational tool.

In general, the normal approach is to use passive identification techniques:

1. Prioritize tracking exceptions by known users when possible (most granular) – this works in authenticated-only sections of the application
2. Consider tracking both known and unknown users in places where authentication is not required, but use the preference of user tracking – works in all locations
3. Utilize system user exceptions in cases where the action is not user-specific or it should be tracked across the whole system, not per-user.

Consider just doing the first of these initially, but design for the case of unknown and system users. Some frameworks may enforce a session identification value even for unauthenticated users. In other situations it may be possible to consider hardware identifiers, or certificates, or a combination of HTTP headers[71] such as User-Agent Accept-Language with the remote IP address (and possibly X-Forwarded-For or Via) for web requests, or user-agent fingerprinting techniques[72,73]. Some of these could be spoofed by the user. Also remember that for web systems, requests from a single user at a fixed location can be drawn randomly from a larger pool of IP addresses, and requests from a single user's mobile device can change source network repeatedly due to switching between mobile network base stations and from mobile network to WiFi and vice versa.

Not all types of event detection always need to identify individual users (e.g. system trends). Additionally AppSensor does not necessarily need to be perfect – just good enough to identify an attack with an appropriate degree of certainty. This level of confidence will depend upon the type of application, degree of assurance required and the types of response actions possible. Ensure the user identification techniques proposed are permitted in the relevant jurisdictions and if user opt-in is required, or opt out allowed.

Sensors

Detection points are instrumentation sensors, normally embedded directly within the application code. While it is possible, and sometimes very desirable, to have detection points in other systems, for the purposes of the current discussion this guide will mainly focus on in-code detection points.

AppSensor can be thought as an input validation pattern for applications. In traditional IDS information may come from network traffic and host logs. In AppSensor's case, the information will typically originate from data input validation practices undertaken by the application. This input validation should be being undertaken anywhere trust boundaries are crossed. So if something is going to be consumed; it must be validated. During the input validation it either passes the criteria the programmer had in mind; or it fails and an exception is thrown – that exception being thrown contains valuable information.

The data/access validation code should often already exist in a securely coded application; it is then only necessary to add "instrumentation" to collect that information together, and act on it. For a whitelist input validation check for example, the primary logic already exists but would be modified to call the AppSensor components (modifications shown in bold).

Figure 2   PSEUDO CODE ILLUSTRATING THE ADDITION OF APPSENSOR DETECTION POINT LOGIC WITHIN EXISTING INPUT VALIDATION CODE

```
if ( Value in Whitelist ) then
    [existing normal process execution];
else
    [send event to AppSensor];
    [existing exception/error handling];
end if;
```

Some detection points may not exist in the existing code at all, as would be the case for many blacklisting input validation checks. In this case all the code would be new (bold).

Figure 3   PSEUDO CODE ILLUSTRATING THE ADDITION OF COMPLETELY NEW APPSENSOR DETECTION POINT LOGIC

```
if ( Value in Blacklist ) then
    [send event to AppSensor];
end if;
```

Part I : AppSensor Overview

The best detection points are custom ones, designed and optimized specifically for how the application works and the risks it faces. But AppSensor has identified over fifty examples which can be used as the basis for defining custom detection points, used "as is" or used as something to help stimulate ideas. The AppSensor detection points are defined with descriptions, considerations and examples on the OWASP website[74], are reproduced in the *Detection Points* section of *Part VI : Reference Materials*.

Thresholds to determine an attack

As discussed above, attack determination must take into account whether each detected event is simply suspicious or actually an attack event. When developing a response policy, it is vital to determine the appropriate thresholds for response actions. The objectives are to select thresholds and response actions that:

- Deter malicious activity
- Prevent determined attackers from successfully identifying vulnerabilities
- Minimize the impact when any false positives are recorded (non-malicious activity)

In general, attack determination should use the approach:

- React immediately to malicious events
- Monitor suspicious events.

This means that every time a detection point that represents a malicious activity is activated, the response should be activated immediately (i.e. the threshold is "1 event"). And typically, a response should be undertaken for a small number of detection point activations that represent suspicious activity (i.e. the threshold is for example "3 events"). These always need to be customized to meet the specific needs of the organization and the application itself. The simplest implementation would be to consider the total number of activations across all detection points, but more granularity in response can be obtained when thresholds are be defined per detection point, per type of detection point or per group of detection points.

Response

Action and inaction

A response policy should be established which sets specific thresholds and response actions based on the detected actions of each user (or all users in a group, or all users). In AppSensor a response is a change in application behavior; it is not any form of retaliation. The term "countermeasures" could be used, but AppSensor used the term "response" to suggest a much wider range of actions than purely offensive ones. The response aims to defend the application, its users and everyone's data:

- Organization data
- User data (sometimes including PII/personal data)
- Data belonging to other parties (e.g. suppliers, customers and partners).

Detection of events is not useful without an automated response to deter and prevent a successful compromise. Some of the most commonly implemented response actions and their pros and cons are shown below.

Table 1   PROS AND CONS OF THE MOST COMMONLY IMPLEMENTED RESPONSES

Responses	Aspect	
User Notification	Description	Provide a visual warning message to the user to deter further attack activity. For example "A security event has been detected and logged".
	Pros	May deter a casual attacker by alerting them that their activities are being monitored.
	Cons	Will not deter a determined attacker and provides the attacker with some knowledge of what events are being detected as malicious.
Account Logout	Description	Log the account out.
	Pros	Causes difficulty with to most automated attack tools since the session will be interrupted after a small number of interactions. Logging out the user also provides a clear indication that the performed actions are being monitored and the application is responding to attacks.
	Cons	Automated tools can be modified to automatically re-authenticate to bypass this response action.
Account Lockout	Description	Lock the user account. The user account could be permanently locked, unlocked automatically after a pre-set period (e.g. 30 minutes), or unlocked manually after the user has contacted the help desk.
	Pros	Locking the account will cease the attack activity (if authentication is required).
	Cons	If the organization or application does not control the creation of accounts, then the attacker could generate numerous accounts and use each one until it is locked.
Administrator Notification	Description	Notify the administrator via email or other methods of the malicious activity.
	Pros	An administrator could take additional actions or enable additional logging capabilities in real time. Notification is especially effective for system trend events which require human analysis.
	Cons	If used too often, this notification could become another type of information overload which is mostly ignored.

Response selection

The definition of thresholds is inherently tied to the selection of response actions. The thresholds and response actions must be customized to meet the specific needs of the application, and normal user behavior. Two contrasting examples are:

- A highly sensitive application operating within a restricted environment may be configured such that even the most subtle suspicious activity is considered to be an

attack (all have threshold "1") where lockout and administrative notification is appropriate
- A public website is regularly scanned by search engines each indexing hundreds pages/day and must not be blocked as it might otherwise affect customers arriving from natural searches, but some sort of limits need to be imposed to prevent competitors copying data off the site to undertake daily price comparisons; some source IP addresses might be excluded from response actions or have very high thresholds, whereas other sources of unauthenticated users have lower thresholds before rate limiting or blocking responses are activated.

The power of AppSensor is its placement within the application for detection, and its ability to respond to malicious activity in real time. The most common response actions are user warning messages, log out, account lockout and administrator notification as noted above. However, since AppSensor is connected into the application, the possibilities of response actions are limited only by the current capabilities of the application, or what it is extended to be able to do.

Other ideas for response actions are documented on the OWASP website[75], are summarized in the *Responses* section of *Part VI : Reference Materials*. There is a useful description of US legal considerations of more invasive responses in the recently published book "Offensive Countermeasures: The Art of Active Defense"[76]. What is legal, moral, or culturally acceptable will be different in other jurisdictions, and also depends on an organization's sector, regulations, industry standards, the type of application users and the purpose/functionality of the application.

The AppSensor pattern

The above ideas are summarized in the conceptual elements below.

Table 2   LIST OF CONCEPTUAL ELEMENTS IN THE APPSENSOR PATTERN

Element	Description
Detection Point	A specific point during the execution of a program that allows event generation
Event	An observed occurrence in an application that is monitored and analyzed to determine attacks
Event Manager	This collects event notifications from the detection points and polls the event analysis engine for any appropriate response actions to execute
Event Analysis Engine	Used for the analysis and processing of incoming event data to compile, store and process them to determine if an attack has occurred
Event Store	The storage mechanism for events
Attack Store	Storage mechanism for attacks, which are produced by the analysis of events
Response	The action taken as a result of attack recognition
Reporting Client	An application that provides data visualization e.g. a dashboard

The terms are defined more fully in the *Glossary*, and are illustrated in the figure below.

Figure 4 SCHEMATIC ARRANGEMENT OF APPSENSOR CONCEPTUAL ELEMENTS

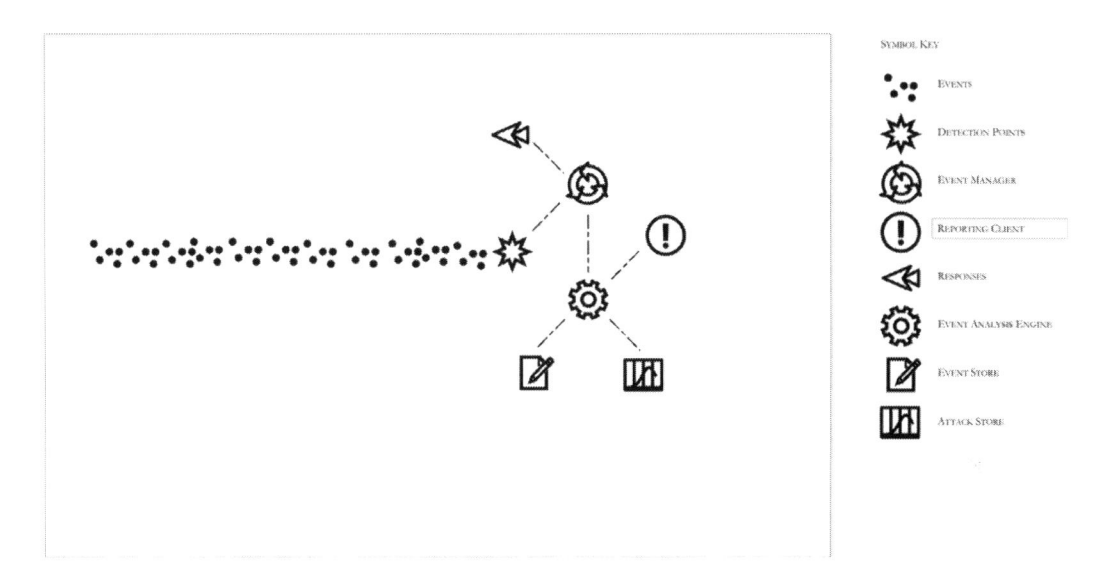

Figures based on this schematic arrangement are included later in the guide.

Part I : AppSensor Overview

Part II : Illustrative Case Studies

On the following pages examples of how AppSensor can be used for a range of different software application architectures and business risk.

Part II : Illustrative Case Studies

Chapter 5 : Case Study of a Rapidly Deployed Web Application

Table 3   PROPERTIES FOR THE CASE STUDY OF A MINIMAL APPSENSOR IMPLEMENTATION FOR A SMALL RAPIDLY-BUILT WEB APPLICATION THAT ALREADY HAS A STRONG INPUT VALIDATION MODULE

Background	An entrepreneurial micro business has developed a web product to help financial service companies. All web application functionality requires the users to be authenticated. There are no public parts of the application except for the log in page. The company will publish the web product to market as soon as possible but also needs to demonstrate robust defenses to its customers who will want to perform their own penetration testing. The business's own development team has created a parameter input validation framework that checks every single request's URL, parameter names and parameter values. The web application's entry points are known and are defined in an existing database table which is updated at each release. The team has decided to use AppSensor-like capabilities to warn them about forced browsing to invalid URLs, missing mandatory parameters, the submission of additional or duplicated parameters, and invalid parameter value data types. Note that additional input validation exists, but initially this will not be linked into the attack detection and response system. Just URL, parameter names and value data types.
Objectives	1. Immediately identify any non-normal use of the application 2. Slow down an attack using compromised user credentials.
Detection points	The detection points only need to be added within the existing global input validation module. The detection points selected are shown below. All exist within the application code. | Area	ID	Scope	Detection Description	AppSensor Refs
---	---	---	---	---
Request	*i*	Every request	Invalid URL	ACE3, IE2
	ii	Every request	Invalid parameter names	RE5, RE6
	iii	Every request	Invalid parameter value type	RE8, IE2	 *i* also occurs for "404 not found" responses.
Response actions and thresholds	All events share the same response. Thresholds are all one (i.e. immediately, so there is no need to undertake counts over time periods). Only one SMS alert will be sent per request/response cycle (i.e. not per parameter). 	ID (from above)	Threshold	Response Description	AppSensor Refs
---	---	---	---
i, ii, iii	Any 1 event	Log out authenticated user and send SMS alert to the dev-ops team	ASR-J, ASR-B	 This will require the ability to: • Initiate a response for each detection point event • Terminate user sessions, log out users, and send SMS alerts • Whitelist certain IP addresses to suppress the response actions (e.g. external vulnerability scanner, the company's own penetration testers).

Chapter 6 : Case Study of a Magazine's Mobile App

An implementation that takes into account mobile-specific risks.

Table 4 PROPERTIES FOR THE CASE STUDY OF A MAGAZINE'S MOBILE APP TO IDENTIFY AUTHENTICATION ATTACKS, ACCOUNT-SHARING AND BLATANT XSS ATTEMPTS

Background	A well-respected business magazine has developed a new mobile application with a native front end to support the needs of it's existing client base as well as reach new customers. Most application functionality requires the users to be authenticated, which is undertaken via server-side components. There is a small public portion of the application that shows a portal-style page with headlines from the top stories.
	This is the first mobile application written by the internal development team. The team is made up of a mix of web developers and back-office developers. The business customer has two serious concerns: • Loss of revenue due to users sharing accounts • Loss of readership due to defacement of magazine content. In addition, the development team has another concern: • The authentication and authorization framework used is new to the team since they are accustomed to the typical web session handling (cookie) model, whereas the new model uses access tokens. Authentication will require communication with the magazines internet-facing systems to minimize critical functionality in the application itself. Some magazine content is stored locally on the devices to improve response times. The team has decided to use AppSensor-like capabilities to warn them about account sharing, code injection attempts, and to monitor access to the authentication portion of the application closely.
Objectives	1. Detect attacks against the authentication component; the team intends to start with the authentication component, and add monitoring to the authorization component if necessary in the future 2. Identify account-sharing between users 3. Detect XSS attempts that could lead to defacement.

Table 4 continued...

Part II : Illustrative Case Studies

Detection points	The detection points need to be added to the authentication component and within the existing global input validation module. The detection points selected are shown below. All exist within the application code. Geo-location as a detection point has to be used carefully. There are many use cases where geo-location may change for a completely valid reason. | Area	ID	Scope	Detection Description	AppSensor Refs
---	---	---	---	---
Authentic ation	i	Every auth attempt	Use of Multiple Usernames	AE1
	ii	Every auth attempt	Multiple Failed Passwords	AE2
	iii	Every auth attempt	High Rate of Login Attempts	AE3
	iv	Every auth attempt	Utilization of Common Usernames	AE12
	v	Every auth attempt	Deviation from normal geo-location	AE13
Request	vi	Every server request	Cross-site scripting (XSS) attempt	IE1
Local cache	vii	Every cache read	Data integrity fault	IE4	
Response actions and thresholds	The thresholds are set high enough to ensure the activity is likely malicious, and so the responses are more strict. Detection points monitoring events occurring at the magazine's servers have more authority than events detected locally on the device hosting the app. 	ID (from above)	Threshold	Response Description	AppSensor Refs
---	---	---	---
i, ii, iii, iv	Any 10 events	Alert operations staff	ASR-B
	Any 25 events	Block IP address (and customer account if known) for whole site (manual reset by operational administrator)	ASR-L, ASR-K
v	Any 1 event within 1 hour of previous access	Notify user of invalid usage, log user out	ASR-E, ASR-J
	Any 5 events within 1 month	Block IP address (and customer account if known) for whole site (manual reset by operational administrator)	ASR-L, ASR-K
vi	1 event	Block request	ASR-G
	Any 3 events	Log user out	ASR-J
	Any 6 events by user and/or individual IP address	Block IP address (and customer account if known) for app (manual reset by operational administrator)	ARS-L, ASR-K
vii	Any 3 events	Alert operations staff	ASR-B	 Non singular event thresholds refer to per user rolling 24 hour periods unless specified otherwise. This will require the ability to: - Notify the operations staff via email/SMS - Perform blocking of IP addresses - Verify a user's geo-location at a high level (maybe accurate within 200-300 miles).

Chapter 7 : Case Study of a Smart Grid Consumer Meter

Gas and electricity smart meters are beginning to replace traditional meters. These allow remote usage monitoring and configuration, and can offer some benefits to both the supplier and consumer.

Table 5   PROPERTIES FOR THE CASE STUDY OF A SMART GRID CONSUMER METER FOR THE DETECTION OF ATTEMPTED AND ACTUAL TAMPERING.

Background	Remote connectivity may use an embedded SIM card to connect with a mobile network provider, or in the case of broadband-connected home, utilize the existing WiFi connection. Customers often have concerns about privacy, confidentiality of data, difficulties in changing their supplier, and health due to the use of mobile phone and WiFi technology.
	Mobile technicians connect to smart meters using an infrared optical port which is more reliable in the many different locations that the meters can be installed in. The technicians use security codes to authenticate and then may alter the configuration or collect information. The long, highly random, security codes could be identified by brute force and dictionary attacks.
	Identical functionality is available remotely, but the optical port is much more exposed.
Objectives	1. Identify attacks against authentication functions 2. Detect other extremely unusual activity.
Detection points	The detection points must be built in to the meter's logic.

Area	ID	Scope	Detection Description	AppSensor Refs
Optical port	i	Every auth attempt	>10 attempts per minute	AE3
	ii	Every auth attempt	6 failed security codes	AE2
Configuration	iii	Each access	Updated	UT1
Configuration	iv	Every flash image	Update received	-
Communications	v	Each outbound connection	Connection made to unapproved destination	IE2
Cover	vi	Enclosure opened	Physical tamper switch to detect enclosure removal	RP2

Response actions and thresholds	The automated response actions must not disrupt consumers' supplies under any circumstance. Logging an alert messages to the supplier's head-end systems are the only response actions.

ID (from above)	Threshold	Response Description	AppSensor Refs
(All)	1 event	Log locally	ASR-A
i, ii, iii, v	Any 3 events	Alert message to head-end system with copy of configuration and recent log items	ASR-B
iv, v	1 event	Alert message to head-end system	ASR-B

These require local logging and alert message signaling capabilities. Non singular event thresholds refer to rolling 24 hour periods. No more than one alert message to be sent in any 60 minute period.

Part II : Illustrative Case Studies

Chapter 8 : Case Study of a Financial Market Trading System

An example of detection capabilities for misuse of inherent application functionality.

Table 6   PROPERTIES FOR THE CASE STUDY OF A FINANCIAL MARKET TRADING SYSTEM FOR THE DETECTION OF COLLUSION BETWEEN TRADERS.

Background	The operator of a financial trading tool is concerned about collusion between buyers, between sellers, and between buyers and sellers. They may attempt to manipulate prices to inflate them, perform insider trading, and undertake accommodation trading.
	The company cannot track user-to-user communications through other channels (e.g. instant messaging, telephone, email and SMS) but has complete insight into the activities undertaken using a client-server software application developed internally.
	By building detection capabilities directly into the software application, it reduces the requirement for centralized collection, logging and complex event analysis.
Objectives	1. Detect signs of collusion for further investigation 2. User-specific monitoring but must take into account the actions of other users.
Detection points	All detection points are related to trading activities. Detection point *iii* requires an examination of multiple group relationships to identify similar patterns.

Area	ID	Scope	Detection Description	AppSensor Refs
Trading	*i*	Every trade	Unexpectedly low price	-
	ii	Every trade	Unexpectedly high price	-
	iii	Every trade	Similar actions taken by pairs or groups of users	-
	iv	Every trade	High trading speed	UT2
	v	Every trade	Unexpected trading pattern	UT4

	Many other types of fraud detection could be implemented in a similar in-application manner.
Response actions and thresholds	No disruption to trading is permitted. All actions are recorded to an audit trail.

ID (from above)	Threshold	Response Description	AppSensor Refs
i, ii, iv	Any 10 events	Alert anti fraud team	ASR-B
iii, v	1	Alert anti fraud team	ASR-B

The thresholds can be adjusted on a per-user basis so that suspected misbehavior can be watched more closely. The compliance team also review the event data periodically.

Chapter 9 : Case Study of a B2C Ecommerce Website

This example illustrates an initial standalone implementation where the development team have embedded the detection points into their own business-to-consumer (B2C) ecommerce website source code.

Table 7   PROPERTIES FOR THE CASE STUDY OF A B2C ECOMMERCE WEBSITE

Background	The retailer's ecommerce channel accounts for 25% of their turnover. The website is comprised primarily of a product catalogue, shopping basket and check-out system, customers must register to check-out and pay, but can then also manage their accounts, submit reviews and take part in focus group discussions. The website is custom built and maintained in-house. The application has been through a number of recent revisions to remove identified vulnerabilities. There are no centralized input validation and exception handling modules.
Objectives	1. Identify generic attacks as soon as possible so they can be monitored. 2. Detect specific attacks against the custom logic in the product catalogue, shopping basket, checkout and payment functions 3. Identify attacks against database content.
Detection points	In this initial implementation, the development team want to limit the number of detection points to less than ten, albeit some of these will occur in multiple instances. For example all requests will have some generic blacklist detection points, and all database query results sets will be validated against expected record count ranges (e.g. always none, always one, 2-10, 11-100 and 101+). The detection points selected are shown below. All exist within the application code, except for the last one (*ix*) which is implemented as triggers in the database that initiate a special web service call to the application. There are no site-wide (all user) thresholds. | Area	ID	Scope	Detection Description	AppSensor Refs
---	---	---	---	---
Request	*i*	Every request	Invalid/incorrect HTTP verb	RE1, RE2, RE3, RE4
	ii	Every request	SQL injection attempt	CIE1
	iii	Every request	Cross-site scripting (XSS) attempt	IE1
Catalogue	*iv*	Product display	Product value mismatch	IE4
Basket	*v*	Basket handling	Basket value mismatch	IE4
Payment	*vi*	Payment authorization	Card authorization failure	(Custom)
	vii	Order completion	Price mismatch between order & payment	IE4
Database	*viii*	Every SELECT query	Returned record set size incorrect	CIE2
	ix	-	Database table integrity fault	IE5	 The events are recorded in a database application log table.

Table 7 continued...

Part II : Illustrative Case Studies

Response actions and thresholds	The response actions were selected to block blatant abusers of the site and use alerting to operations staff for most other detected events. Threshold comparisons (per IP address and per user) will only include events in the previous 24 hours.		

ID (from above)	Threshold	Response Description	AppSensor Refs
i, ii, iii	Any 1 event	Block request	ASR-G
	Any 3 events by user	Log out authenticated user	ASR-J
	Any 6 events by user or and individual IP address	Block IP address (and customer account if known) for whole site (manual reset by website administrator)	ASR-L, ASR-K
iv, v	Either 1 event	Alert operations staff	ASR-B
	Any 2 events	Block IP address for dynamic areas (1 day auto-reset)	ASR-I
vi	3 events	Alert operations staff, and redirect back to shopping basket summary	ASR-B, ASR-G
vii	1 event	Alert operations staff, put order on hold, and block future order check-out for the customer (manual reset)	ASR-B, ASR-D, ASR-I
viii	1 event	Alert operations staff, abort the current process, display an error page, and block the customer account (manual reset)	ASR-B, ASR-G, ASR-E, ASR-K
ix	1 event	Alert DBA and operations staff	ASR-B
(All)	1 event	Increase application logging granularity and indicate on monitoring dashboard	ASR-A, ASR-C

This will require the ability to:

- Count detection points events for each threshold per IP address, and per user, and do this for every request
- Change application logging level, raise alerts to operations staff, change the status of an order, terminate website user sessions, redirect responses, block individual requests, disable check-out functionality for individual users, block access to the whole website for an IP address and for individual IP addresses, reset blocks
- Display events on a monitoring dashboard.

Chapter 10 : Case Study of B2B Web Services

AppSensor applied to a system that has a small number of strongly authenticated (system) user accounts.

Table 8 PROPERTIES FOR THE CASE STUDY OF B2B WEB SERVICES

Background	A manufacturer exposes selected suppliers to its acquisition systems via web services.
	The permitted web service request source locations are controlled by network firewall rules which are monitored and which have robust change control processes. Additionally customers must have a current, valid and non-revoked X.509 certificate.
	Security requirements were defined at the start of the implementation of the services, and were verified during design reviews, static code analysis (code review), dynamic testing. An independent specialist security company undertakes penetration testing at each release. There is ongoing external and internal vulnerability assessment scanning daily.
	Suppliers have strict security obligations placed on them and their development processes. However, the manufacturer is concerned about misuse of the web services by a rogue insider within any of the supplier organizations.
Objectives	1. Block clearly malicious requests to allow time for further investigation.
Detection points	The detection points are primarily built into the application's input validation module, but detection points *i* and *ii* rely on an internal logging module. Checking the result of the XML parser *vi* is a separate output validation step that had to be added.

Area	ID	Scope	Detection Description	AppSensor Refs
Requests	*i*	Every request	Invalid API entry point	ACE3, IE2
	ii	Every request	High rate requests	UT2
XML parsing	*iii*	Every request	Does not match schema	IE4
	iv	Every request	Invalid signature	IE4
	v	Every request	Invalid values/attributes	IE2
	vi	Every request	Parser error returned	CIE2

Response actions and thresholds	Suppliers are not allowed access to the production systems until their methods of interaction have been tested and approved. The threshold before response is therefore strict.

ID (from above)	Threshold	Response Description	AppSensor Refs
(All)	Any 3 events	Terminate request, log user out, lock user account, raise syslog event, and send email alert to service owner and operations team	ASR-G, ASR-J, ASR-K, ASR-C, ASR-B

The threshold comparison reviews all events in the previous 7 day period.

Part II : Illustrative Case Studies

Chapter 11 : Case Study of a Document Management System

AppSensor applied to an internal client-server application containing very sensitive information, which could affect national security if compromised.

Table 9 PROPERTIES FOR THE CASE STUDY OF A DOCUMENT MANAGEMENT SYSTEM

Background	A government agency gathers a large amount of information from disparate sources and stores this in a document management system, which is only available to known, strongly-authenticated users on an internal private network. The information is tagged with a custom classification system and access rights are strictly enforced. However, the agency is still concerned with the amount of data and the possibility of rogue employees going beyond the needs of their assigned work, mining the data for personal gain, or on behalf of organized crime or other nation states. The agency is confident in the authentication and authorization security controls enforced in the document management system, but have decided to add AppSensor functionality to detect suspicious usage of valid functionality.
Objectives	1. Monitor users behavior 2. Identify suspicious usage.
Detection points	The detection points are added into the access control library. | Area	ID	Scope	Detection Description	AppSensor Refs
---	---	---	---	---
Access Control	i	Every document access request	Rate of document access	UT2
	ii	Every search	Frequency of use	UT4
	iii	Every document display	Frequency of use	UT4	 The agency has identified a potential detection point external to the application – an existing data loss prevention (DLP) system – but have decided to implement that in a later phase. The events are logged to a high-integrity database.
Response actions and thresholds	Only responses that are transparent to the employee are implemented. The 	ID (from above)	Threshold	Response Description	AppSensor Refs
---	---	---	---
i	48 per hour	Alert operations staff	ASR-B
ii, iii	+1,000% over 5 d	Alert security staff	ASR-B	 Once the DLP integration is undertaken, it is intended use disabling of functionality (ASR-I) when an attack is detected to limit the impact as much as possible.

Chapter 12 : Case Study of a Credit Union's Online Banking

A statistical approach applied to customer-facing banking web applications where there was a significant concern regarding malware-infected customer desktop and mobile devices.

Table 10   PROPERTIES FOR THE CASE STUDY OF A CREDIT UNION'S ONLINE BANKING

Background	A credit union is redeveloping its online banking systems. It has mature software development practices where security is considered at many stages of the development lifecycle, and has made a significant investment in infrastructure protection. In the redevelopment the credit union wants to take the opportunity to build in advanced attack impact-minimizing techniques to protect the web applications. The primary concerns are customers whose own computers have been compromised by malware (e.g. Citadel, KINS, SpyEye, Zeus), and secondly other fraudulent activity. The credit union maintains data flow diagrams for each business process and has identified all the state-changing steps deemed to be higher risk. This has been complemented by an analysis of known web security incidents from other banks[77] in order to define placement of detection points that can feed event information into an existing fraud prevention analysis engine, developed by the credit union's statisticians and actuaries, but which currently lacks the user and context specific information available from the online customer systems.
Objectives	1. Detect early signs of attacks 2. React in order to minimize the impact of the attack.
Detection points	Request detection points are numerous and are of two main types; these are complemented by reputational data from other internal and external anti-fraud systems.

Area	ID	Scope	Detection Description	AppSensor Refs
Request	-	Every request	Usage of a process step	UT1
	-	Every request	Per-request token integrity check	IE4
	-	Every request	Known trojanized browser attack	IE3
Reputation	-	Every request	Address, IP and card blacklists	RP2
	-	Each session	Customer profiling	RP2
	-	Each session	Third party fraud scoring	RP2

The events are sent to the centralized fraud analysis engine that uses a highly customized stochastic model to identify malicious behavior. In this case, the events recorded are not only misuse, but also per-user usage patterns.

Response actions and thresholds	The response action is determined in real time at each and every detection point activation whether to allow the process to continue, or to perform some other action.

ID (from above)	Threshold	Response Description	AppSensor Refs
(All)	(Probabilistic)	Proceed	ASR-P
		Proceed but track	ASR-A, ASR-D
		Prevent transaction	ASR-G
		Log user out	ASR-J
		Flag for further investigation	ASR-C
		Redirect customer to free AV	ASR-E

Part II : Illustrative Case Studies

Part III : Making It Happen

This section describes the process of planning, implementing and operating application-specific attack detection and response. The process is technology agnostic and attempts to be descriptive rather than prescriptive, providing awareness, describing the problem set, outlining different approaches at a higher level, and some generic approaches. Success comes down to many details and the process should be adapted to an organization's own culture, its working practices and, most importantly, the risks it faces.

Part III : Making It Happen

Chapter 13 : Introduction

The process to implement AppSensor should not be long and complex, and it is important to focus on a minimal set up that provides sufficient detectability of attacks. There is no need to be overwhelmed by all the attacks possible. Keep in mind AppSensor should not be trying to detect all malicious behavior – AppSensor only needs to detect enough obviously behavior to make a decision about the intent of a user as to whether they are malicious or not.

The previous illustrative case studies in Part II can also be used as short-cut design patterns. Further inspiration is available in *Chapter 1 : Application-Specific Attack Detection & Response - Technique adoption*, and the examples in *Part IV : Demonstration Implementations*. The remaining content of this Part III provides information to build knowledge more about the concepts, to implement a more formal process, to gain a deeper understanding, and to learn from experience gained with actual production implementations.

Process, culture and technology agnostic

In this guide no particular development methodology is required or assumed. The suggested process can be adapted to local methods and culture, and to suit each organization's business processes. For many organizations, the steps can be built into applications through a process of continual improvement and are well-suited to Agile methodologies.

The methodology described here does not identify which technologies should be used. If in doubt, initially teams should use what they know best and are familiar with.

Begin with a pilot application

Organizations thinking about AppSensor often begin with a pilot application to learn the techniques and build up attack detection skills. This is sometimes an internal application only used by developers or created as a proof-of-concept trial. Consider utilizing non-disruptive response actions only and log everything. However, do give consideration to the issues raised in the remainder of this Part III to help ensure a successful, and extensible, pilot.

Suggested method

Part I described how real-time detection and response to be built into applications. Whenever possible, AppSensor capabilities should be defined in project requirements from an early stage, but software can also be refactored or its capabilities enhanced. The additional coding should be subject to the same secure development process as another other software changes. This includes risk analysis, design, code review, testing, operational enablement, etc.

The recommended approach is to include the following aspects within the organization's own software development practices, in whatever way they are structured, ordered and practiced:

- Design
    - Strategic requirements
    - Detection point selection
    - Response action selection
    - Threshold definition
- Implementation
- Verification
- Deployment
- Operation.

This method leads to the creation of requirements, user stories and test cases. For more formal development practices and for procurement documentation, further reference materials may be required such as schedules of detection points, thresholds and responses.

AppSensor and security in the software development life cycle

If organizations already have, or are in the process of building, a comprehensive programme[60],[61] to include security throughout the development life cycle (SDLC), considerations for AppSensor should be addressed in the same program.

Some more common secure SDLC (S-SDLC) are cross-referenced in the four tables below. The mappings indicate where the use of AppSensor is likely to require changes to existing application security practices. At the time of writing this version of the AppSensor Guide the relatively new ISO/IEC 27034[50] is neither complete nor mature enough to provide a similar cross-reference.

Of course, these illustrative mapping are not the only activities that are needed to develop secure software – a requirement before even considering AppSensor (see *Part I : AppSensor Overview - Chapter 3 : The AppSensor Approach - Stop! Develop and operate secure applications first*).

Part III : Making It Happen

The most relevant activities from the Open Software Assurance Maturity Model (Open SAMM)[41] version 1.0, that align with aspects for using AppSensor, are shown in the table below:

Table 11 APPSENSOR ASPECTS MAPPED TO OPEN SAMM ACTIVITIES

AppSensor Aspect	OWASP Open SAMM Function	Security Practice	Activity Code and Description
Design	Governance	Policy & Compliance	PC 1.A Build and maintain compliance guidelines
			PC 2.A Build policies and standards for security and compliance
		Education & Guidance	EG 1.B Build and maintain technical guidelines
	Construction	Threat Assessment	TA 1.A Build and maintain application-specific threat models
			TA 1.B Develop attacker profile from software architecture
			TA 2.A Build and maintain abuse-case models per project
			TA 3.B Elaborate threat models with compensating controls
		Security Requirements	SR 1.A Derive security requirements from business functionality
			SR 1.B Evaluate security and compliance guidance for requirements
			SR 2.A Build an access control matrix for resources and capabilities
			SR 2.B Specify security requirements based on known risks
			SR 3.A Build security requirements into supplier agreements
		Security Architecture	SA 1.B Explicitly apply security principles to design
			SA 2.B Identify security design patterns from architecture
			SA 3.A Establish formal reference architectures and platforms
	Verification	Design Review	DR 1.A Identify software attack surface
Implementation	Governance	Policy & Compliance	PC 2.B Establish project audit practice
Verification	Construction	Security Architecture	SA 3.B Validate usage of frameworks, patterns, and platforms
	Verification	Design Review	DR 1.B Analyze design against known security requirements
			DR 2.A Inspect for complete provision of security mechanisms
		Security Testing	ST 1.A Derive test cases from known security requirements
Deployment	Deployment	Vulnerability Management	VM 1.B Create informal security response teams
			VM 2.A Establish consistent incident response process
		Operational Enablement	OE 1.A Capture critical security information for deployment
			OE 1.B Document procedures for typical application alerts
Operation	Deployment	Environment Hardening	EH 1.A Maintain operational environment specification
			EH 3.A Identify and deploy relevant operations protection tools
		Operational Enablement	OE 2.B Maintain formal operational security guides

The most relevant activities from the Building Security In Maturity Model (BSIMM)[57] version 6, that align with aspects for using AppSensor, are shown in the table on the following page.

Table 12 APPSENSOR ASPECTS MAPPED TO BSIMM ACTIVITIES

AppSensor Aspect	BSIMM Domain	Practice	Activity Code and Description	
Design	Governance	Strategy and Metrics	SM1.6	Require security sign-off
		Compliance and Policy	CP1.3	Create policy
			CP2.3	Implement and track controls for compliance
			CP2.4	Paper all vendor contracts with software security SLAs
			CP3.2	Impose policy on vendors
	Intelligence	Attack Models	AM1.1	Build and maintain a top N possible attacks list
			AM1.3	Identify potential attackers
			AM1.4	Collect and publish potential attack stories
			AM2.1	Build attack patterns and abuse cases tied to potential attackers
			AM2.2	Create technology-specific attack patterns
		Security Features and Design	SFD1.2	Engage SSG with architecture
			SFD3.1	Form a review board or central committee to approve and maintain secure design patterns
		Standards and Requirements	SR1.1	Create security standards
			SR1.3	Translate compliance constraints to requirements
			SR2.2	Create a standards review board
			SR2.5	Create SLA boilerplate
			SR3.2	Communicate standards to vendors
Implementation	Intelligence	Security Features and Design	SFD1.1	Build and publish security features
	SSDL Touchpoints	Architecture Analysis	AA1.1	Perform security feature review
			AA1.2	Perform design review for high-risk applications
Verification	SSDL Touchpoints	Architecture Analysis	AA2.1	Define and use AA process
		Code Review	CR2.2	Enforce coding standards
		Security Testing	ST1.1	Ensure QA supports edge/boundary value condition testing
			ST1.3	Drive tests with security requirements and security features
			ST3.5	Begin to build and apply adversarial security tests (abuse cases)
Deployment	Deployment	Software Environment	SE2.2	Publish installation guides
		Configuration Mgmt and Vulnerability Mgmt	CMVM1.1	Create or interface with incident response
Operation	Governance	Compliance and Policy	CP3.3	Drive feedback from SDLC data back to policy
	Intelligence	Attack Models	AM1.5	Gather attack intelligence
	Deployment	Software Environment	SE1.1	Use application input monitoring
			SE3.3	Use application behaviour monitoring and diagnostics
		Configuration Mgmt and Vulnerability Mgmt	CMVM1.2	Identify software defects found in operations monitoring and feed them back to development
			CMVM3.3	Simulate software crisis

Part III : Making It Happen

The high-level areas from the BITS Financial Services Roundtable Software Assurance Framework[45] January 2012 version, that align with aspects for using AppSensor, are shown in the table below.

Table 13 APPSENSOR ASPECTS MAPPED TO BITS SOFTWARE ASSURANCE FRAMEWORK AREAS

AppSensor Aspect	BITS Framework Area
Design	Threat Modelling
Implementation	Security Software Assurance Development Standard
	Coding Practices
Verification	Security Testing
Deployment	Pre-Implementation Practices
Operation	Post Implementation Phase Controls

The high-level processes from Microsoft Security Development Lifecycle (MS SDL)[55] Process Guidance version 5.2, that align with aspects for using AppSensor, are shown in the table below:

Table 14 APPSENSOR ASPECTS MAPPED TO MS SDL PROCESSES

AppSensor Aspect	MS SDL Phase	Process
Design	Requirements	Establish security requirements
		Security and privacy risk assessment
	Design	Analyze attack surface
		Threat modelling
Implementation	-	-
Verification	Verification	Attack surface review
Deployment	Release	Incident response plan
Operation	Response	Execute incident response plan

Next steps

The following two chapters describe the most typical AppSensor implementations. The following chapters can also be read to provide additional ideas and considerations for a more formal approach and/or complex AppSensor deployment.

Implementation issues are also discussed in the comparative research and experiment undertaken independently by Pål Thomassen "AppSensor: Attack-Aware Applications Compared Against a Web Application Firewall and an Intrusion Detection System"[33]. This paper also includes a large number of useful references for further reading.

Chapter 14 : Design and Implementation

The design stage includes identifying strategic considerations, sensor selection and positioning, and determination of the appropriate type of response to block or mitigate attacks based on an analysis of business risk, process criticality and user experience requirements.

Management support

The implementation of AppSensor should not be undertaken in isolation from other information security initiatives. Consideration should be given to the effects on all users and especially any legal, regulatory and contractual obligations. Clearly low-risk, internal only applications with a small user base may well have many fewer considerations, but even with these aspects like monitoring of staff could be an issue. In all cases the event data is likely to be valuable and could contain intellectual property.

Existing change management processes that include security, privacy and compliance risk assessment should be leveraged to gain management understanding and support. After all, implementing AppSensor should be a success story so give everyone a chance to be part of the success story.

Organizational policy

It is helpful to agree some sort of high-level guidance on what automated actions are deemed to be acceptable – determined by a range of appropriate stakeholders such as business and product managers, development management, software architects, lead developers and legal/compliance officers. The stakeholders could include representatives from human resources, customers or partner organizations depending upon the types of users. This is necessary even if a very Agile development method is used. The "policy" should consider the organization's risk tolerance and the desired user experience (e.g. acceptability of changes to service level and function availability, changes to usability, legality).

Remember "users" are not always people and can be other information systems. The selected response actions will also depend on the purpose of the application such as whether it is a sales channel, a marketing asset, a service for citizens, a high-availability process or safety critical system.

The important point to re-emphasize is that AppSensor-like functionality must never affect normal users. This is quite difficult for conventional defensive mechanisms, and should be straightforward for applications. Therefore any concerns about the effect on (normal) users can often be discounted, to allow the group to focus on what the business considers is unreasonable and at what point it should take action and how. An organization's

Part III : Making It Happen

information security policy and incident response plan may help determine the approach, but often consideration of application response is unlikely to have occurred previously.

A policy is mainly focused on the acceptable responses, but in turn this can help define what type of attack detection is required. Here are some different, and sometimes contradictory, points of view various organizations may have:

- Only allow a few security events that are obviously attacks or several minor events which are just suspicious
- Do not prevent users doing anything, but log, monitor and alert fervently
- Never log out or lock out site administrators, but ensure they are aware of all suspicious and attack events, and know that their own activity is being recorded in tamper-evident audit logs with any AppSensor alerts being sent to their supervisors
- Any two attacks each with more than 75% certainty that it is an attack must log the user out and lock their account immediately, and this can only be reset by two administrators from different locations acting together
- Never disable any functionality
- Authenticated administrators who have access to the most functionality and the greatest data access permissions should have the strictest thresholds before a response action is undertaken
- Active (against the user) responses will only be used for (malicious) users external to the corporate network
- Active responses will only be used for (malicious) users internal to the corporate network
- Application functionality will not be changed unless the user's source location is in a higher-risk country
- Ensure the (malicious) user is oblivious to the response actions being taken
- Nothing must be done which might affect WCAG 2.0 Level AA Conformance
- Public unauthenticated users are the least trusted and should have the most strict thresholds (i.e. lowest number of events before an attack is determined).

Some AppSensor policy requirements can usually be gleaned from existing application requirements. For example, it may be necessary to ensure that the response actions do not:

- Undermine advertising claims about service provision (e.g. capacity, rate of use)
- Contradict the organization's culture, mission or approach
- Contravene contractual obligations such as service level agreements (e.g. uptime)
- Conflict with a corporate policy or other mandate
- Break a regulatory requirement
- Perform any illegal act in the jurisdiction of the application and/or the users.

It can be productive to discuss the examples above in a workshop-style discussion to help define some high-level policies before attempting to specify appropriate detection points, responses and related thresholds. The facilitator should be able to steer the group so that relevant aspects are covered.

Another approach to developing a high-level policy is to work through the main entry points or functionality for the target application(s) and, from the perspective of each user role, write some general rules for response that are allowed and appropriate. Take into consideration the effect the response actions might have on users and other systems, as well as the particular application. At this stage it is better to focus less on technical issues such as "how do we do this", and more on user experience and business risk viewpoints.

Try to define 10-15 rules that apply to all users. However it is likely there will be demands for greater granularity in the response actions, and architects and developers may want to allow for this in their specifications and designs.

Architecture

Another factor in what is achievable using AppSensor is how the functionality can be implemented. The architecture of the target application(s), environments, and availability of source code all influence what is possible. Code can be completely custom-built or it could consume demonstration code produced for the OWASP AppSensor Project. For a new application, AppSensor functionality can be defined in requirements documentation for in-house (e.g. functional specifications) or out-sourced development using an invitation to tender (ITT), request for proposal (RFP), functional specification associated with a draft contract, etc.

The key components required are:

- Detection points within the execution path of an application's program that allows event generation when a tracked observable occurrence takes place
- Event store to record events
- Event analysis engine that analyses incoming event data to determine whether an attack is taking place, based on a specified policy (of detection point activity and related time-dependent thresholds)
- Event manager that monitors the event analysis engine for any appropriate response actions to execute
- Responses taken as the result of attack recognition
- Reporting client for presentation of data stored in the event analysis engine.

The detection points generally need to be located within the application code base, and where there are existing modules performing centralized input valid and output validation, this can reduce the impact of additional code. In certain cases there may be sufficient event

Part III : Making It Happen

information in application logs, and those could be used for attack determination by an event analysis engine. But the use of existing logs alone is unusual and if the granularity of event information is so good, the detection points probably already exist.

Attack determination logic will need to be developed. This would typically be in local code, using a standalone service engine or using some form of events and log management system such as for Security Information Event Management (SIEM), threat information store, other continuous monitoring systems, or fraud detection systems. If source code is not available or cannot be changed, consider whether application logs can be used as a source of event data – but these are not normally adequate. Otherwise consideration could be given to externalizing the detection to a proxy (e.g. a proxy such as a web application firewall, filter or guard). For more inspiration see the example implementations in *Part IV : Demonstration Implementations*.

When an application is deployed using multiple hosts and there is a centralized analysis engine, consideration about how events from multiple hosts are aggregated, correlated and analyzed.

Where necessary, integration with other systems must be considered as early as possible. These may include:

- Network firewalls and used for blocking response actions
- Intermediate network points (e.g. local stations, aggregators, collectors, proxies, traffic and load balancers)
- Application firewalls as detection points and/or response actions
- Electronic mail and other messaging systems for alerts
- Systems providing information as reputational detection points
- Related applications as detection points
- Security vulnerability information, reporting, virtual patching[78,79] and related management systems
- Other operational logging, monitoring and management information systems.

For inter-system communication, ensure there is adequate system identification assurance and that sufficient protection exists for the confidentiality and integrity of messages.

Detection point selection

A full list of example detection points is included in *Table 30* in *Part VI : Reference Materials - Detection Points - Listing*. At first consider implementing just 5-10 detection points for most applications. In many cases a "single" detection point could actually monitor many different URLs (e.g. input validation exception in a centralized module that checks every parameter name and value). In other cases a single generic type of detection point may need to have multiple specific instances (e.g. validating the output of database queries).

The six best detection point types

Detection points for the following six types of event are considered to be very good attack identifiers and should be considered first:

- Authorization failures (e.g. resource or action requested with insufficient privileges)
- Client-side input validation bypass (e.g. data format mismatch or missing mandatory values)
- Whitelist input validation failures (e.g. invalid data type or data length/range)
- Authentication failures (e.g. password change failures, re-authentication failure)
- Blatant code injection attack (e.g. common SQL injection strings)
- High rate of function use (e.g. requests/pages/views/windows per 5 minutes).

Part II : Illustrative Case Studies provides additional inspiration for detection points. Many additional ideas for detection point selection are provided in *Chapter 16 : Advanced Detection Points*.

Document the aims and requirements of each detection point selected, like any other software requirement.

Thresholds and responses

If possible, begin implementation of AppSensor in areas of the application where users are already authenticated such as customers, clients, colleagues or citizens. By default, use the following attack detection thresholds:

- 3 events due by any detection points activated by a single user in a 24 hour period
- 6 events due by any detection points activated by a single user in a 4 hour period

And, initially perhaps only consider the following responses:

- Account log out
- Account lock out for a fixed time period
- Administrator notification

The thresholds and actions can then be combined. For example:

- If any 3 detection points are activated in 24 hours, create a support event ticket and send an email alert to operations team
- If any 6 detection point are activated in 4 hours, log the user out and lock the account for 2 hours

To begin with operate only with alert responses until the number of such situations becomes known and confirmed that it does not affect any normal application usage.

Part II : Illustrative Case Studies shows other thresholds and responses. Many additional ideas and considerations are provided in *Chapter 17 : Advanced Thresholds*, where the use of existing application functionality for responses is also discussed.

Planning for operation

In whatever way the threshold and response selection are implemented, ensure they can be easily customized through future configuration changes rather than code modification. Example alterations that should be allowed for are:

- Amending an existing attack detection threshold (e.g. the number of events and/or the time period)
- Amending the response action of an existing threshold (e.g. to another one or more supported actions)
- Adding new thresholds across single, all or any group of detection points (e.g. any N events across detection points A and B only in period P)
- Deleting an attack detection threshold.

It may also be necessary to clear or reset all event data. Some broader questions to consider when considering the implementation are:

- Should there be an option to overrule all responses so that they log only?
- Could this "log only" option for certain source locations (e.g. an IP address) which applies to only certain strongly authenticated users and is of limited time duration, raises administrative alerts when set, removed or expires, and includes a process for management approval?
- Can AppSensor data be exported into risk management and vulnerability management systems?
- Can AppSensor data be exported in real time to security integration manager (SIM) systems?

An AppSensor implementation that detects attacks in real time is likely to cause significant difficulties for functional and security testing. The "log only" concept mentioned above could be utilized for these situations. Further considerations are discussed in the advanced discussions in *Chapter 16 : Advanced Detection Points* and *Chapter 17 : Advanced Thresholds*.

Implementation

Altering existing code always introduces risks, and future maintainability must be considered. Where possible build for an extensible architecture so that the minimum amount of effort is used for changes to other applications or during the design and implementation of AppSensor for new applications. Consider if a service-orientated approach can be designed, such as illustrated in the example implementation described in *Chapter 20 : Web Services (AppSensor WS)*.

The implementation is always application, framework, language, deployment and architecture specific. The detection points are usually highly integrated within the application, but the event store, event analysis engine, attack detection and response selection may be less so. The types of response actions chosen may mean changes to the application code unless they are all externalized (e.g. to network devices).

For all code modifications, ensure these follow the same software development life cycle practices as other application code, including secure coding practices. In particular, assume tuning of all settings and thresholds will be required. Develop test cases or unit tests for each detection point, threshold activation and response.

For outsourced development, identify who owns code and any intellectual property.

Threshold and response selection configuration settings must have sufficient protection to prevent them being modified by the application itself or by unauthorized users. Consider restricting knowledge about the precise detection points and configuration.

Part III : Making It Happen

Chapter 15 : Verification, Deployment and Operation

Introduction

This chapter looks at the key steps for a successful deployment of AppSensor to a production environment.

Verification

Like for all software development, ensure AppSensor's correct implementation is verified (the correct detection points are activated, event data are recorded, attack detection occurs as planned and the correct responses take place) through the use of testing processes in development, in QA, at deployment, at launch and periodically thereafter. AppSensor is part of the application's codebase. If possible unit tests be created during the specification or design stages, but a mixture of approaches is recommended:

- Unit tests written for the AppSensor functionality
- Using example attacks
- Running an application security scanner against the application
- Mimicking the behavior of desirable search engine robots
- Replaying actual valid application traffic (if existing).

AppSensor functionality should be included in integration and system test plans. Any settings that can be used to change or override AppSensor behavior (e.g. to set all actions to "log only") must also be tested.

It is also useful to have AppSensor enabled during usability testing so that any concerns about the impact on normal application usage can be addressed, and evidence gathered to document these concerns to be unwarranted.

Do not attempt to verify AppSensor by testing the implementation with known one-shot attacks (e.g. exploits of known weaknesses). Fix the issue instead, or otherwise mitigate it. AppSensor does not protect vulnerable applications. Its purpose is not to detect every attack possible, but only to detect enough to identify a user as an attacker, and then respond in an appropriate manner.

Deployment

Utilize existing change control processes for deployment. Build in time to allow tuning of the system, especially to configure response thresholds. AppSensor event timestamps must be synchronized with trusted time sources to allow cross-system event correlation and to support incident investigations. Additional defenses in production environments may change or could mask information that would be identified as malicious events by the

AppSensor detection points. Therefore, re-run verification checks to ensure the deployed application responds in the same manner as in non-production systems.

Operation

Logging, signaling, monitoring and reporting

Where possible event and attack data should be incorporated into centralized logging and monitoring systems. These data can complement other event logging information from network and host devices.

It is recommended that standards-consistent logging formats are utilized whenever possible. But where nothing exists, or application-specific logs are required. See *Part III : Making It Happen - Chapter 18 : AppSensor and Application Event Logging*.

Signaling may also be required to forward event, attack and response data to other devices such as network firewalls, application firewalls, traffic management devices, and other business systems including management reporting, CRM and correlation engines (e.g. fraud management). Furthermore signaling of information can be used to share attacker data within industry exchanges, or with regulators, or open Computer Emergency Response/Readiness Teams (CERTs).

The data format suitable for signaling is context-specific but for compatibility could use industry and government formats such as one of the following.

- Common event format (CEF)[80]
- The XML schema Incident Object Description Exchange Format (IODEF)[81] and email format X-ARF (Extended Abuse Reporting Format)[82] for sharing computer security incident information by Computer Security Incident Response Teams (CSIRTs)
- Structured Threat Information eXpression (STIX)[83] for cyber threat intelligence information, sponsored by the office of Cybersecurity and Communications at the U.S. Department of Homeland Security
- The schema Cyber Observable eXpression (CybOX)[84] for the specification, capture, characterization, and communication of events or stateful properties that occur in the operational cyber domain, also sponsored by the office of Cybersecurity and Communications at the U.S. Department of Homeland Security
- Industry-specific standards (e.g. ANSI C12.22[85] message services for smart grids, Automated Copyright Notice System[86] for copyright infringement notices)
- Vendor-specific standards (e.g. Vocabulary for Event Recording and Incident Sharing[87] common language for describing security incidents).

The protocol/format selected should be compatible with an organization's own standards and the receiving systems, or allow automated conversion using a filter into such a format. Consideration must be given to the adequate identification of event and attack data sources, and to prevent modification, interception, deletion and replay of data. The sensitivity of data included in the signaled information should also be considered to determine the necessary measures to prevent unauthorized access while in transit and at rest.

Organizations that deploy AppSensor-like capabilities are encouraged to tag event data with the example detection point and response types, so that data has greater future inter-operability.

AppSensor has defined the following formats for signaling:

- Events:
    - JSON – AppSensor Event Format (AEF)
    - AppSensor event data using Common Event Format (CEF)

Attacks and responses may be defined in the future. The syntaxes are enumerated in *Part VI : Reference Materials - Data Signaling Exchange Formats*.

AppSensor event and attack data should arise infrequently in a well-designed and properly verified implementation. Thus the requirements for logging, monitoring and reporting on these data may be different than other sources of security event data:

- Usage by normal users should not generate any event data
- Attack event data has a very high degree of confidence

Consequently there is no need to examine large quantities of data to identify attacks. This alters the requirements for reports and visual dashboards. Combining AppSensor data with other noisier source may mask important information. However, combining data provides a wider view of all types of attack (network, host and application).

Dashboards

By its nature, the high-confidence attack data and application insight available using AppSensor tends to be a different from many other types of security event data. A pure AppSensor-only dashboard for a single application ought to look like the mock-up shown in *Figure 5* below i.e. empty. This is because the actions of normal users, even non-malicious users making mistakes, should not usually be AppSensor events.

Figure 6 illustrates how specific an AppSensor attack determination event should be. And *Figure 7* shows how data could be shared with other applications such as a CRM in real time.

Chapter 19 : AppSensor and PCI DSS for Ecommerce Merchants

Figure 5   AN IMAGINARY APPSENSOR DASHBOARD UNDER NORMAL OPERATIONAL CONDITIONS I.E. BLANK

AppSensor Dashboards > Supplier Portal

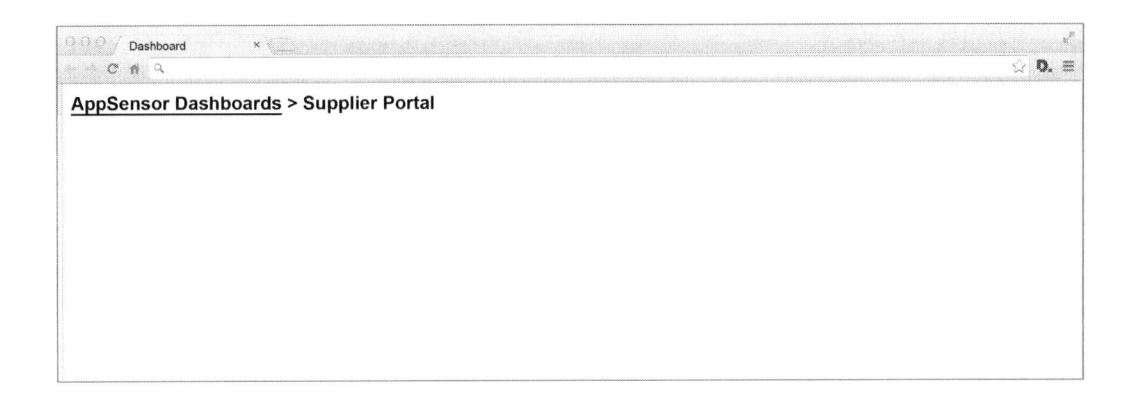

Figure 6   THE IMAGINARY APPSENSOR DASHBOARD WHEN A USER IS IDENTIFIED AS AN ATTACKER

AppSensor Dashboards > Supplier Portal

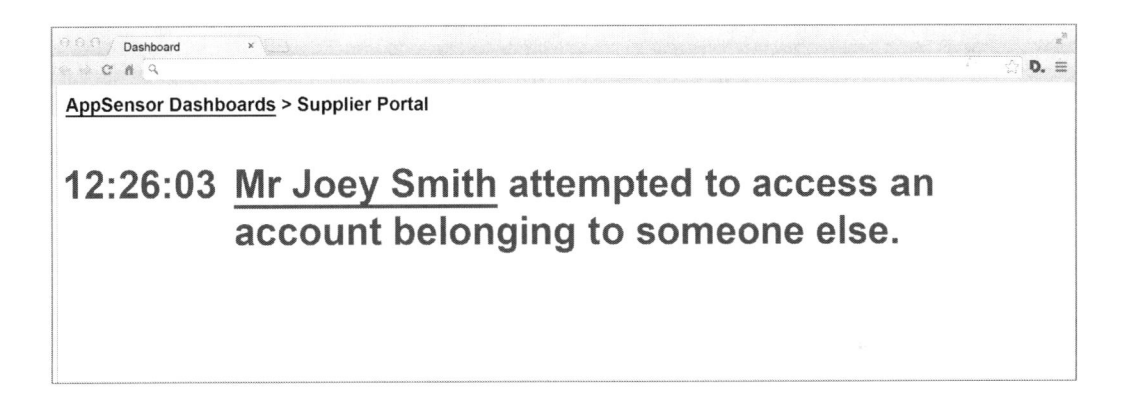

12:26:03 Mr Joey Smith attempted to access an account belonging to someone else.

Figure 7   THE IMAGINARY APPSENSOR DASHBOARD DEMONSTRATING APPSENSOR CROSS-SYSTEM INTEGRATION

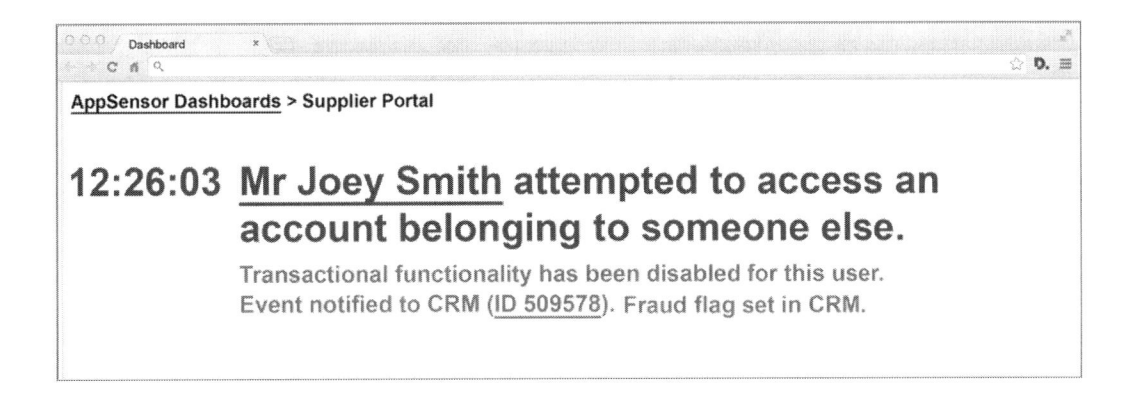

AppSensor Dashboards > Supplier Portal

12:26:03 Mr Joey Smith attempted to access an account belonging to someone else.

Transactional functionality has been disabled for this user.
Event notified to CRM (ID 509578). Fraud flag set in CRM.

These present very clear information and no drill down is required. Actions have already been undertaken automatically to the defined policy. Of course, some ability to view multiple and past events is needed. This is quite different to the usual view of security event dashboards, where large volumes of data need to be aggregated, collated, analyzed and presented in an understandable manner.

However, AppSensor dashboards can be created using the functionality built into popular security event management tools and log visualization tools like Logstash with Kibana, OSSEC with Analogi, Loggly, Solar Winds and Splunk. OWASP does not endorse or recommend any commercial products or services and most products classified as Security (Incident) Event Management (SIEM) systems are also capable of consuming AppSensor event and attack data when suitably formatted and sent. See *Part V : Model Dashboards - Chapter 27 : Security Event Management Tools* for some examples. But as mentioned above, it may be necessary to segregate AppSensor data from the noise of other less-specific event data. Some organizations use AppSensor data primarily to enhance the analysis of other security event data.

Application-specific dashboards rendering AppSensor data have already been created and demonstrated. Furthermore, where event and attack data are being gathered primarily using the ModSecurity web application firewall, or that format has been used to log such data elsewhere, the jwall.org Audit Console[88] or WAF-FLE[89] could be used. For ideas about using these, see *Part V : Model Dashboards*.

Bug, defect and vulnerability tracking systems can also be used to expose knowledge from AppSensor data. See *Part V : Model Dashboards - Chapter 29 : Application Vulnerability Tracking* for further ideas.

Operational tuning

Attack detection thresholds and responses will need to be amended during operation. This may be due to selecting incorrect values during planning, or due to unknown information related to the application and its users, or due to changes in the application's functionality or usage over time. See the advanced discussions in *Chapter 16 : Advanced Detection Points - Optimization* and *Chapter 17 : Advanced Thresholds and Responses - Threshold tuning*.

The work to ensure the thresholds and response configuration can be configured separately from the code will be vital here. All changes must of cause go through relevant risk assessment and change management processes to ensure they do not have an adverse effect on normal users, the security of the application and its data, any compliance or other business mandates. Where possible, real application usage should also be replayed through test systems to assess the changes. Even with complete regression testing of an application, it is still advisable to allow new and updated AppSensor detection points to only use non-disruptive responses initially (e.g. logging changes, alerting administrators), or consider only applying them to a subset of users to confirm the dynamics in production systems.

Review, change control and remodeling

There should be a periodic review of the AppSensor implementation to ensure it is operating correctly. Consideration of AppSensor should be built into change management practices so that software releases do not adversely impact upon AppSensor and that opportunities for additional detection points can be considered.

Control validation

Periodically run AppSensor unit tests against the production environment to ensure the defensive measures are in place, working as expected and that event information flows through to the appropriate operational and management reports.

Incident management

Consider how event and attack data from AppSensor should be incorporated into centralized incident identification and management processes, and update the incident response plan to take into account the automatic actions undertaken by AppSensor. Build AppSensor-sourced events into incident response plan scenarios and tests.

When application security incidents occur, consideration should always be given to how the root cause could have been prevented or the "kill chain" broken. The first reaction should not be to alter AppSensor detection points, thresholds and responses to match a particular attack. It is certainly valid to consider how the incident circumvented all controls, and whether the attacker could have been detected sooner, but the root cause is usually related to activities earlier in the SDLC.

Part III : Making It Happen

Chapter 16 : Advanced Detection Points

Introduction

This chapter examines a more formal approach to the selection and definition of detection points.

Approach

In more advanced AppSensor implementations, the aim should also be for simplicity, not complexity. It is important not to be overwhelmed by the many choices available; the ideas in *Part II : Illustrative Case Studies* show how detections points can be used in practical implementations.

Additional code increases complexity. However if an existing application has already been developed with security built in, obvious locations for detection points are likely to already exist (e.g. input validation, exception handing, logging) and similarly some local response actions may already be being used (e.g. reject the input, ask the user to re-enter text, log the user out, etc).

At first, consider the detection requirements to create an initial model, and then look at how to optimize this model and check it using attack analysis before considering the response actions in *Chapter 17 : Advanced Thresholds and Responses*.

The analysis is suitable both for consideration during procurement, as well as development processes. Outsourced development and services could be asked to implement AppSensor and provide access to the event data.

Inspirational detection points

Many standard example detection points have been documented. The detection point IDs and titles are summarized in *Table 30* in *Part VI : Reference Materials - Detection Points - Listing*. They are also arranged there in various categorizations.

Each example detection point type is described in more detail in the subsequent tables. Some of the terminology, considerations and examples tend to be web application biased due to the significant proportion of software applications that are now delivered in this manner. However, the approaches can be used in many other sorts of architectures and technologies, and just need to be viewed in an alternative manner.

The reputation detection points could be treated in one of two ways.

- Like any other detection point contributing to the count of suspicious events
- Used to alter threshold levels, or associated response actions such as logging level.

The former should be used with caution since they could lead to event data collection where the confidence in knowing these are attack events is reduced.

Detection point requirements

Given the strategic requirements such as a policy and architectural approach (discussed previously), the scope of the application(s) must be understood. Existing applications should have documentation relating to their structure and functionality; these may be some of the artifacts produced during design and/or risk assessment processes. Where possible ensure the following are known:

- The different roles users fall into, and how these are allocated
- All the valid application entry points (e.g. for desktop applications all user interface controls, for web applications whether POST and/or GET should be used and whether SSL/TLS is mandatory, optional or prohibited)
- Which of the entry points change state
- Which users/roles have access to these entry points
- The broad functionality blocks and trust boundaries (e.g. data flow diagrams)
- The various inputs for each entry point (form, URL query string and path parameters, HTTP headers including cookies), and their data types and acceptable values
- Which of the inputs may be manipulated by users and whether the interface for doing that is constrained (e.g. radio buttons and select elements) and whether there is any client-side validation for any of the elements
- Whether there is functionality relating to authentication and session management.

Additionally, access to source code of an existing application can aid detection point selection and positioning, since there will be greater knowledge about data flow and security mechanisms that already exist.

Firstly it is necessary to identify possible (candidate) detection points. The candidate detection points can be selected using application risk classification, threat assessment (e.g. attack surface modeling, threat analysis, misuse/abuse cases, common attack patterns) or combinations of these.

A broad-brush approach to select candidate detection points is to base it solely on the category types most appropriate for various application risk ratings. For example: "All Class X applications will have whitelist input validation detection points". Risk is organization dependent and may change as threats alter. However, this type of approach is not recommended until a number of applications have been "instrumented" so that the organization has sufficient experience, and has been able to adjust the detection points to match its own risk needs. The knowledge can then be applied to target other applications in the organization's portfolio with a similar risk profile. It is a good way to extend a tried and tested approach.

Part III : Making It Happen

The actual threats, possible vulnerabilities and the potential impacts can also be used to select candidate detection points. Remember it is not always the best approach to use AppSensor to detect individual specific attacks - keep in mind the need to look for clearly malicious general behavior (before an actual vulnerability is discovered and an exploit created). In an earlier implementation guide[90] there is a multi-part chart cross-referencing the detection points with two well-known classifications:

- Web Application Security Consortium (WASC) Threat Classification[91]
    - Attacks
    - Weaknesses
- OWASP Top Ten 2010 - The Ten Most Critical Web Application Security Risks.

These can be used with individual application threat assessments and other forms of risk analysis to identify candidate detection points from the standard examples. Consideration should also be given to additional custom detection points for specific business logic threats that have been identified.

The OWASP Cornucopia[92] card game, which helps enumerate security requirements, has cross-references between the requirements, AppSensor detection points and other information sources.

Further ideas can be found in the recent book "Web Application Defender's Cookbook: Battling Hackers and Protecting Users"[93] which discusses how ModSecurity can be used to protect applications.

Model creation

Once there is a list of candidate detection points, they should be specified further to define:

- Purpose
- General statement of its functionality
- Details of any prerequisites
- Related detection points.

The examples and considerations in the schedule of example detection points (*Part VI : Reference Materials*) can be used as a guide here. Each application may require multiple versions of the same detection point e.g. IE3 whitelist validation of parameter names, IE3 whitelist validation of IP addresses, etc.

For each point begin a specification sheet like the examples in *Figure 38* and *Figure 39* in *Part VI : Reference Materials - Detection Points - Detection point specification sheets*. These should identify the AppSensor identity code and the more specific purpose for the particular application.

The "Series" number in the figures will be used as the starting point numbering for sequential numbering of each detection point instance e.g. IE1-1001, IE1-1002, etc. It is possible to have identical AppSensor detection point identity codes (e.g. IE1) but with different purposes (e.g. the whitelist is source IP addresses rather than parameter values) and those should have a different series numbering e.g. 1000, 2000, etc. Where data will be aggregated by some other system, rather than just locally, it will be necessary to differentiate the event sources, and some form of identity standard should be considered. The shorthand might be IE1-1012, but the full identity might include the host, application name as well. For example, "WEB05-WEBSHOP-IE1-1012".

At this stage, these specification sheets should be independent of where the detection points will be located, and should not include any consideration of response actions.

Aggregating detection points need slightly different specification. The trend and comparison period for each detection point must also be identified. For example these might include both technical and business tests:

- 5 different usernames tried in 30 minutes (AE1)
- The source location changes to any other continent (SE5)
- Number of orders placed in 1 hour (UT1)
- Number of logouts in 5 minutes (STE1)
- Number of new site registrations in 15 minutes (STE3)
- Number of shopping carts abandoned in 1 hour (STE3).

Once the draft specification sheets are complete, it can be useful to also create a high-level overview of the application showing the main processing blocks/functionality perhaps in the style of a data flow diagram. Then, using a list of the site's functionality and/or different usage scenarios together with the specification sheets, mark up the approximate positions of the various detection points identified. Many usage scenarios will have very similar data flows and can be grouped together.

Identify other systems the application exchanges data with and optionally include an indication of known trust boundaries. Examine the charts and look for additional detection point requirements. For example, consider input validation and the number of returned records (CIE2).

These should begin to show how it makes sense to undertake the discrete generic pre-processing detection points in centralized functionality since it will be common to almost all requests. The discrete business layer detection points will be associated with particular application functions.

Create a summary sheet that defines the proposed detection point locations for each type such as the examples in *Figure 40* and *Figure 41*. In these, whitelist input validation (a discrete business layer detection point) may occur in very many locations in the application code, and discrete generic pre-processing detection points are likely to exist in very much fewer, and possibly a single, locations. The content of these schedules is entirely dependent on what is necessary for the particular organization, and in some cases not everything will be finalized at this stage.

This is the initial AppSensor model for an application, comprising the specification sheets and optional diagrams.

Optimization

The candidate detection points should now have initial specifications. It is necessary to make sure the purposes and descriptions created perform correctly. Beginning with the specification sheets and data flow diagrams, optimize the detection point model in three ways:

- To maintain a high confidence in attack identification through adjusting the sensitivity
- To consider relationships with other systems and the effects these may have on detection points
- To determine if any detection points can be removed to eliminate overlaps and duplicates.

High confidence in attack identification

During this stage, consider what could go wrong with input data. Ensure that the detection points are tuned to detect malicious behavior and not just user errors – some could be specified in a way that leads to events occurring due to normal behavior. In *Figure 1* the range of user behavior was used to illustrate that malicious attacks are different to normal application use. *Figure 8* below shows how this approach can be applied to individual input values where the type and format of an acceptable value may have some tolerance between what is acceptable and what is unacceptable:

Figure 8 THE SPECTRUM OF APPLICATION ACCEPTABLE USAGE ILLUSTRATING HOW NORMAL USE REQUIRES INPUT VALIDATION TO CATER FOR A RANGE OF USER-PROVIDED INPUT

Some "invalid" user data examples are shown in *Figure 9* on the following page. Users may copy and paste information into form fields, or put the data in the wrong field, or use an unexpected format such as when entering a phone number. Applications should allow some degree of variation in user behavior and thus allow for normal user error. It is necessary to check the proposed detection points will not inadvertently flag what might be normal behavior as an attack. For each detection point, examine possible scenarios where the detection point might be fired by normal, or non-malicious use. This will help tune the system helping us choose appropriate response actions. For each detection point consider:

- Automated non-malicious systems (e.g. web crawlers)
- Human error (misunderstanding, typographical)
- Input device errors (e.g. conversion of voice to text, truncation of a URL in a link)
- Specificity of error threshold (e.g. space, hyphen and parentheses characters in a telephone number, past/future application changes such as old URLs, forms)
- Network configuration and architecture.

For example, an application's entry points are well defined and a detection point is chosen to be activated when a request is made for any other URL (e.g. force browsing, URL whitelisting). The application may be able to monitor HTTP "not found" (response status code 404) errors and other invalid URLs using an internal module or it could consume such data from another device (e.g. web server logs or a web application firewall) if this can be done in real time. But a public web application is likely to receive a large number of non-malicious 404s and these will not normally be attacks. The ability for AppSensor to maintain a high degree of confidence in attack identification in this example this depends upon the way the detection point and response are specified.

Another example would be an invalid ID parameter. If the options are provided to the user in a constrained interface element like a form select element, it is more suspicious than if there are some unexpected characters in a form text element.

Figure 9   THE SPECTRUM OF APPLICATION ACCEPTABLE USAGE SHOWING HOW SOME UNACCEPTABLE DATA INPUT ARE MUCH MORE LIKELY TO INDICATE A MALICIOUS USER

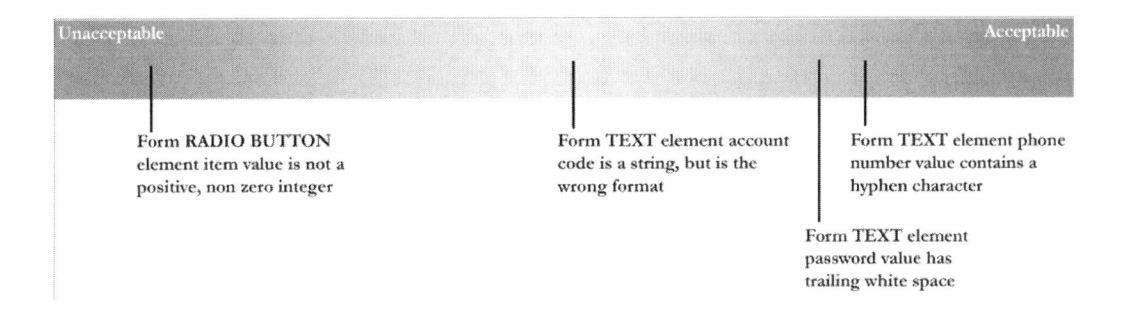

Unacceptable		Acceptable
Form RADIO BUTTON element item value is not a positive, non zero integer	Form TEXT element account code is a string, but is the wrong format	Form TEXT element phone number value contains a hyphen character
		Form TEXT element password value has trailing white space

Part III : Making It Happen

Some examples for detection points which could be susceptible to these types of sensitivity problems are expanded upon in *Part VI : Reference Materials - Detailed descriptions of detection points*. Consider these in the target application(s) and the way in which the input aspect (URL, headers, parameter name or value) might conceivably be provided by the user.

The actual context is also important. If a data entry form has some presentation-layer (client-side) validation in addition to equivalent matching server-side validation, and the submitted data includes problems which the presentation-layer validation should have caught, the acceptability of the inputs may be different. If there is also type and format and lengthy validation on the client side, the above diagram changes considerably as shown in *Figure 10* below.

Figure 10 THE SPECTRUM OF APPLICATION ACCEPTABLE USAGE SHOWING HOW APPLICATION-SPECIFIC KNOWLEDGE INCREASES THE ABILITY TO DIFFERENTIATE BETWEEN NORMAL AND MALICIOUS INPUT

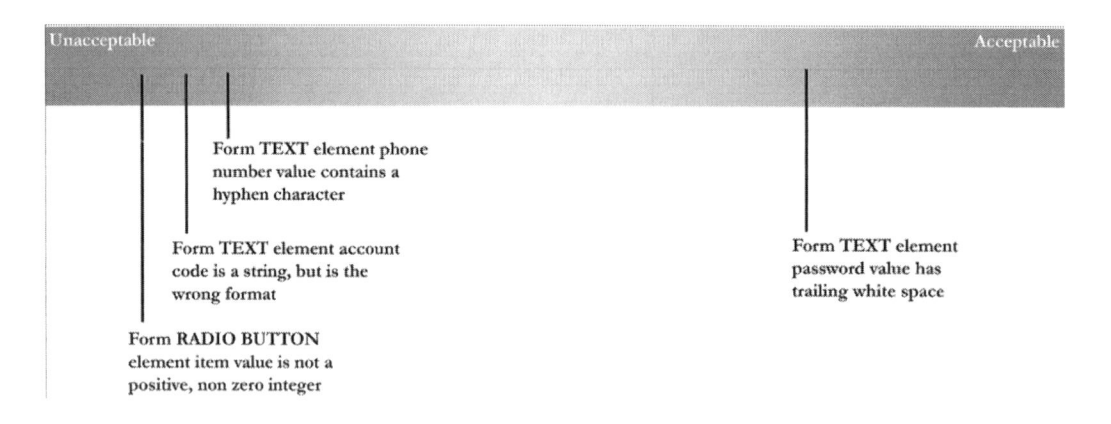

Unacceptable / Acceptable

- Form TEXT element phone number value contains a hyphen character
- Form TEXT element account code is a string, but is the wrong format
- Form RADIO BUTTON element item value is not a positive, non zero integer
- Form TEXT element password value has trailing white space

Relationships with other systems

Similarly, if a request or data are received from a trusted information system, the standard of tests to validate the data could be stricter. XML data which has been validated by an XML Firewall should be of higher quality, and less prone to human errors, than that in an RSS feed pulled directly from another website. Do not trust either source completely, but consider the seriousness of a detection point being activated from a more reliable source.

Therefore consider the original source of data being processed. Was it user-generated content, or was it retrieved from a reliable source; if the latter what verification has already been performed? This analysis may lead to the creation of additional detection point instances of the same detection point identity code, but they have different requirements and are used on different types of input.

Overlaps and duplicates

Finally, it is necessary to remove any duplication of effort - using the same detection point more than once on the same input or using another detection point which does not add any further value.

This process is undertaken by examining the model to check that detection points with the same functionality are not being repeatedly called on the same data. Note that the same detection points may correctly occur many times within the processing of a request such as when each parameter value is checked against a whitelist.

It is also possible that some detection points have been specified in a manner which negates the need for others. Check whether a very specific detection point is already tested in a less specific detection point. For example if AE10 (adding additional POST variables) is proposed for the application's authentication module and broad request validation includes RE5 (additional/duplicated data in request) it may be possible that AE10 is not adding any further detection. Provided these are given identical priority, there is no need for both, or the RE5 could be modified to capture the functional area or purpose, which might them be used to affect the response action. But note it may still be useful to record that the action was the more specific AE10 (as well as RE5), and another option would be to alter the specification for RE5 so it can activate AE10 type events at the same time, if it knows it is an authentication request.

Figure 37 (in *Part VI : Reference Materials - Detection Points - Related types*) uses link arrows to show possible inter-relationships between detection points. Depending upon how the detection points have been specified, the source of a link arrow might be a more generic version of the destination of the link arrow. This does not mean the source necessarily caters for all possibilities, but can be useful in avoiding duplication. But check that removing a detection point does not mean that an aspect is left uncovered in another attack. Then update the specifications and charts with any changes required.

Next create test cases for requests that should activate the detection points. Try to create separate tests for each detection point, and this may mean hundreds of test cases since they will include at least one for every parameter submitted in requests.

Lastly, review application design/functionality that changes the flow through code and especially any blocking actions (e.g. redirects, session termination, custom error page display). Check whether any of these circumvent or prevent detection points from being activated. For example the application might already lock an account for 20 minutes after three invalid passwords are provided in a 24 hour period but AE2 (multiple failed passwords) may have been specified requiring a different number.

Part III : Making It Happen

Attack analysis

The last stage recommended for detection point selection is to undertake an attack analysis. Although this step can be bypassed, it is useful to work through what will happen in real attack situations. Select attacks that have been identified from threat assessments, or if this is not available consider those from, for example:

- Common Attack Pattern Enumeration and Classification (CAPEC)[68]
- WASC Threat Classification v2.0[91]
- Studies of attack methods[69,92,94,95,96,97,98].

Use both likely attacks identified during risk assessments as well as feasible but much less likely attacks. Remember, AppSensor is concerned with identifying and stopping attacks against unknown vulnerabilities such as:

- SQL injection point introduced during a change to the application which was missed due to insufficient testing
- Zero day vulnerability in a code library used by the application.

For each attack, consider a range of valid and invalid application entry points, and check the model through using the real attacks. Examine all the detection points which might be activated, ignoring for the moment what their response may be. List all the detection points for each attack scenario and determine whether these are reasonable, and provide sufficient coverage. Then consider if it is possible for human or transmission errors to generate the same situation. If so, re-assess the detection points proposed.

If necessary, re-iterate through detection point selection steps to finalize the selection of detection points. This process creates the following artifacts:

- Detection point specifications
- Schedule of detection point locations
- Test cases.

See also the comments about testing in *Chapter 15 : Verification, Deployment and Operation*.

The attack detection thresholds and responses can now be defined.

Chapter 17 : Advanced Thresholds and Responses

Introduction

This chapter presents additional detail on defining attack determination thresholds and choosing responses appropriate to the business and the application users.

Approach

In AppSensor a response is an action taken as the result of attack recognition i.e. a change in application behavior; it is not any form of retaliation. The response aims to defend the application, its users and everyone's data:

- Organization data (e.g. business data, intellectual property, source code)
- User data (sometimes including PII/personal data)
- Data belonging to other parties (e.g. suppliers, customers, clients, partners).

Having defined a policy (see *Chapter 14 : Design and Implementation*), this should include a small number of high-level rules, and the type of acceptable response actions will already be largely defined.

Conventional defenses vs. AppSensor defenses

Traditional defensive mechanisms are often much more limited in the types of automated response actions possible. They might only include simple allow or deny:

- No change (e.g. continue logging/monitoring)
- Process terminated (e.g. reset connection).

The capabilities of AppSensor are potentially much wider – whatever the application does or could be coded to do. A full spectrum of responses might very feasibly include:

- No change (same as traditional defenses)
- Logging increased
- Administrator notification
- Other notification (e.g. other system)
- Proxy
- User status change
- User notification
- Timing change
- Process terminated (same as traditional defenses)
- Function amended

- Function disabled
- Account log out
- Account lock out
- Application disabled
- Collect data from user.

Additionally, since an application has knowledge about the user's roles and permissions, it is entirely possible to define response actions that target individual users, groups of users or all users. There could even be multiple tiers of response, dependent upon the user's actions over periods of time.

AppSensor can be used flexibly and does not need to do everything itself. Response actions could be undertaken by:

- Application itself
- Another system (e.g. application firewall, network firewall, another application).

While the process is primarily interested in real-time responses, the (actual or planned) capabilities of the application and related system components should be considered first. It may be possible to leverage these existing capabilities, or extend them, to provide the selected response actions.

The recommended approach is to consider the general countermeasures required, rather than the specifics for each detection point. Threshold definition (later) can link multiple detection points with multiple response actions.

Built-in potential

Many applications already have discrete (unconnected) security control responses built in. This might include functionality such as:

- Terminating a request when blacklisted inputs are received
- Fraud detection
- Adding time delays to each successive failed authentication attempt
- Locking a user account after a number of failed authentication attempts
- Application honey pot functionality
- Logging a user out when they utilize the browser's "back" button
- Terminating a session if a user's geo-location changes
- Blocking access by certain IP addresses when malicious behavior is detected
- Recording unexpected actions.

But these are usually implemented as isolated processes and some may be undertaken reactively to events, or using post transaction processes, or performed largely in a manual way. AppSensor needs to focus and formalize these approaches.

The above functionality might be able to be used, or converted into modules which a centralized analysis engine could call to invoke response. Therefore, do try to identify the following capabilities in functional specifications and deployed code:

- Application logging (e.g. security events, audit trails)
- Changes to logging level
- Alerting (e.g. email, SMS)
- User messages
- User logout
- Account lockout
- Redirects (web).

Other things like disabling individual functions or disabling the whole application are much less likely to exist.

Inspirational responses

Table 45 in (*Part VI : Reference Materials - Responses*) lists examples of some common AppSensor responses categorized by their effect on the user i.e. from the user's viewpoint. These range from responses which are transparent from the user's point of view, to passive, and then to more disruptive active responses, and ultimately intrusive.

The subsequent *Table 46* categorizes these by their general purpose (logging, notifying, disrupting, blocking). It also shows the broad purposes, whether the target of the response affects a single user or all users and the duration of the action. The full definitions are maintained on the OWASP website[99], and are reproduced in the *Responses* section of *Part VI : Reference Materials*.

Many other actions can be mapped to one of the example responses listed, but there may be other special types of action a particular application, or related system, can perform.

Attack identification threshold definition

Initially exclude the consideration of detection points in the modifying class, since these are normally used to adjust default thresholds and actions. Thresholds need to be set for how many events are allowed to be created before an attack event is confirmed and the predefined response is made. There are other considerations for thresholds, discussed below, and in practice a mix of threshold settings will usually be required.

Part III : Making It Happen

For initial implementations, such as for a pilot, simply set an overall threshold for a count of all detection point events over a time period. It is also possible to set thresholds for individual responses for single or groups of detection points.

Threshold period

Any threshold of more than "1" only has meaning over a certain time period. For example with a threshold of "3" events, if a user performs three suspicious actions in a short period of time, this might be significant and a response undertaken. But if these three actions occur over the course of several days, it may be considered a much lower risk.

Therefore for each threshold greater than "1", define the period. For user-specific detection points (as opposed to application-wide "all user" ones), normally use "previous 24 hours" as the threshold period. Beware of using terms like "today" or "this week" in threshold definitions because events just before the period rollover (e.g. just prior midnight) might not be counted against the threshold. The time period over which each threshold applies needs to be long enough to cater for slow attacks, but will need to be selected with consideration of any active responses that have time factors such as lockout period.

Note that it may make sense to use other time periods in each application. If a threshold period is tied to session length, a log out response (if used) will reset the period. Also consider how/when session-related data are stored and cleared in the application.

Tiered responses

Some AppSensor implementations set a number of different response actions to occur, even for a single detection point activation. For example, it might make sense to display a warning message to the user each time this occurs (i.e. at "1 event") and log them out the fifth time it occurs (e.g. at "5 events over the last 14 days").

Overall user threshold ("One user")

If a user activates many different detection points, it might be they do not trigger any individual detection point threshold (assuming they are all greater than "1"). Consider setting another threshold (more than 1) for all cumulative detection point activations for each user. For example "Any 12 events over the last 24 hours".

Fuzzed responses

Some attackers may try to avoid attack detection capabilities built into applications. This may not be an issue if the detection points provide sufficient coverage, but another approach is to introduce some degree of randomness into the response selection so an attacker cannot necessarily determine whether they have been detected.

Beware of complexity

The following discussion mentions many possibilities and considerations. Overly complex response rules and interactions are:

- Difficult to understand
- Cause unforeseen side-effects
- Can lead to bypass situations.

Response threshold definition defined on a per detection point basis, or detection point type basis, allows for more fine-grained tuning.

Thresholds for aggregating detection points

Some detection points require multiple user interactions to occur before they can be activated, such as:

- Use of Multiple Usernames (AE1)
- Multiple Failed Passwords (AE2)
- Detect Large Number of File Uploads (FIO2)
- Speed of Application Use (UT2)
- High Number of Logouts Across the Site (STE1)
- etc.

These were referred to as "aggregating" detection points previously. These should all have a response threshold of "1", but within the detection point itself some view needs to be taken of what "multiple", "large number", "speed", "high number", etc mean – and over what sampling periods.

Unless the application has only a few users, system trend detection points monitoring "all users" (e.g. STE1, STE2, STE3) are usually best defined with percentage changes over a particular time period (e.g. "200% increase over one hour"). Such trend monitoring will not be useful without an automated response, as the value of this monitoring is in actively identifying and stopping an attack. It will be necessary to collect usage data over a period of time before setting the thresholds, and the thresholds may need to change as use of the application varies due to interest, time of day, seasons and external events.

Thresholds for user event and user trend detection points

It is important to separate the application's own responses from those of AppSensor. An application may lock accounts due to multiple failed authentication attempts or it might block requests using a disallowed HTTP method. But AppSensor still needs to record and monitor these to undertake responses in addition to the application's normal behavior.

Part III : Making It Happen

Two approaches need to be considered:

- Whether the responses are dependent upon user role (e.g. authenticated versus unauthenticated)
- Whether responses are set on a per-detection point basis, or a per application basis.

The high-level rules should provide guidance on the first of these. If AppSensor is only implemented for the authenticated part of an application, or there is only one role, this question needs no further consideration. Applying different thresholds to different roles does create additional complexity, and some detection points and responses may not be valid for certain roles (e.g. authentication and session management exception types).

Further to the previous discussion, consider using the rule that three suspicious events is equivalent to a single attack event. This weighting could be altered for each detection point, rather than just on suspicious versus attack, but the recommendation is not to alter weightings and instead alter thresholds (number and period) only.

It may be undesirable to repeatedly count identical events over time. Some example could be:

- Multiple use of the same wrong password for a single account name
- Repeated reload of the same web page with exactly the same invalid data.

Each detection point will have its own threshold of a small number of security events before a response action is taken. Then also consider the total number of security events generated by all detection points – the latter should normally all be set with the same period e.g. one day. Sample individual and overall thresholds are shown in *Table 15* and *Table 16* below.

Table 15   EXAMPLE THRESHOLDS AND RESPONSES FOR INDIVIDUAL PER USER DETECTION POINTS

Detection Point	Role	Threshold	Period	Response	Response Code
RE1-001	Authenticated	2	1 hour	Request terminated + Account lockout 30 minutes	ASR-G, ASR-K
	Public	5	1 day		
RE6-102	Authenticated	10	5 minutes	Security violation message + Account logout	ASR-E, ASR-J
CIE1-001	Authenticated	3	15 minutes	Security violation message + Function disabled	ASR-E, ASR-I
HT3-005	Authenticated	1	NA	Admin alert + Proxy to alternative system	ASR-B, ASR-N

A threshold of "1" or a percentage comparison, such as shown for the HT3 detection point in *Table 15* above, means the threshold is reached immediately, and no time period needs to be defined. The longer the period, the stricter is the policy.

Response threshold definition based on a per detection point basis allows more fine-grained tuning. However it is usual to have both thresholds for each detection point and an overall limit on the total number of any detection points activated in a time period. The time period over which each threshold applies needs to be long enough to cater for slow attacks, but will need to be selected with consideration of any active responses that have time factors such as lockout for a period. Having the overall limit can help allow the individual thresholds to be much more tightly set.

Table 16　EXAMPLE MULTIPLE THRESHOLDS AND RESPONSES FOR THE OVERALL NUMBER OF EVENTS PER USER IN A SINGLE FIXED TIME PERIOD

Detection Points	Threshold	Period	Response	Response Code
(All)	5	24 hours	Security violation message	ASR-E
(All)	30	24 hours	Security violation message + Account logout	ASR-E, ASR-J
(All)	45	24 hours	Security violation message + Account lockout 5 minutes	ASR-E, ASR-K
(All)	60	24 hours	Security violation message + Account lockout 30 minutes	ASR-E, ASR-K
(All)	100	24 hours	Security violation message + Account lockout indefinite	ASR-E, ASR-K

Consideration also needs to be given to situations where multiple detection points are activated with a single user action ("event landslides"). This is not unlikely and two examples are:

- A SQL injection attack leads is detected as a Command Injection exception (CIE1), but also fails Input Exception whitelist checks (IE2) and Request Exception due to other missing parameters (RE6)
- Separate Input Exception validation checks may identify problems with many different parameter values (e.g. IE2, IE2, IE2, IE3, IE4, IE4).

In these cases, one request could lead to an individual detection threshold being exceeded more rapidly than expected or even the overall threshold being reached very quickly. It is important to record every event, but for some applications one mitigation against event landslides could be to limit the contribution to the overall threshold as only one security event per user interaction (e.g. request/response cycle, key depress, process activation, message). If possible, make this a configurable setting.

In a more advanced implementation may be able to track the exact event details, so that duplicate suspicious security events are not necessarily counted twice. For example, if a user submits an authentication form with the same wrong password twice, that doesn't usually provide twice as much evidence of an attack i.e. if AE5 (Unexpected Quantity of Characters in Password) is activated twice with the same value, this may be less significant than two AE5 activations by the same user but with different values.

Security event logs may include a confidence rating, defining how certain the event identification is. In AppSensor, the detection points should have been selected and their sensitivity tuned so that the confidence is very near 100% all the time. In other words, weighting based on confidence should not be required.

It may therefore be appropriate instead to define multiple overall thresholds, each with different time periods.

Table 17 EXAMPLE RESPONSE THRESHOLDS FOR THE OVERALL NUMBER OF EVENTS PER USER FOR A RANGE OF TIME PERIODS

Detection Point	Threshold	Period	Action	Response Code
(All)	5	1 day	Security violation message	ASR-E
(All)	6	2 days	Security violation message	ASR-E, ASR-J
(All)	8	1 week	Security violation message + Account lockout indefinite	ASR-E, ASR-K

Different thresholds and response actions could be based on the application's risk classification.

These might also have permutations for different roles. Initially keep thresholds simple, but allow for multiple thresholds over different time periods for different user roles, even if they are not implemented initially.

Thresholds for system trend detection points

It is difficult to provide general guidance on system trend response actions. But having an automated response to a sudden significant shift in system activity is one of the benefits of using AppSensor. "Significant" is application, business, environment dependent. It may also be time and season dependent.

The thresholds to initiate a response need to be considered once the range of normal behavior has been examined over a period of time. This also needs to consider special situations that could alter the normal patterns of usage such as vacations, time of day, newsworthy events and marketing activities, so that benign but variable site usage is not flagged as an attack. Therefore thresholds would usually include administrator notification levels before disabling a particular feature or the whole site. The existing AppSensor documentation provides a good example of this:

Table 18 EXAMPLE RESPONSE THRESHOLDS FOR A SYSTEM TREND DETECTION POINT MONITORING THE USAGE RATE OF AN APPLICATION'S "ADD A FRIEND" FEATURE

System Trend Delta	Action	Response Code
+1000% (5 minutes)	Administrator notification	ASR-B
+200% (15 minutes)	Administrator notification	ASR-B
+200% (60 minutes)	Administrator notification	ASR-B
+500% (15 minutes)	Administrator notification	ASR-B
+1000% (15 minutes)	Temporarily disable Add a Friend feature	ASR-I

System trend events should not be included in the overall (user) threshold mentioned above. By their nature they are very specific and will rarely add anything to knowledge about an individual user. Similarly there is no need for an overall system trend threshold.

Thresholds for modifying detection points

The reputational detection points (RP1-4) can be used to dynamically alter thresholds in real time. For example if an organization tracks the national terror threat level and such aspects are considered relevant to the application, the thresholds could alter in response to this (RP4). However, the degree of trust in the source, availability and accuracy of information needs to be considered with each detection point. Some (like the national terror threat example) would require a threshold of "1" if the intention is to make a change in AppSensor's response as soon as the event occurs.

Any change that disables a user, feature or the whole application could be used to perform a denial-of-service attack, and therefore responses to activation of detection points in the modifying class should be chosen conservatively.

Overall summary

For all thresholds, define whether counts are ever reset, e.g. at the end of a session, when an application is restarted.

Figure 44 in *Part VI : Reference Materials - Responses* shows part of an example schedule documenting the application's threshold settings. This shows that some of the session management exceptions only have meaning for a period that equals the session length, and that some aggregating detection points will have thresholds of "1" where they act like an off/on switch.

Threshold tuning

Once the thresholds and actions have been determined, final tuning of the model should be undertaken to ensure that the combined model behaves as required. Tuning is usually best accomplished by facilitating a discussion which includes members from various parties concerned with the application.

For each of the attacks defined in threat models, or the attacks reviewed when defining detection points, examine whether the responses are as desired.

1. Examine typical user activities and introduce all types of input which could be accidental to check how much tolerance there is for:
   a. Misunderstandings
   b. Typing errors
   c. Copying and pasting formatted text
   d. Navigation changes such as using bookmarks, partial links or the back and forward buttons
2. Consider slow and fast use of the application, and how often each function might be requested
3. Consider the response to static content (e.g. RSS feeds, style sheets, video, images, JavaScript files, HTML files) requests
4. Consider requests for missing content
5. Examine carefully activities that can lead to active responses that disable part or all the application
6. How do the range of available responses affect the wider system and related systems (interdependencies and interoperability)?
7. Identify situations where multiple detection points might all occur with a single users interaction (e.g. a single web request, an individual button click) and ensure the response actions are appropriate
8. Consider the effect of the planned responses on other metrics such as uptime of the application and other systems, application response times, user satisfaction, throughput requirements and other business measures.

Some organizations may be able to use information from usability testing studies to assist with the second item. For example, disabling the whole application could stop further recording of security events and even prevent an administrator from re-enabling the application if that function is usually undertaken using a web interface that is part of the application.

Modify the detection points, attack thresholds and responses if necessary.

See also the comments about testing in *Chapter 15 : Verification, Deployment and Operation*.

Chapter 18 : AppSensor and Application Event Logging

Introduction

Application security event logging and audit trails are not a requirement to adopt AppSensor, but they should already be present in securely designed applications. For further information see the OWASP Application Logging Cheat Sheet[100].

AppSensor is not directly concerned with the wider needs for application event logging. It is not necessary to have application logging to implement AppSensor. However, there is some synergy in that well implemented application event logging could be used or extended to be an AppSensor event store.

Application event logging is necessary but not equivalent to its AppSensor counter part. Another way of thinking about this is that if the application throws an exception it logs it and continues execution. Where AppSensor differs is that it analyzes these exceptions and potentially alters the application's behavior. In AppSensor there is already a very high confidence in the events because they are baked into the application. Event logs of these activities contain high-value information for centralized logging and monitoring systems.

Application event logs

Application logs sometimes neither record sufficient security events nor adequate detail about these. Whenever a detection point is activated it is necessary to capture and record that information. The minimum information that should be collected for each event is:

- Date and time
- Entry point (e.g. the event activated by a user such as clicking a button, URL for a web application)
- User identity (e.g. authenticated user ID, location, IP address, token)
- Any data submitted
- Malicious activity
- Whether it is suspicious or an attack.

In practice, a wider range of information can be beneficial both for attack determination, and for other operational activities such as user experience, performance monitoring, error investigation and incident response. Some suggestions for comprehensive combined application security event logging with AppSensor detection point information capture is shown in *Table 19* below. Further explanation and guidance is available[101,102,103,104,105,106].

It is useful to ensure events can be grouped by request (multiple events may occur for a single request/response) by recording a unique action/request ID in the logs, including details of which AppSensor detection points were activated if applicable (code location and

Part III : Making It Happen

instance) and including any AppSensor response actions taken and the final status. These might be added to the normal application security event logging, or be recorded in supplemental files/data stores. For a web application, the fields might be as shown below (see the references at the end of the previous paragraph for a description of these fields).

Table 19   TYPICAL EVENT LOGGING PROPERTIES FOR WEB APPLICATIONS

Logged information	Property	Logged information	Property
When	Event date/time	AppSensor detection	Sensor ID
	Log date/time		Sensor location
Security event	Type		AppSensor Detection Point ID(s)
	Severity		Description
	Confidence		Message
	Custom classification(s)	Optional supporting details	Request headers
	Owner		Request body
Location	Host		Response headers
	Service/application name		Response body
	Port		Error stack trace
	Protocol		Error message
	HTTP method		Other system response
	Entry point	Result (including AppSensor response)	Status
	Request number		Reason for status
Request	Purpose		HTTP status code
	Target		AppSensor Result Response ID(s)
User	Source		Description
	Identity		Message
	HTTP user agent	Record integrity	Identity
	Client fingerprint		Hash

Similar properties could be defined for other types of application.

With such logged event data, and suitable detection points calling the logging mechanism, these could then be analyzed to determine attacks. See also *Chapter 15 : Verification, Deployment and Operation - Operation - Logging, signaling, monitoring and reporting*.

For AppSensor event data, where there is a high level of knowledge about the event, consider also recording additional Security Content Automation Protocol (SCAP)[107] meta data:

- Common Weakness Enumeration (CWE)[108]
- Common Configuration Enumeration (CCE)[109]
- CAPEC[68] attack identifiers,
- Common Misuse Scoring System (CMSS)[110].

Additionally perhaps use Software Identification (SWID) Tags[111,112] to assist source labeling.

Web server logs

On the topic of existing logs, the question of using web server logs is often raised since these are often enabled by default. Common Log File Format[113] includes insufficient information, but Extended Log File Format[114] is widely supported by web servers are will usually be configured to provide the following information for each request:

- Event date/time
- URL path
- HTTP method
- Source IP address
- Source user agent
- Query string
- Bytes transferred
- Response status code.

Given only this data, and without adding any further detection points, it may be possible to implement a subset of AppSensor detection point categories simply by mining the web server logs. The detection points that could be implemented in this manner, without any further knowledge of the application, are shown in *Table 20*.

Table 20 POSSIBLE DETECTION POINTS IF THE ONLY EVENT SOURCE ARE WEB SERVER LOGS

Detection Point Category	ID	Title
Request Exception	RE1	Unexpected HTTP Command
	RE2	Attempt to Invoke Unsupported HTTP Method
Authentication Exception	AE3	High Rate of Login Attempts
File IO Exception	FIO1	Detect Large Individual File
	FIO2	Detect Large Number of File Uploads
System Trend Exception	STE1	High Number of Logouts Across The Site
	STE2	High Number of Logins Across The Site
	STE3	High Number of Same Transaction Across The Site

The main difficulty is the lack of attribution to user identity apart from IP address and possibly a fingerprint that includes the user agent. By tuning the application to use specific status codes for different events it may be possible to extend the use of web server logs further, but if the application is to be modified, implementing application event logging would be a better approach.

Part III : Making It Happen

Additionally web server logs are generally voluminous. This combined with the lack of detailed application-specific attack intelligence makes them generally very unsuitable for AppSensor-like attack detection. Therefore this method is not discussed further in this guide.

Chapter 19 : AppSensor and PCI DSS for Ecommerce Merchants

Introduction

Merchants with web-facing ecommerce applications need to protect cardholder data, whether or not a hosted payment page solution has been implemented.

Requirement 6.6

The Payment Card Industry (PCI) Security Standards Council requires in-scope public facing web applications to address new threats and vulnerabilities on an ongoing basis PCI Data Security Standard (DSS) in requirement 6.6. One of the two options to meet this requirement is to undertake reviews using manual or automated application vulnerability security assessment tools or methods, at least annually and after any changes. The other option is to detect and prevent attacks continuously. In PCI DSS version 2.0 (issued October 2010), this method was worded as follows:

> *[by] Installing a web-application firewall in front of public-facing web applications*

In PCI DSS version 3.0[115] (issued November 2013), the wording was updated to:

> *[by] Installing an automated technical solution that detects and prevents web-based attacks (for example, a web-application firewall) in front of public-facing web applications, to continually check all traffic.*

In the related document Summary of Changes from PCI DSS Version 2.0 to 3.0[115], this change is described as a clarification and:

> *Increased flexibility by specifying automated technical solution that detects and prevents web-based attacks rather than "web-application firewall." Added note to clarify that this assessment is not the same as vulnerability scans required at 11.2.*

This does suggest that a web application firewall (WAF) is not the only option to be considered to meet this requirement, and that it is possible that AppSensor-like approach could also be used. The relevant testing procedure is stated as:

> *Examine the system configuration settings and interview responsible personnel to verify that an automated technical solution that detects and prevents web-based attacks (for example, a web-application firewall) is in place as follows:*
> *- Is situated in front of public-facing web applications to detect and prevent web-based attacks.*
> *- Is actively running and up to date as applicable.*
> *- Is generating audit logs.*
> *- Is configured to either block web-based attacks, or generate an alert.*

The choice of WAF, AppSensor or a synergistic combination should be discussed with the merchant's acquiring bank, PCI Qualified Security Assessor[116] (QSA), or Internal Security Assessor (ISA). All the above features of running, being up-to-date, generating logs and configured to block and/or alert would also be a required part of the implementation.

SAQ A and SAQ A-EP

The PCI DSS self-assessment questionnaires (SAQs) A and A-EP are sometimes used by ecommerce merchants where cardholder data functions are fully or partially outsourced respectfully.

AppSensor may be the best way to detect malicious behavior in and around payment forms, during checkout, on payment pages and even on payment service provider's hosted payment pages.

Regardless of the eligibility criteria and which SAQ is appropriate, AppSensor can help provide additional assurance about the website's integrity and give early warning of attacks, possibly before they become anything more serious. AppSensor is a valuable application security measure regardless of its compliance contribution.

Part IV : Demonstration Implementations

A large proportion of this guide has been dedicated to a description of the concept to provide analysts, architects, designers and developers with the knowledge to implement this approach in their own systems. This is because the approach is application-specific and therefore, there is no single implementation method or single best-suited out-the-box solution. Part IV provides practical examples of how the concept can be deployed, including some standalone components that could be utilized within an organization's own deployments, or to act as inspiration. The OWASP code portion of the project described in the next two chapters aims to build a reference implementation that can be used to implement the concepts conveyed in this guide.

Chapter 20 : Web Services (AppSensor WS)

Introduction

This is a reference implementation and is a development branch included within the scope of the OWASP AppSensor Project called "AppSensor WS". This more recent implementation introduces a service-based model, using either XML/SOAP or JSON/REST, instead of both the detection/response and attack analysis code being combined as in the initial "AppSensor Core" (version 1) demonstration implementation - see *Chapter 21 : Fully Integrated (AppSensor Core)* below.

AppSensor WS was begun as part of the Google Summer of Code (GSoC) 2012[117,118] by Rauf Butt with mentoring by John Melton and Kevin W Wall, building upon the code for "AppSensor Core". The OWASP GSoC[119] initiative was promoted and administrated by Fabio Cerullo and Jason Li. Subsequently it has been developed further by John Melton.

Description

The application being protected is the client application. It detects events and/or attacks and sends them to the analysis engine using web services. It then receives responses (either via polling or some push mechanism like websockets) to execute.. The detection points, event monitor and responses have to be built into the client application at appropriate points in the logic. Code from AppSensor WS is executed on demand when the web services are called.

The web services are:

- /events
    - POST with JSON event data
    - GET with query string "earliest=[SOME_TIMESTAMP]"
- /attacks
    - POST with JSON event data
    - GET with query string "earliest=[SOME_TIMESTAMP]"
- /responses
    - GET with query string "earliest=[SOME_TIMESTAMP]"

The format for the JSON event data is described in *Part VI : Reference Materials - Data Signaling Exchange Formats*.

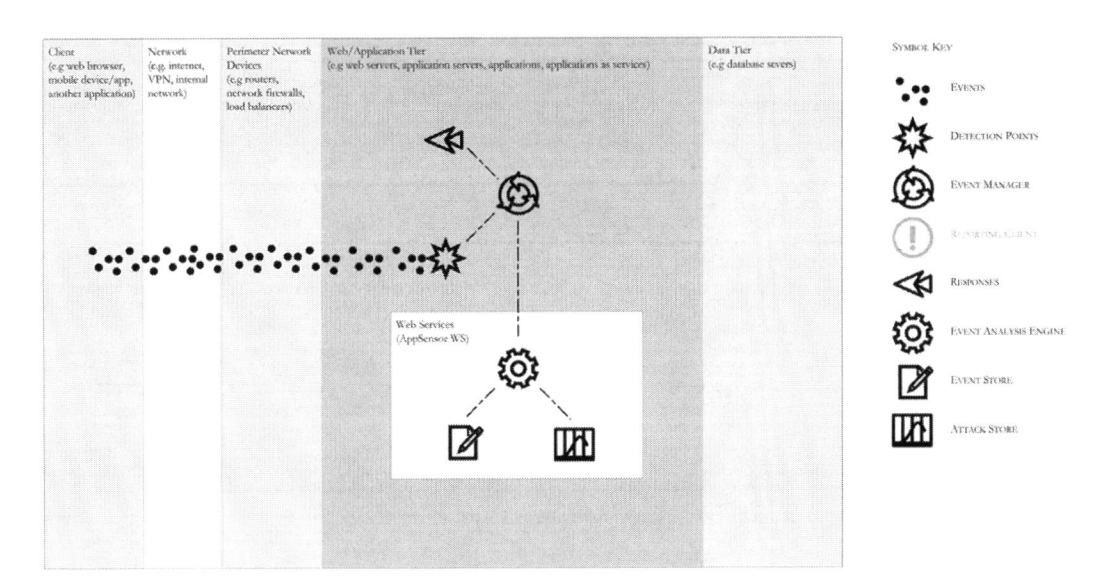

Figure 11 SCHEMATIC ARRANGEMENT OF THE APPSENSOR WS REFERENCE IMPLEMENTATION

There is also a "local mode" for java projects that does not use web services, but rather native API calls within the JVM. The analysis engine could be ported to other languages, but the intention is for the analysis engine to stay in Java and be accessed using web services by any language that can do JSON/REST and/or XML/SOAP. The intention is to build reference code in a few popular languages showing how this works.

AppSensor scope

Like AppSensor Core (described in the next chapter), the selection of detection points, where they are added, and how the software responds, are (client) application and organization dependent. The client application determines the detection point and signals us that it has occurred. The analysis engine simply evaluates this against the policy and generates attacks/responses as appropriate. Thus all detection point and response categories are potentially supported by the analysis engine web services (the server). See *Table 30* and *Table 45* in *Part VI : Reference Materials* for the complete listing.

Source code

The code is currently being developed and further extended. The latest source code is available from:

```
https://github.com/jtmelton/appsensor
```

The previous source code and appsensor.jar file are available from:

Part IV : Demonstration Implementations

```
http://mvnrepository.com/artifact/org.owasp.appsensor/AppSensor/0.1.3
.5
```

```
http://repo1.maven.org/maven2/org/owasp/appsensor/AppSensor/0.1.3.5/A
ppSensor-0.1.3.5.jar
```

The version at the time of writing is 0.1.3.5 and is issued under the BSD 3-Clause License[120].

Implementation

A developer guide has been provided at:

```
https://www.owasp.org/index.php/AppSensor-WS_Developer_Guide
```

Considerations

This Java implementation has the following dependencies:

- JUnit Java unit testing
- Mockito Java mocking framework

This AppSensor implementation is currently under development and is subject to change.

Related implementations

Chetan Karande has begun development of a node.js web services client. The code is located at:

```
https://github.com/ckarande/appsensor/tree/master/sample-apps/simple-
nodejs-ws-rest-client
```

Chapter 21 : Fully Integrated (AppSensor Core)

Introduction

Prior to the development of the version 2 demonstration implementation (see previous chapter), Michael Coates and John Melton created a pure integrated Java version. Like the more recent "AppSensor WS", this is a reference implementation and is a development branch included within the scope of the OWASP AppSensor Project called "AppSensor Core".

Description

AppSensor Core handles the collection of event data, and selection of appropriate responses based on a policy defined as a Java properties files. The detection points and responses have to be built into the application at appropriate points in the logic. Code from AppSensor Core is then executed during run time as events occur.

Figure 12 SCHEMATIC ARRANGEMENT OF THE APPSENSOR CORE REFERENCE IMPLEMENTATION

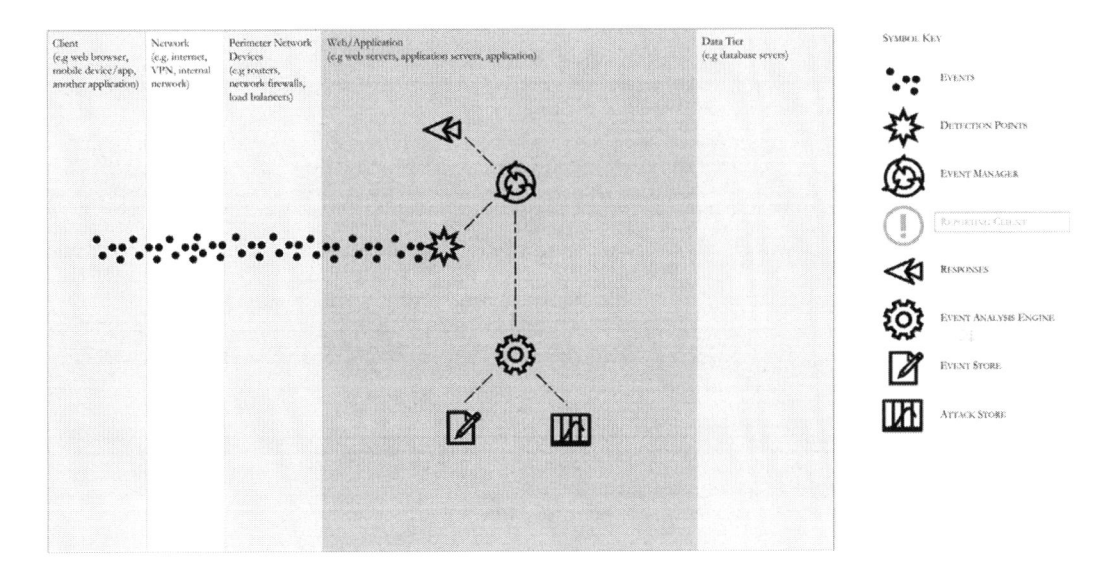

AppSensor scope

The selection of detection points, where they are added, and how the software responds, are application and organization dependent. However, the following detection point and response categories are supported:

Part IV : Demonstration Implementations

Table 21 LIST OF DETECTION POINT CATEGORIES SUPPORTED BY APPSENSOR CORE

Category Description	Detection Point ID	Title
Request Exception	RE1	Unexpected HTTP Command
	RE2	Attempt to Invoke Unsupported HTTP Method
	RE3	GET When Expecting POST
	RE4	POST When Expecting GET
Access Control Exception	ACE1	Modifying URL Argument Within a GET for Direct Object Access Attempt
	ACE2	Modifying Parameter Within A POST for Direct Object Access Attempt
	ACE3	Force Browsing Attempt
Input Exception	IE1	Cross Site Scripting Attempt
System Trend Exception	STE1	High Number of Logouts Across The Site

Table 22 LIST OF RESPONSE CATEGORIES SUPPORTED BY APPSENSOR CORE

Category Type	Description	Response Code	Description
Silent	User unaware of application's response	ASR-A	Logging Change
		ASR-B	Administrator Notification (SMS and email)
Active	Application functionality reduced for user(s)	ASR-I	Function Disabled
		ASR-J	Account Logout
		ASR-K	Account Lockout

The individual interfaces can be extended in order to modify AppSensor for a particular environment, and to support additional detection points and response actions.

Source code

The source code and appsensor.jar file are available from:

    https://code.google.com/p/appsensor/

    https://code.google.com/p/appsensor/downloads/detail?name=AppSensor-0.1.3.jar

The version at the time of writing is 0.1.3 and is issued under the BSD 3-Clause License[120].

Implementation

A developer guide has been provided at:

    https://www.owasp.org/index.php/AppSensor_Developer_Guide

Considerations

This Java implementation has the following dependencies:

- OWASP ESAPI Java library
- JavaMail libraries (activation and mail jar files)
- Servlet/JSP libraries
- Logging API library (log4j by default).

This AppSensor implementation is no longer under development.

Related implementations

This Java implementation method was utilized in the comparative research and experiment undertaken independently by Pål Thomassen "AppSensor: Attack-Aware Applications Compared Against a Web Application Firewall and an Intrusion Detection System"[33]. A description of how AppSensor Core was implemented on SimpleShiroSecuredApplication has been written by Mária Jurčovičová [121].

The AppSensor Core implementation has also been ported to .Net by Luke Briner and is available to download at:

https://www.owasp.org/index.php/File:AppSensor_Core_-_dotNet.zip

This AppSensor Core (version 1) implementation model will still be available in version 2 – called "local mode" (as opposed to REST or SOAP).

See also *Chapter 24 : Invocation of AppSensor Code Using Jni4Net*.

Part IV : Demonstration Implementations

Chapter 22 : Light Touch Retrofit

Introduction

In this demonstration implementation, an application has been instrumented with custom code to show how AppSensor functionality can be retrofitted to an existing project. The implementation does not make use of any AppSensor Project's library code (as described in the previous two chapters above).

The application used in this example is the bulletin board application phpBB[122], released under the GNU General Public License[123]. The implementation was performed in a manner that affected as little of the original code as possible.

This demonstration implementation does not form part of the core development efforts within the OWASP AppSensor Project.

Description

Detection points were added by the additional of minimal additional PHP code without altering the phpBB source code. Additional fields were added to some of the application's database tables together with new tables for the event and attack stores. An existing phpBB feature which allows "banning" of submissions by individual users was utilized as one response by inserting records into the relevant database table; a second response was added external to the code base by using the host firewall to block IP addresses.

Figure 13 SCHEMATIC ARRANGEMENT OF EXAMPLE LIGHT TOUCH RETROFIT TO EXISTING CODE

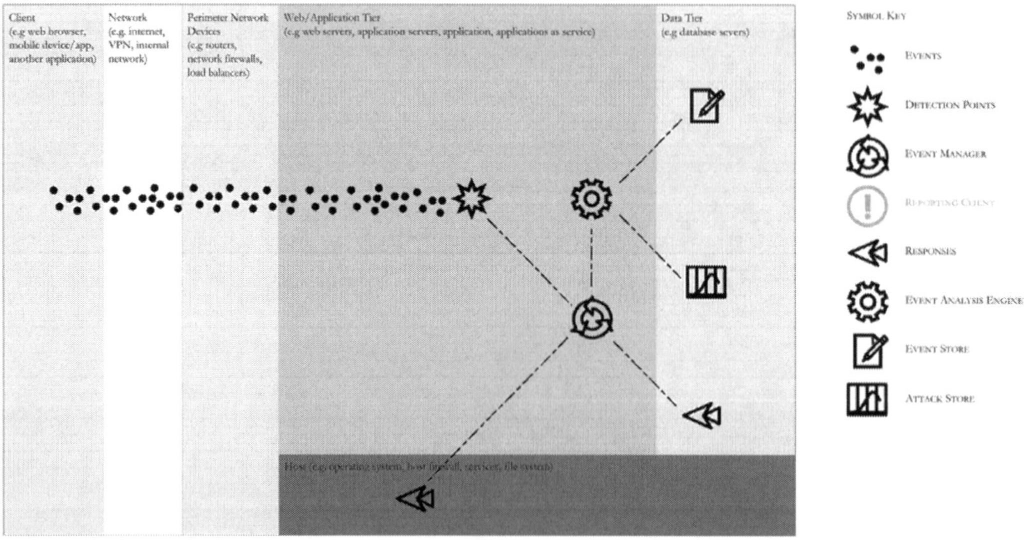

AppSensor scope

The following detection point and response action categories are included:

Table 23 LIST OF DETECTION POINT CATEGORIES IMPLEMENTED IN THIS EXAMPLE LIGHT TOUCH RETROFIT

Category Description	Detection Point ID	Title
Authentication Exception	AE1	Use of Multiple Usernames
	AE2	Multiple Failed Passwords
Access Control Exception	ACE3	Force Browsing Attempt
Input Exception	IE2	Violation Of Implemented White Lists
	IE3	Violation Of Implemented Black Lists
File IO Exception	FIO2	Detect Large Number of File Uploads
Honey Trap	HT2	Honey Trap Resource Requested
	HT3	Honey Trap Data Used
User Trend Exception	UT4	Frequency of Feature Use

Table 24 LIST OF RESPONSE CATEGORIES IMPLEMENTED IN THIS EXAMPLE LIGHT TOUCH RETROFIT

Category Type	Description	Response Code	Description
Active	Application functionality reduced for user(s)	ASR-I	Function Disabled
		ASL-L	Application Disabled

In this case, the response to disable the functions utilizes phpBB's inherent "block" functionality and the response to disable the application is accomplished by blocking an IP address using the host network firewall level. In this implementation, it was accomplished by using the "netsh advfirewall firewall" command[124] for Windows Firewall, but iptables could be used on *nix systems, and similarly for other operating systems; an external network device could also be used.

Source code

The phpBB bulletin board application can be downloaded at:

    https://www.phpbb.com/downloads/

PHPIDS as a blacklist input exception detection point. PHPIDS, default_filter.xml and converter.php can be downloaded from:

    https://phpids.org/downloads/

Part IV : Demonstration Implementations

The additional database SQL scripts and PHP files can be downloaded at:

    https://www.owasp.org/index.php/File:Appsensor-demo-
    lighttouchretrofit.zip

This is proof of concept code and is neither optimized nor production-ready.

Implementation

Developer notes are included within the file containing the source code.

Considerations

The PHP implementation of the event manager needs permissions to perform real-time changes to the host-based firewall. This could be changed to signal a separate network firewall instead.

This implementation is no longer under development.

Related implementations

None.

Chapter 23 : Ensnare for Ruby

Introduction

Ensnare[125] is a gem plugin for Ruby on Rails developed to allow the rapid configuration and deployment of a basic malicious behavior detection and response scheme.

It was created by Andy Hoernecke and Scott Behrens and uses a combination of honey traps to entice malicious users, and a configurable suite of responses to confuse, allude, delay, or stop an attacker. The documentation states Ensnare was partially inspired by Ryan Barnett's blog posts about honey traps[126,127]. Ensnare has no connection with the OWASP AppSensor Project, but appears to be a close relative.

This production implementation does not form part of the core development efforts within the OWASP AppSensor Project.

Description

Ensnare uses honey trap type of detection points referred to as "traps" which can be benign cookies, parameters, bad paths, or even regular expressions of known attack signature such as from a scanner. When a trap is triggered, the event ("violation") is logged. When predefined threshold of violations is reached for a user, based on username, session or IP address, the predetermined response is deployed into the response.

Figure 14 SCHEMATIC ARRANGEMENT OF THE ENSNARE IMPLEMENTATION

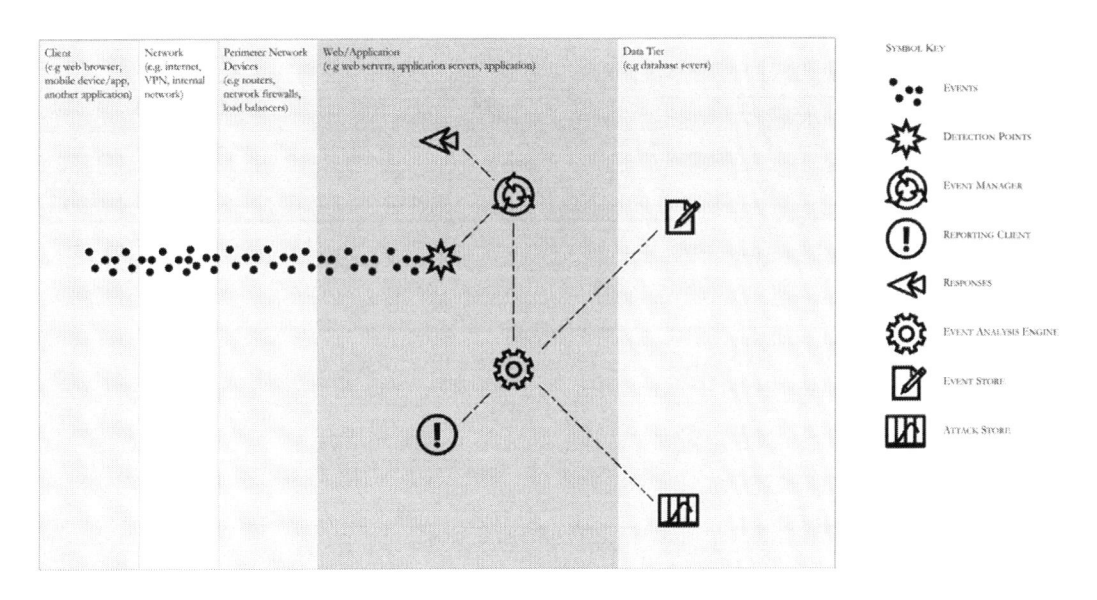

Part IV : Demonstration Implementations

Custom traps can also be created in the application, and Ensnare allows violation logging from anywhere in the application.

AppSensor scope

The following detection points are available as standard:

Table 25   LIST OF DETECTION POINT CATEGORIES IMPLEMENTED IN ENSNARE

Category Description	Detection Point ID	Title
Honey Trap	HT1	Alteration to Honey Trap Data
	HT2	Honey Trap Resource Requested
	HT3	Honey Trap Data Used

However custom detection points can be created and, for example, the project's documentation mentions violations of the application's authorization controls.

The following response action categories are defined in Ensnare:

Table 26   LIST OF RESPONSE CATEGORIES IMPLEMENTED IN ENSNARE

Category Type	Description	Response ID	Titles
None	No response	ASR-P	No Response
Passive	Changes to user experience but nothing denied	ASR-E	User Notification
		ASR-F	Timing Change
Active	Application functionality reduced for user(s)	ASR-G	Process Terminated
		ASR-H	Function Amended
		ASR-I	Function Disabled

Source code

Ensnare's source code is located at:

    https://github.com/ahoernecke/ensnare

Implementation

Documentation for Ensnare can be found at:

    https://github.com/ahoernecke/ensnare/wiki

Considerations

The detection, attack determination and response steps are implemented as a "before_filter" that runs for every request.

This implementation is currently under development and is subject to change. The Ensnare project wiki[128] requests help with:

- Rails 4 Edition
- More trap types (GET parameters, other headers, Http Methods like Trace)
- Optional config to delay a user entering a threshold (to make it harder to correlate which requests resulted in an application state change)
- Whitelisting
- More response types
- Filtering/queuing on violation data
- More metrics with graph and query functionality.

Related implementations

None.

Part IV : Demonstration Implementations

Chapter 24 : Invocation of AppSensor Code Using Jni4Net

Introduction

Dinis Cruz has used the OWASP O2 Platform[129] C# REPL scripting environment to invoke Java AppSensor and ESAPI methods from an existing .NET application using Jni4Net[130]. Like the application described in *Chapter 22 : Light Touch Retrofit,*, it is another example of retrofitting AppSensor to an existing project. However it does utilize the AppSensor Project's library code.

This demonstration implementation does not form part of the core development efforts within the OWASP AppSensor Project. The O2 Platform has its own mailing list[131].

Description

The core development efforts in Java are consumed within a .Net application which exposes all the same capabilities.

Figure 15 SCHEMATIC ARRANGEMENT OF EXAMPLE APPSENSOR CODE INVOCATION USING JNI4NET

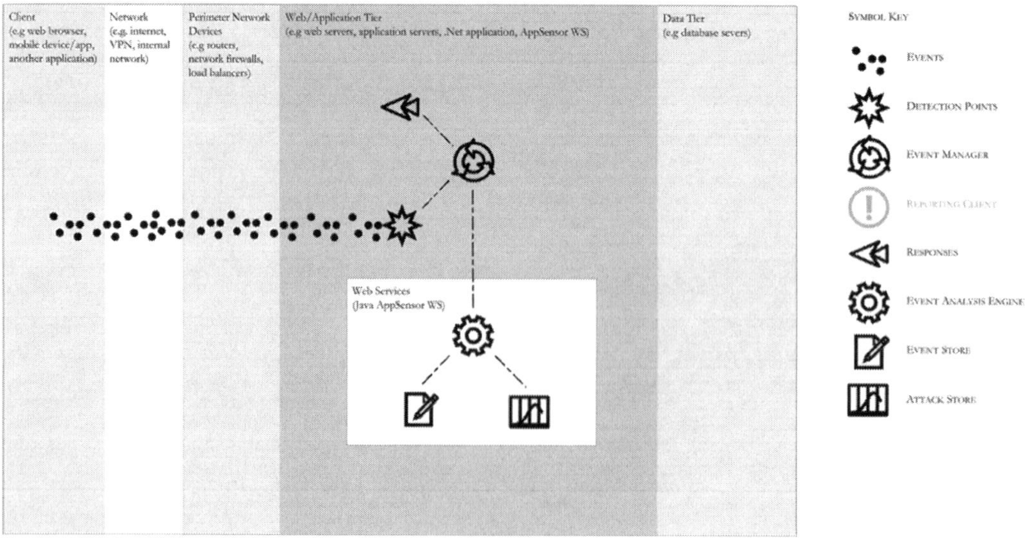

AppSensor scope

The detection points and response actions are identical to those described for AppSensor Core above.

Source code

The source code for the pilot demonstration can be found at:

```
http://github.com:DinisCruz/TeamMentor_3_3_AppSensor
```

This is proof of concept code and is neither optimized nor production-ready.

Implementation

The method of implementation is described at:

```
http://blog.diniscruz.com/2013/06/another-step-in-use-of-esapi-
and.html
```

A video of Denis Cruz's presentation of the concept is available at:

```
http://www.youtube.com/watch?v=dzj3llZ9G6I
```

Considerations

This is purely demonstration code that illustrates an alternative method of implementation.

Related implementations

There is a .Net port of the Java AppSensor Core implementation - see *Chapter 21 : Fully Integrated (AppSensor Core)*.

Part IV : Demonstration Implementations

Chapter 25 : Using an External Log Management System

Introduction

An external log management system can be used to aggregate event data and generate some types of responses such as alerts or network changes. An organization with a large number of applications that already has some form of Security Information and Event Management (SIEM) or other Continuous Security Monitoring (CSM) may benefit from this type of approach.

This demonstration implementation does not form part of the core development efforts within the OWASP AppSensor Project.

Description

Detection points are added into each application's source code like a standard AppSensor implementation. But information from the detection points are sent to an external log aggregation and event management system. The external system is responsible for determining the attack and initiating responses.

Events collected by detection points are sent to a centralized system using Common Event Format[132] (CEF) over syslog protocol.

Figure 16 SCHEMATIC ARRANGEMENT OF EXAMPLE EXTERNAL LOG MANAGEMENT SYSTEM

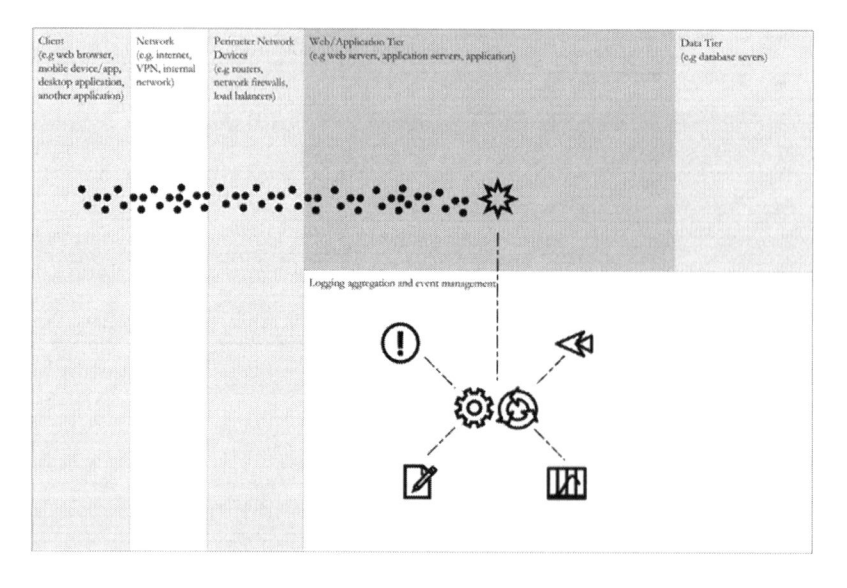

AppSensor scope

Any detection points capable of being added to the application(s) and elsewhere could provide event data to the external system.

Although potentially any response is possible, assume the signaling is one-way from the application(s) to the external system,. Then the most likely responses supportable via the network are:

Table 27 LIST OF RESPONSE CATEGORIES POSSIBLY AVAILABLE TO AN EXTERNAL LOG/EVENT MANAGEMENT SYSTEM

Category Type	Description	Response Code	Description
None	No response	ASR-P	No Response
Silent	User unaware of application's response	ASR-A	Logging Change
		ASR-B	Administrator Notification
		ASR-C	Other Notification
Active	Application functionality reduced for user(s)	ASR-L	Application Disabled

Of these, administrator notification is the most common (and not necessarily the most effective use of AppSensor capabilities).

Source code

No source code is available.

Implementation

This method still requires the addition of detection points to application code, which is application dependent. All other conceptual elements are undertaken external to the application(s).

An example message structure is shown on the next page. This utilizes predefined and custom key-value pairs in the extension part of CEF:

- User agents string
- Application detection point identifier
- AppSensor detection point category
- HTTP status code
- Request ID (a unique identifier for each application request)
- Local log identifier
- Degree of confidence (in the example 100%).

Figure 17 EXAMPLE USE OF COMMON EVENT FORMAT FOR EVENT SIGNALING

```
src=10.25.102.65
suser=W0005

proto=TCP
dpt=80
dproc=httpd
request=/catalogue/showProduct/
requestMethod=GET
deviceExternalID=AppSensor06
msg=Cross site scripting attempt in parameter prodid
cat=detection
act=block

cs1Label=requestClientApplication cs1=Mozilla/5.0 (Macintosh; U; Intel Mac OS X
10.6; en-GB; rv:1.9.2.17) Gecko/20110420
cs2Label=AppSensorDetectionPointID cs2=R03
cs3Label=AppSensorDetectionType cs3=IE1
cs4Label=StatusCode cs4=403
cn1Label=RequestID cn1=000070825566
cn2Label=AppSensorLogID cn2=1650833
cn3Label=Confidence cn3=100
```

Considerations

This method may not be completely "real time" nor provide feedback information for the application(s) to adapt to the attack. See also *Chapter 18 : AppSensor and Application Event Logging* for a discussion about generic application event logging and *Part VI : Reference Materials - Data Signaling Exchange Formats*.

AppSensor data might simply be used to enhance attack and threat intelligence for fraud detection or advanced persistent threat identification.

Related implementations

Similar logging ideas could be implemented using the open source OSSEC or many commercial log management systems.

Existing security monitoring systems should always be considered as a recipient of AppSensor data, regardless of where the event analysis and event management is being undertaken. Signaling AppSensor event and attack data to an event monitoring system adds valuable information to an organization's threat and attack knowledge.

Chapter 26 : Leveraging a Web Application Firewall

Introduction

OWASP ModSecurity Core Rule Set is a free set of generic application protection rules for the open source ModSecurity[35] web application firewall (WAF). A number of rules implement AppSensor behavior, albeit separate from the application's source code.

When there is no permission or ability to modify an application, the use of a WAF can accommodate some AppSensor-like behavior. This in fact, may be the only available way to apply the concept to some legacy or commercial applications where the source code cannot be altered. WAFs have other valuable uses as well, and may already exist in the application's environment.

This implementation does not form part of the core development efforts within the OWASP AppSensor Project. Instead, please refer to the actively maintained and supported OWASP ModSecurity Core Rule Set Project[36,133] which has its own mailing list[134].

Description

ModSecurity can be deployed embedded within the existing web server infrastructure, out of line listening passively or as a reverse proxy server on the network. The latter has been used in this example so that it can protect multiple back-end web servers. In this pure WAF implementation, all AppSensor-like functionality is undertaken within the WAF.

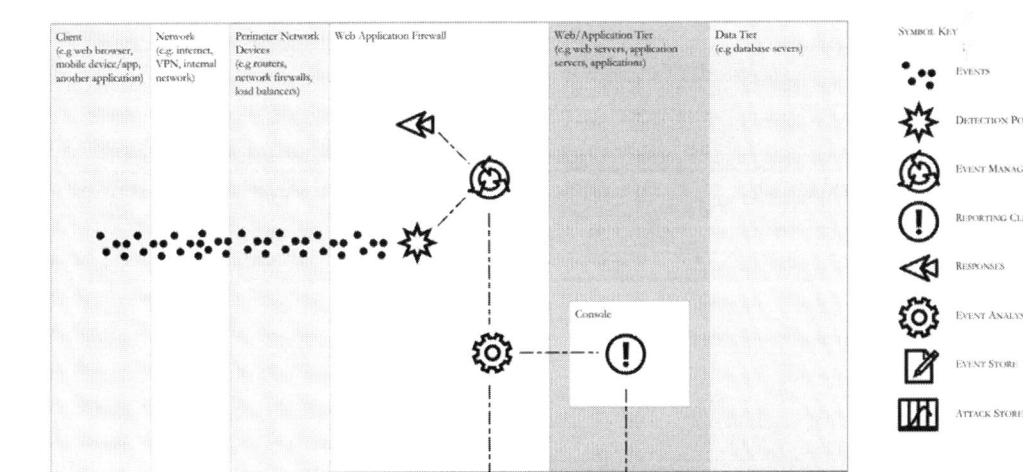

Figure 18 SCHEMATIC ARRANGEMENT OF EXAMPLE LEVERAGING A WEB APPLICATION FIREWALL

Part IV : Demonstration Implementations

AuditConsole[135] is used to browse the event data (indicated in the above diagram as accessible to both the event manager and the reporting client).

In this implementation, only the AppSensor-relevant rules (see below) were enabled, with all other rules disabled or removed. This was so the effect of AppSensor-like functionality alone can be assessed without having to consider the effect of other WAF capabilities.

AppSensor scope

The following detection points have been implemented within in the Core Rule Set (CRS) at the time of writing:

Table 28   LIST OF DETECTION POINT CATEGORIES IMPLEMENTED IN MODSECURITY CORE RULE SET

Category Description	Detection Point ID	Title
Request Exception	RE1	Unexpected HTTP Command
	RE2	Attempt to Invoke Unsupported HTTP Method
	RE5	Additional/Duplicated Data in Request
	RE7	Unexpected Quantity of Characters in Parameter
	RE8	Unexpected Type of Characters in Parameter
Input Exception	IE1	Cross Site Scripting Attempt
Encoding Exception	EE2	Unexpected Encoding Used
Command Injection Exception	CIE1	Blacklist Inspection for Common SQL Injection Values
	CIE4	Carriage Return or Line Feed Character in File Request
Honey Trap	HT1	Alteration to Honey Trap Data
Reputation	RP3	Suspicious Client-Side Behavior

The rules are spread across the "base" and "experimental" directories included in the CRS.

Application-specific custom ModSecurity rules can be written to extend these detection points further. Some AppSensor detection points may be difficult to implement within the WAF due to lack of access available to user information and application context. Having said that, ModSecurity contains a Lua API that can be used to directly query back end data sources.

ModSecurity can be configured to execute a response based on an individual event or as a result of an aggregated (anomaly) score.

All AppSensor example response actions are potentially possible using ModSecurity as listed in the next table.

Table 29 LIST OF RESPONSE CATEGORIES IMPLEMENTED IN MODSECURITY CORE RULE SET

Category Type	Description	Response Code	Description
None	No response	ASR-P	No Response
Silent	User unaware of application's response	ASR-A	Logging Change
		ASR-B	Administrator Notification
		ASR-C	Other Notification
		ASR-N	Proxy
Passive	Changes to user experience but nothing denied	ASR-D	User Status Change
		ASR-E	User Notification
		ASR-F	Timing Change
Active	Application functionality reduced for user(s)	ASR-G	Process Terminated
		ASR-H	Function Amended
		ASR-I	Function Disabled
		ASR-J	Account Logout
		ASR-K	Account Lockout
		ASR-L	Application Disabled
Intrusive	User's environment altered	ASR-M	Collect Data from User

Source code

ModSecurity, the OWASP ModSecurity CRS and AuditConsole respectively can be downloaded at:

    http://www.modsecurity.org/download/

    https://github.com/SpiderLabs/owasp-modsecurity-crs

    http://download.jwall.org/AuditConsole/current/

Implementation

Follow the instructions included within the downloaded archive. More information available at:

    http://www.modsecurity.org/documentation/

    http://blog.spiderlabs.com/modsecurity/

    http://www.jwall.org/web/audit/console/index.jsp

Considerations

ModSecurity is available for Apache, IIS, Java and Nginx - see the download page listed above.

Part IV : Demonstration Implementations

Related implementations

Other WAFs may not be as configurable as the example here – AppSensor cannot be implemented satisfactorily with only a generic negative security model inspecting individual transactions. In order to trigger detection points from either the User Trend Exception (UTE) or System Trend Exception (STE) categories, the security system must be able to track data across multiple requests. A small number of more advanced load balancers that understand the HTTP protocol could support some similar functionality. But note the comments in *Chapter 2 : Protection Measures - Comparison with* .

A web application firewall can also be used for:

- Reputational detection points, for example to send possible attack information to the defended application (detection point type RP2) using HTTP request headers or other signaling
- Responses on behalf of the defended application, for example to perform increased logging (ASR-A), to proxy user requests to another system (ASR-N), to disable functions (ASR-I), to disable the application (ASR-L) and to collect data from a user (ASR-M).

Similarly other application firewalls (e.g. database firewalls) could be used for some detection points and responses.

Part V : Model Dashboards

Data visualization of real-time attack detection and response provides organizations with much needed insight into whether their applications are under attack, and by whom. This part introduces the necessary concepts for visualizing AppSensor data, and presents example application-specific dashboards that have already been created.

Note that OWASP does not endorse or recommend any commercial products or services mentioned.

Part V : Model Dashboards

Chapter 27 : Security Event Management Tools

Introduction

There are many open source and commercial tools for collecting, analyzing and visualizing and exploring security event data. These support common event data formats. As discussed in *Part III : Making It Happen - Chapter 15 : Verification, Deployment and Operation* the many capabilities of event log management tools are not always necessary, since AppSensor data has a high-confidence level and ought to be very information rich already. However, such tools can be used to acquire and present AppSensor data.

Description

In *Part III : Making It Happen - Chapter 15 : Verification, Deployment and Operation - Operation*, and imaginary AppSensor was illustrated.

AppSensor logging and signaling format could be used, but most event log management tools are very flexible and even support event records comprised of simple name-value pairs.

Figure 19 EXAMPLE APPSENSOR EVENT DATA USING DELIMITED NAME-VALUE PAIRS

```
Application=MyPortal|Function=View
Account|Entrypoint=/c/account/view.jsp|UserSaluation=Mr|UserFamilyName=Smith|Us
erPersonalName=Joey|Severity=2|Confidence=100|DetectionPointID=ACE3-
056|DetectionPoint=attempted to access an account belonging to someone
else|ResponseAction1Code=ASR-B|ResponseAction1Description=Syslog event
sent|ResponseAction2Code=ASR-C|ResponseAction2Description=Event notified to CRM
(ID 509578)|ResponseAction3Code=ASR-D|ResponseAction3Description=Fraud flag set
in CRM|ResponseAction4Code=ASR-I|ResponseAction4Description=Transactional
functionality disabled for this user
```

When this data is sent using a system component supporting Common Event Format or other standard format, it can be received by security event management tools.

Users of such tools can then use the in-built capabilities to render, display and visualize the AppSensor data. Other security event management tools can be used in the same manner.

See *Data Signaling Exchange Formats* in *Part VI : Reference Materials* for further information about integrating AppSensor data with security event management tools.

Chapter 29 : Application Vulnerability Tracking

Example: Splunk

An example of Common Event Format in Splunk is illustrated below.

Figure 20 AppSensor Data Feed Addition to Splunk

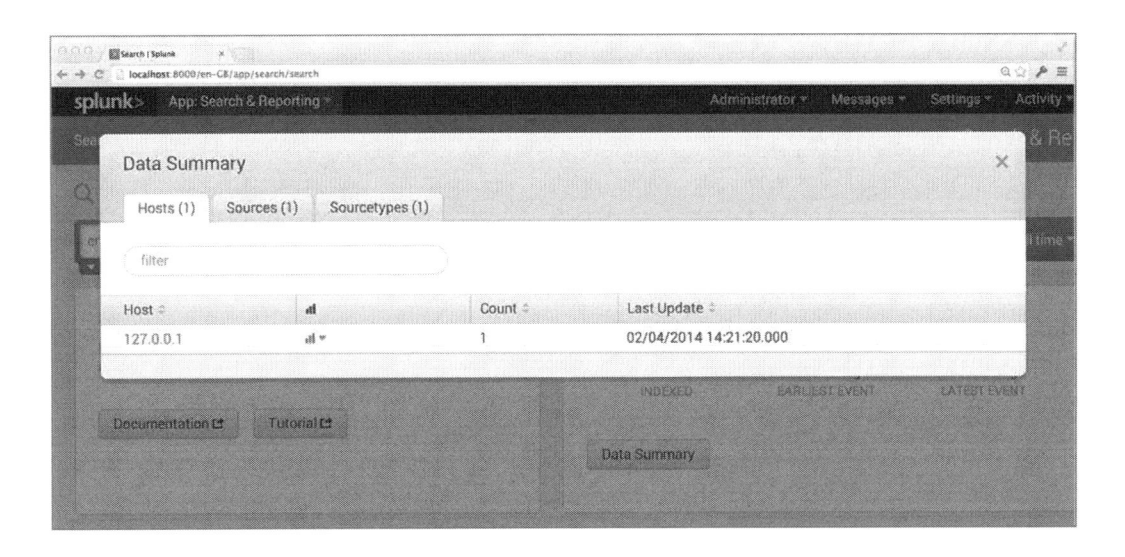

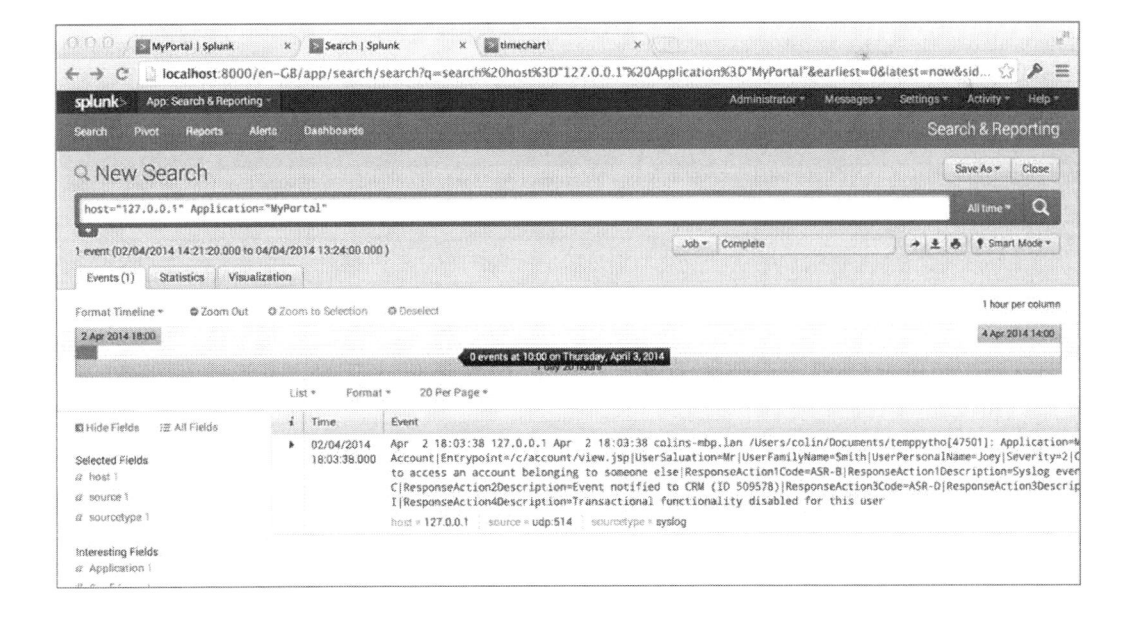

Figure 21 AppSensor Event Summary in Splunk

109

Part V : Model Dashboards

Figure 22 APPSENSOR EVENT DETAIL IN SPLUNK

i	Time	Event			
▼	02/04/2014 18:03:38.000	Apr 2 18:03:38 127.0.0.1 Apr 2 18:03:38 colins-mbp.lan /Users/colin/Documents/temppytho[4750 Account|Entrypoint=/c/account/view.jsp|UserSaluation=Mr|UserFamilyName=Smith|UserPersonalName= to access an account belonging to someone else|ResponseAction1Code=ASR-B|ResponseAction1Descri C|ResponseAction2Description=Event notified to CRM (ID 509578)|ResponseAction3Code=ASR-D|Respo I|ResponseAction4Description=Transactional functionality disabled for this user			
		Event Actions ▼			
		Type	Field	Value	Actions
		Selected	host ▼	127.0.0.1	▼
			source ▼	udp:514	▼
			sourcetype ▼	syslog	▼
		Event	Application ▼	MyPortal	▼
			Confidence ▼	100	▼
			DetectionPoint ▼	attempted to access an account belonging to someone else	▼
			DetectionPointID ▼	ACE3-056	▼
			Entrypoint ▼	/c/account/view.jsp	▼
			Function ▼	View Account	▼
			ResponseAction1Code ▼	ASR-B	▼
			ResponseAction1Description ▼	Syslog event sent	▼
			ResponseAction2Code ▼	ASR-C	▼
			ResponseAction2Description ▼	Event notified to CRM (ID 509578)	▼
			ResponseAction3Code ▼	ASR-D	▼
			ResponseAction3Description ▼	Fraud flag set in CRM	▼
			ResponseAction4Code ▼	ASR-I	▼
			ResponseAction4Description ▼	Transactional	▼
			Severity ▼	2	▼
			UserFamilyName ▼	Smith	▼
			UserPersonalName ▼	Joey	▼
			UserSaluation ▼	Mr	▼
			index ▼	main	▼
			linecount ▼	1	▼
			pid ▼	47501	▼
			process ▼	/Users/colin/Documents/temppytho	▼
			splunk_server ▼	colins-mbp.lan	▼
		Time ○	_time ▼	2014-04-02T18:03:38.000+01:00	
		Default	punct ▼	__:__.__:_-_////[]:_=|=_|=///.|=|=|=|=|=-	▼
		host = 127.0.0.1 source = udp:514 sourcetype = syslog			

Example: AuditConsole

Most security event log tools will support a wide variety of data formats. Some are custom-built for particular data, such as AuditConsole[88] from jwall.org, a web console for managing ModSecurity web application firewall event data imported from audit files or to receive event data using the ModSecurity Log Collector (mlogc) tool. If event data can be saved in this format, or the only event data available is from ModSecurity, AuditConsole can be used.

Figure 23 APPSENSOR EVENT IN THE AUDITCONSOLE DASHBOARD

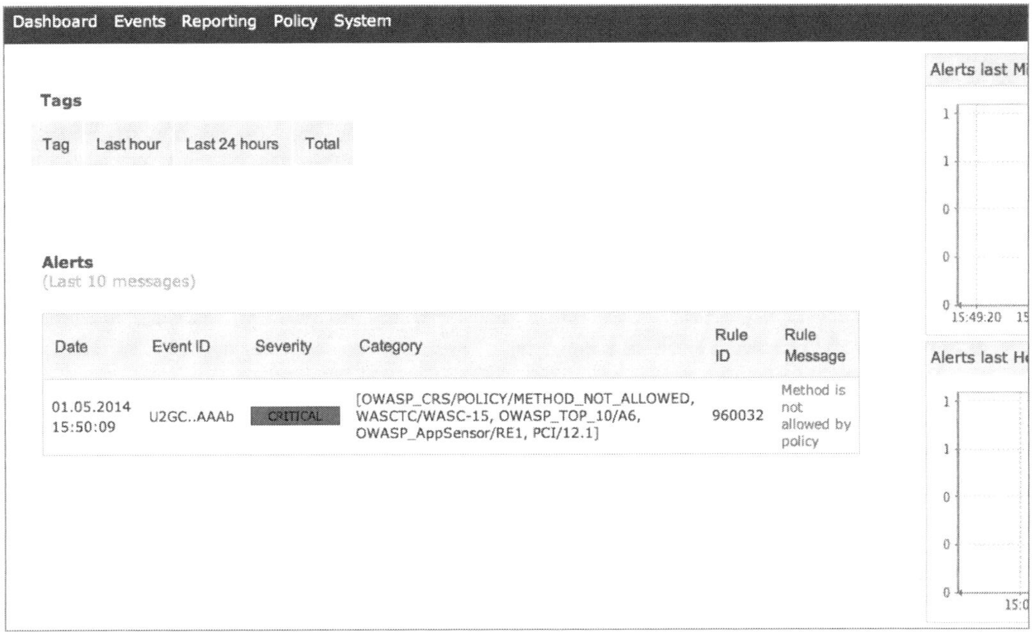

Events can be tagged within AuditConsole, and rules created to send notifications, delete events or call other processes.

AppSensor coverage

Coverage of AppSensor event, attack and response events can be as little or as much as is imported from logging or signaling, but is dependent upon the customization options of the tool.

Part V : Model Dashboards

Chapter 28 : Application-Specific Dashboards

Introduction

A better representation of application attacks can be usually be achieved by building custom dashboards instead of open source and commercial event log management tools. The possibilities are greater, but possibly require more effort. Application-specific attack dashboards are currently an aspect still being developed, and additional ideas and code samples are likely to be available in the near future. Further ideas for information security consoles and dashboards can be found at SecViz[136].

Organizations may have their own application dashboards, and some of the ideas below could be used to extend those.

Description

Example: Streaming Comet

Example application-specific dashboards were demonstrated at OWASP AppSec EU 2011. The demos broadcast example event and attack data to a server which used the Comet model to push real-time updates to an active web page console[137].

Figure 24 AN EXAMPLE APPSENSOR DASHBOARD FOR AN ECOMMERCE WEBSITE

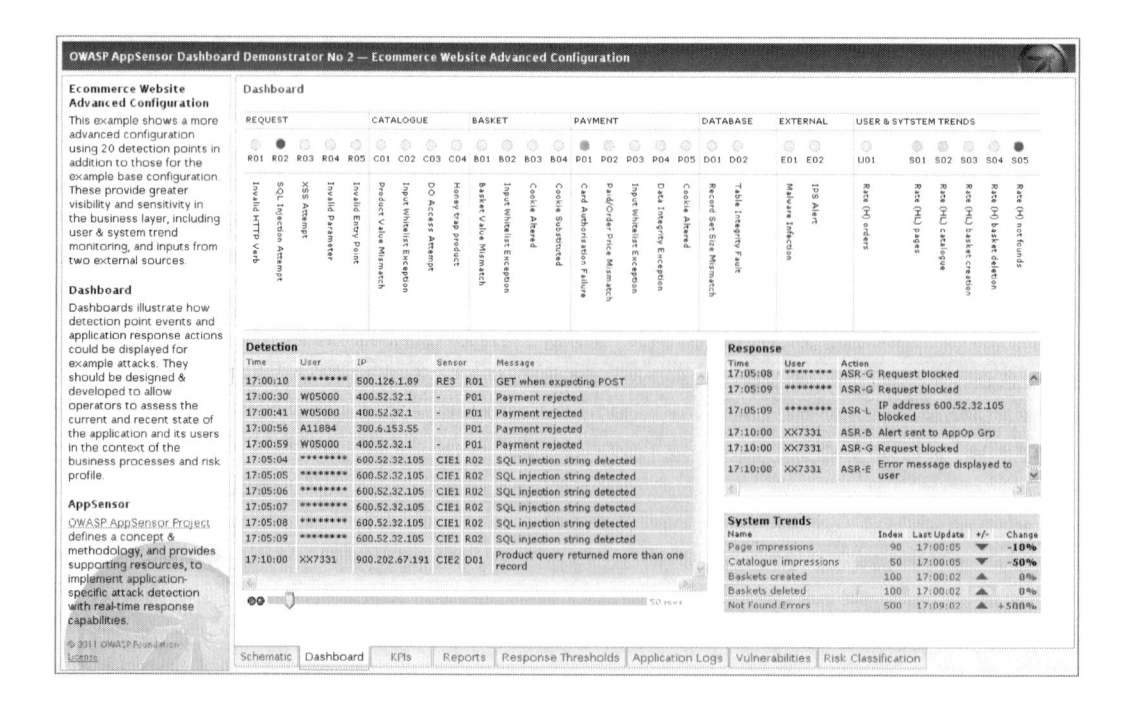

In this the detection points are shown relative to the application's main functional areas are listed across the top with an indicator "light" above each position.

Figure 25 AN EXAMPLE DETECTION POINT INDICATORS ON WEBSITE FUNCTIONALITY MAP

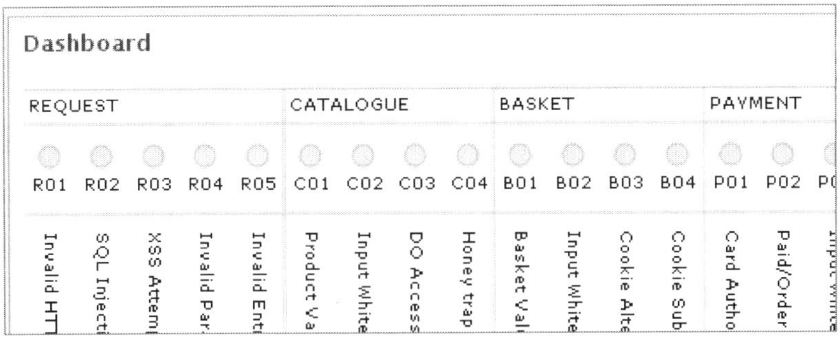

These light up red on attack detection and then fade through orange to yellow and white again over a suitable time period, so they are not completely ephemeral.

Figure 26 ILLUMINATION OF DETECTION POINT INDICATORS

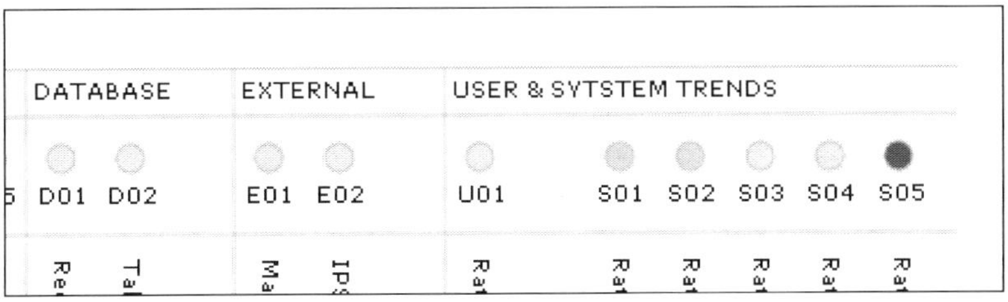

Trend monitoring detection points are showing a separate area at the bottom right of this model dashboard. As data is dynamically updated, the rows change color to indicate refreshes and indicators of trend direction.

Part V : Model Dashboards

Figure 27 SYSTEM TREND DETECTION POINTS

System Trends				
Name	Last	Time	+/-	Change
Page impressions	110	17:00:24	▲	+10%
Catalogue impressions	140	17:00:19	▲	+7%
Baskets created	100	17:00:02	▲	0%
Baskets deleted	100	17:00:02	▲	0%
Not Found Errors	100	17:00:02	▲	0%

Figure 28 HIGHLIGHTING OF CHANGES TO SYSTEM TREND DETECTION POINTS

System Trends				
Name	Index	Last Update	+/-	Change
Page impressions	90	17:00:05	▼	-10%
Catalogue impressions	50	17:00:05	▼	-50%
Baskets created	100	17:00:02	▲	0%
Baskets deleted	100	17:00:02	▲	0%
Not Found Errors	500	17:09:02	▲	+500%

A panel is updated in real time as events occur. In this example where detection points also exist in public areas, there are a larger number of events. The corresponding detection point indicators are illuminated as events appear.

Figure 29 DETECTION POINTS EVENT LOG DISPLAY

Detection					
Time	User	IP	Sensor		Message
17:00:10	********	500.126.1.89	RE3	R01	GET when expecting POST
17:00:30	W05000	400.52.32.1	-	P01	Payment rejected
17:00:41	W05000	400.52.32.1	-	P01	Payment rejected
17:00:56	A11884	300.6.153.55	-	P01	Payment rejected
17:00:59	W05000	400.52.32.1	-	P01	Payment rejected
17:05:04	********	600.52.32.105	CIE1	R02	SQL injection string detected
17:05:05	********	600.52.32.105	CIE1	R02	SQL injection string detected
17:05:06	********	600.52.32.105	CIE1	R02	SQL injection string detected
17:05:07	********	600.52.32.105	CIE1	R02	SQL injection string detected
17:05:08	********	600.52.32.105	CIE1	R02	SQL injection string detected
17:05:09	********	600.52.32.105	CIE1	R02	SQL injection string detected
17:10:00	XX7331	900.202.67.191	CIE2	D01	Product query returned more than one record

50 rows

Chapter 29 : Application Vulnerability Tracking

Automated real-time responses are displayed in another panel.

Figure 30 RESPONSE EVENT LOG DISPLAY

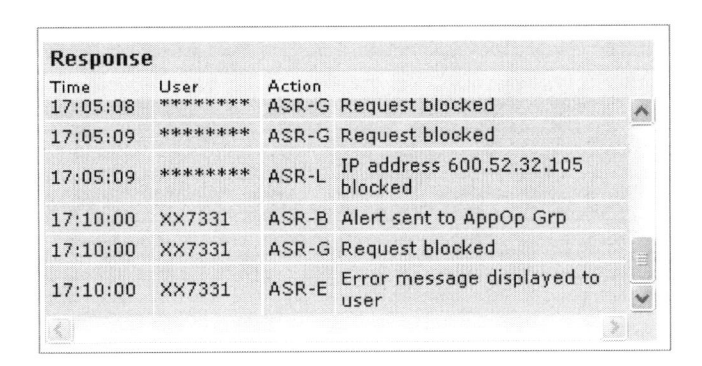

Response			
Time	User	Action	
17:05:08	********	ASR-G	Request blocked
17:05:09	********	ASR-G	Request blocked
17:05:09	********	ASR-L	IP address 600.52.32.105 blocked
17:10:00	XX7331	ASR-B	Alert sent to AppOp Grp
17:10:00	XX7331	ASR-G	Request blocked
17:10:00	XX7331	ASR-E	Error message displayed to user

This is of course all completely custom to the application and the individual organization's view of threats.

Example: Ensnare

The Ensnare Ruby gem includes raw details of the "violations" and summary metrics. See *Part IV : Demonstration Implementations - Chapter 23 : Ensnare for Ruby*.

The following two screen captures are reproduced from the Ensnare project wiki[128].

Figure 31 ENSNARE VIOLATIONS LISTING

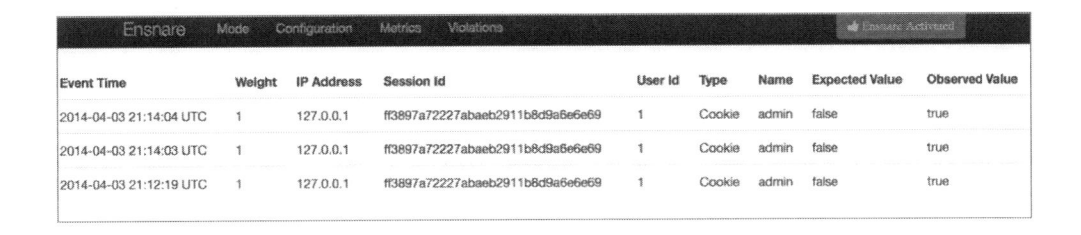

Event Time	Weight	IP Address	Session Id	User Id	Type	Name	Expected Value	Observed Value
2014-04-03 21:14:04 UTC	1	127.0.0.1	ff3897a72227abaeb2911b8d9a6e6e69	1	Cookie	admin	false	true
2014-04-03 21:14:03 UTC	1	127.0.0.1	ff3897a72227abaeb2911b8d9a6e6e69	1	Cookie	admin	false	true
2014-04-03 21:12:19 UTC	1	127.0.0.1	ff3897a72227abaeb2911b8d9a6e6e69	1	Cookie	admin	false	true

Part V : Model Dashboards

Figure 32 ENSNARE METRICS PAGE

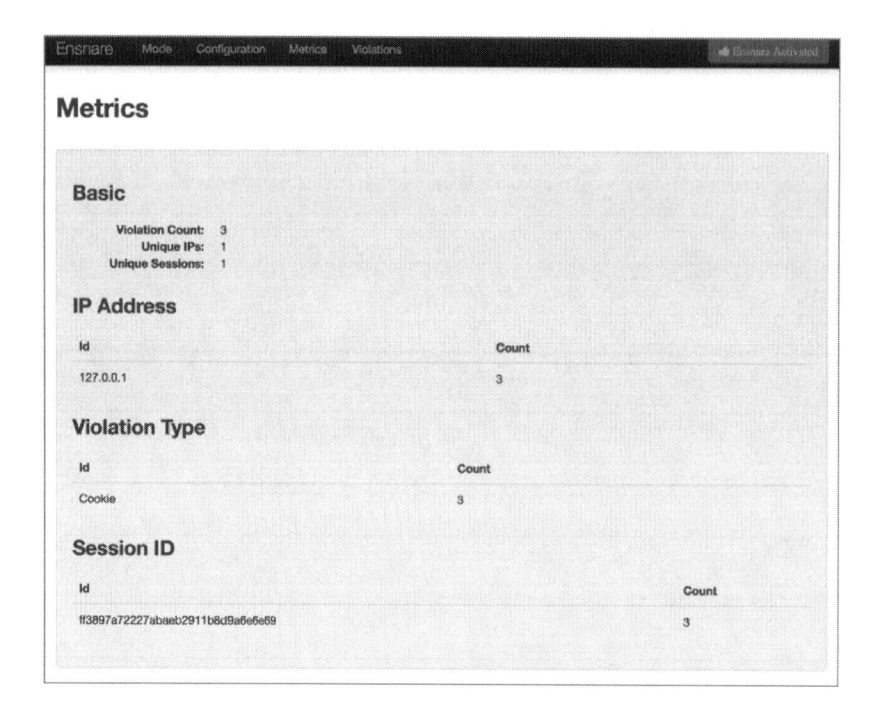

Example: AppSensor WS

The AppSensor WS reference implementation demonstrates how simply information from the Event Analysis Engine can be rendered in a web page. See *Part IV : Demonstration Implementations - Chapter 20 : Web Services (AppSensor WS)*.

AppSensor coverage

Coverage of AppSensor event, attack and response events can be as little or as much as is imported from logging or signaling, but is dependent upon the customization options of the tool. But with all of these model examples, code can be developed to produce a custom dashboard by the organization to suit their own business needs.

Chapter 29 : Application Vulnerability Tracking

Introduction

Software bug/defect/vulnerability tracking systems can also consume AppSensor data to add intelligence for severity rating and prioritization. Knowledge about actual attacks and how attackers may be getting close to vulnerabilities scheduled for mitigation is valuable information. This class of software will usually have multiple methods of data import, and will be preconfigured to consume data from commonly used commercial and open source information security risk and vulnerability software.

Description

Application vulnerability tracking software usually supports a portfolio of projects or applications.

Example: ThreadFix

An open source tool in this area is ThreadFix[138] that facilitates the import, aggregation, analysis and management of vulnerability data from security verification activities throughout the software development lifecycle. This has the additional capability of creating web application firewall (WAF) rules that can be deployed while vulnerabilities are being investigated, corrected, tested, deployed and verified.

The default dashboard in ThreadFix displays vulnerabilities grouped by severity and by most common by CWE[108]. It is possible to imagine how the very specific AppSensor data could be overlaid to provide insight into which types of vulnerability might be being actively targeted by different groups of users. This would not generally work as well with less specific, and more voluminous, data from network devices.

Figure 33 and *Figure 34* on the following page, illustrate a mock overlay of attacks grouped by user group. Note the logarithmic scale. These could potentially also be made into more detailed reports. ThreadFix and other tools in this class of software do not yet support this capability, but could be extended to do so.

In practice, some of the most common CWEs such as configuration and information leakage issues may not be included in AppSensor attack detection, and it may not be simple to provide a mapping from detection points to CWEs.

Part V : Model Dashboards

Figure 33 THREADFIX DASHBOARD SHOWING MOCK UP OF CWE VS ATTACK CHART OVERLAY

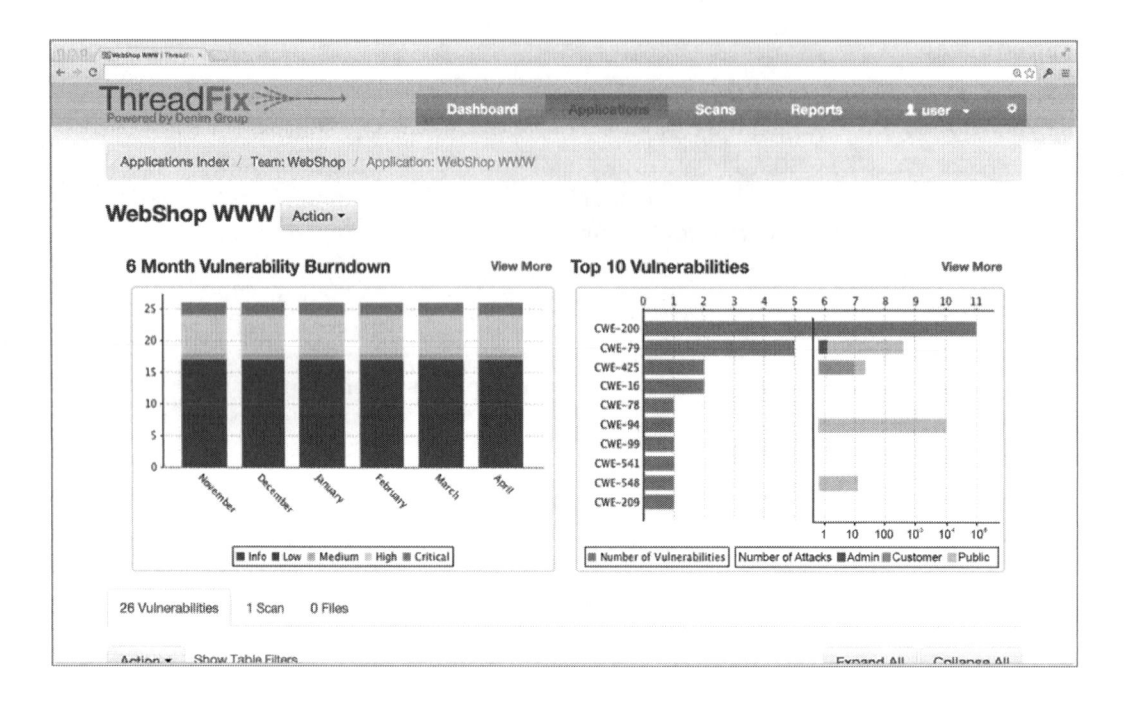

Figure 34 DETAILED VIEW OF CHART OVERLAY MOCKUP

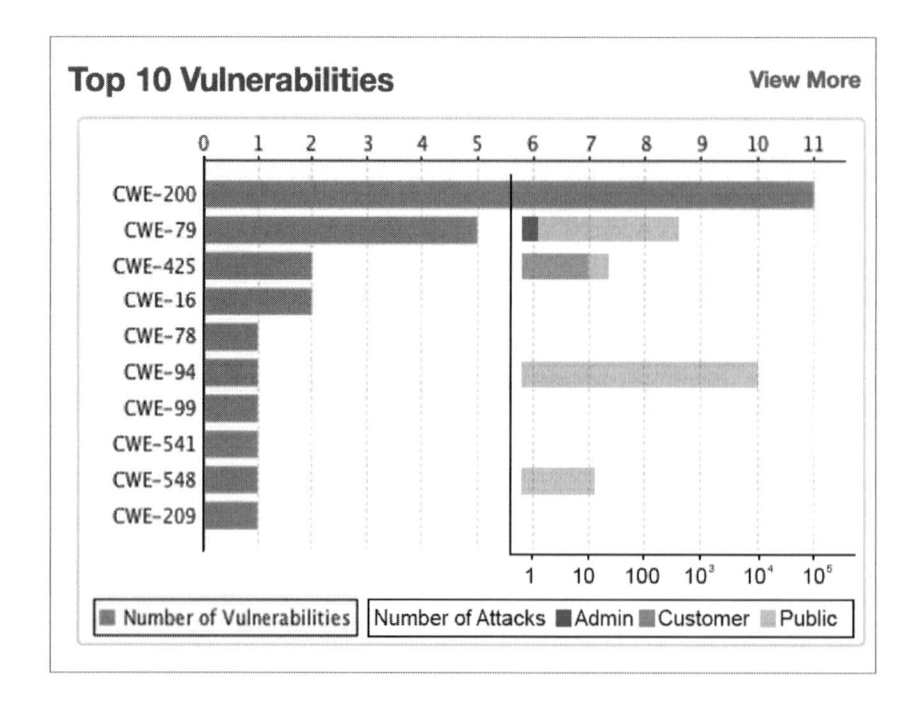

Chapter 29 : Application Vulnerability Tracking

Since tools like this also import static analysis (code review), a more useful possibility is identifying attacks against particular filters, modules or functions. These could be mapped during the detection point design specification stage, and saved in AppSensor logs or included in AppSensor event signaling (see *Data Signaling Exchange Formats* in *Part VI : Reference Materials*).

Similarly if application logging records the entry point (i.e. URL path), this could be used to cross reference attacks and vulnerabilities. A mock-up of this addition to ThreadFix's vulnerability report drill down is shown below.

Figure 35 MOCKUP ILLUSTRATING HOW URL PATHS COULD BE USED TO MATCH VULNERABILITIES IDENTIFIED THROUGH SECURITY SCANNING CORRELATE WITH WHERE ATTACKS ARE OCCURRING

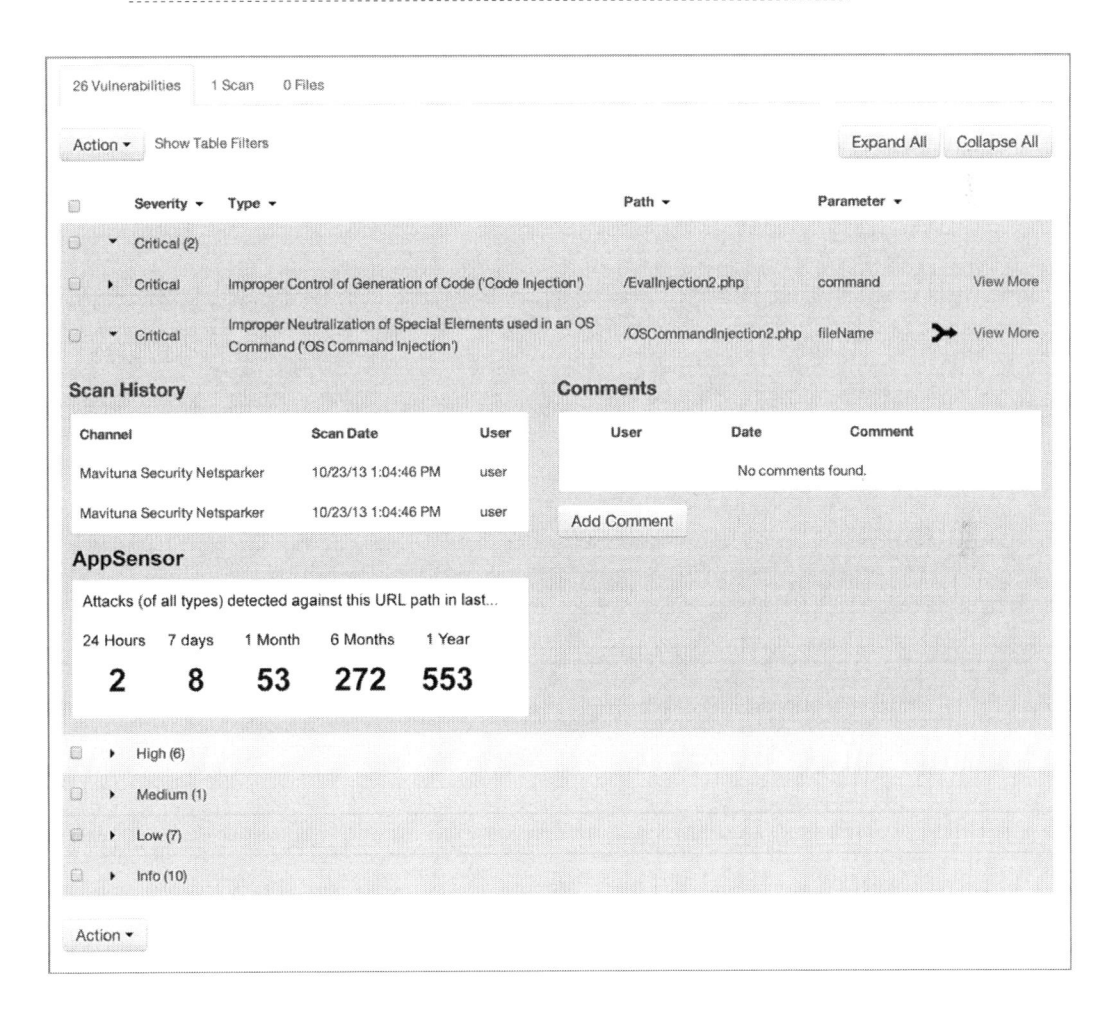

Part V : Model Dashboards

AppSensor coverage

Coverage of AppSensor event, attack and response events can be as little or as much as is imported from logging or signaling, but is dependent upon the customization options of the tool.

Part VI : Reference Materials

In this section, the primary information sources are included. Updates and reference materials are maintained on the OWASP AppSensor Project website[1].

Glossary

A glossary of terminology has been produced for the project to define what particular terminology means in the context of application layer attack detection and prevention. In some cases existing intrusion detection terminology is not consistent with an application specific approach, is implementation specific, or has an alternative meaning in software development that could lead to confusion.

Resources from US Committee on National Security Systems (CNSS)[139], MITRE Corporation[140] and National Institute of Standards and Technology (NIST)[27] were used to find and determine names. Adopters are encouraged to use terminology that is consistent with their own in-house standards and which are familiar to development teams.

Access Controller	The access controller component performs the authorization function in the **event analysis engine**. Based on the authenticated **user** (**client application**/reporting client), the access controller determines what functions and data are available to said **user** and enforces access to those.
Attack	Any kind of malicious activity that attempts to collect, disrupt, deny, degrade, or destroy information system resources or the information itself. Specifically within the context of AppSensor, an attack is a collection of **events** that violates a specified policy.
Attack Store	The attack store is the storage mechanism for **attacks**, which are produced by the analysis of **events**.
Authenticator	The authenticator is the component that performs user authentication. This functionality lives within the event analysis engine. Note: This component is used to authenticate **client applications** and reporting clients, NOT end users to the **client applications** or reporting clients.
Client Application	The client application is the business application that is being protected by AppSensor. This is the application that will be annotated with **detection points**, and will be protected by responses.
Correlation	Correlation refers to the determination of relation between **events** based on some common set of data. For example, two seemingly unrelated **events** generated by two different **application clients** may be determined to be correlated together due to their being caused by end **users** sharing a common username.
Credential(s)	The credential represents the object associated with identity

	assertion for **client applications** and reporting clients when authenticating to the **event analysis engine**.
Detection Point	A detection point is a specific point during the execution of a program that is instrumented in a way that allows event generation. In practice, the execution of the program could involve components that are architecturally separate from the running client application. For instance, a web application (A1) could use a detection point in a WAF that is protecting A1. This would still be considered a detection point for A1.
Event	An event is any observable occurrence in a system and/or network. Specifically within the context of AppSensor, an event is an observed occurrence that is monitored, especially within the application itself, with the intention that the occurrence be considered in the set of occurrences analyzed to determine **attacks**.
Event Analysis Engine	The event analysis engine is the component of the AppSensor architecture that represents the analysis and processing of incoming **event** data. The **events** are compiled (and stored) in the analysis engine, then processed to determine if and when response actions are appropriate. All of the service level APIs represented by "AppSensor WS" are exposed by this component.
Event Manager	The event manager collects **event** notifications from the client application detection points and polls the **event analysis engine** for any appropriate **response actions** to execute.
Event Store	The event store is the storage mechanism for **events**.
Intrusion	An intrusion is a successful **attack**.
Reporting Client	The reporting client is the architectural component of AppSensor that represents the data visualization e.g. a dashboard. In general, this component views, but does not produce, the data stored in the **event analysis engine**. This is meant as a set of functionality to provide a useful representation of the AppSensor data.
Response	A response is the action taken as a result of **attack** recognition. The goal of executing a response could be to gain or store more information about the attack and/or prevent further attacks.
Resource	A resource is a defined component of the application. This could be at various levels of granularity, but generally represents an accessible subset of the application (specific component, specific URL, etc.)

Role	A role is an attribute assigned to a user that ties membership to function. When an **user** has a given role, the **user** is granted the rights of that role. When the **user** loses that role, those rights are removed. The rights given to the role are consistent with the functionality that the **user** needs to perform the expected tasks.
Threshold	A threshold is a value that sets the limit between normal and abnormal behavior.
Trend	A trend is the determination of a pattern or tendency of a series of data points moving in a certain direction over time.
User	An entity that has access to the protected application. This could represent a human or a system, or possibly a collection of either.

Detection Points

Listing of detection points

The example AppSensor detection points are listed in *Table 30* below with additional details and examples for each category in the summary table below and subsequent twelve tables. As discussed in *Part III : Making It Happen*, AppSensor only needs to detect enough obviously malicious behavior to make a decision about the intent of a user, it does not need to detect all malicious behavior. Thus only a small subset of detection points is usually ever implemented for each application.

Table 30 SUMMARY OF APPSENSOR DETECTION POINT IDENTIFIERS AND TITLES GROUPED BY EXCEPTION CATEGORY

Category Description	Detection Point ID	Title
Request Exception	RE1	Unexpected HTTP Command
	RE2	Attempt to Invoke Unsupported HTTP Method
	RE3	GET When Expecting POST
	RE4	POST When Expecting GET
	RE5	Additional/Duplicated Data in Request
	RE6	Data Missing from Request
	RE7	Unexpected Quantity of Characters in Parameter
	RE8	Unexpected Type of Characters in Parameter
Authentication Exception	AE1	Use of Multiple Usernames
	AE2	Multiple Failed Passwords
	AE3	High Rate of Login Attempts
	AE4	Unexpected Quantity of Characters in Username
	AE5	Unexpected Quantity of Characters in Password
	AE6	Unexpected Type of Character in Username
	AE7	Unexpected Type of Character in Password
	AE8	Providing Only the Username
	AE9	Providing Only the Password
	AE10	Additional POST Variable
	AE11	Missing POST Variable
	AE12	Utilization of Common Usernames
	AE13	Deviation from Normal GEO Location
Session Exception	SE1	Modifying Existing Cookie
	SE2	Adding New Cookie
	SE3	Deleting Existing Cookie
	SE4	Substituting Another User's Valid Session ID or Cookie
	SE5	Source Location Changes During Session
	SE6	Change of User Agent Mid Session

Table 30 continued…

Part VI : Reference Materials

Category	Detection Point	
Detection Point Category	ID	Title
Access Control Exception	ACE1	Modifying URL Argument Within a GET for Direct Object Access Attempt
	ACE2	Modifying Parameter Within A POST for Direct Object Access Attempt
	ACE3	Force Browsing Attempt
	ACE4	Evading Presentation Access Control Through Custom POST
Input Exception	IE1	Cross Site Scripting Attempt
	IE2	Violation Of Implemented White Lists
	IE3	Violation Of Implemented Black Lists
	IE4	Violation of Input Data Integrity
	IE5	Violation of Stored Business Data Integrity
	IE6	Violation of Security Log Integrity
	IE7	Detect Abnormal Content Output Structure
Encoding Exception	EE1	Double Encoded Character
	EE2	Unexpected Encoding Used
Command Injection Exception	CIE1	Blacklist Inspection for Common SQL Injection Values
	CIE2	Detect Abnormal Quantity of Returned Records
	CIE3	Null Byte Character in File Request
	CIE4	Carriage Return or Line Feed Character in File Request
File IO Exception	FIO1	Detect Large Individual File
	FIO2	Detect Large Number of File Uploads
Honey Trap	HT1	Alteration to Honey Trap Data
	HT2	Honey Trap Resource Requested
	HT3	Honey Trap Data Used
User Trend Exception	UT1	Irregular Use of Application
	UT2	Speed of Application Use
	UT3	Frequency of Site Use
	UT4	Frequency of Feature Use
System Trend Exception	STE1	High Number of Logouts Across The Site
	STE2	High Number of Logins Across The Site
	STE3	High Number of Same Transaction Across The Site
Reputation	RP1	Suspicious or Disallowed User Source Location
	RP2	Suspicious External User Behavior
	RP3	Suspicious Client-Side Behavior
	RP4	Change to Environment Threat Level

This list, and the details in the later tables are maintained on the AppSensor website's list of detection points[74]. Always check there for the most recent information.

Categorization of detection points

It is also useful to categorize these example detection points in other ways than exception category.

Suspicious/Attack

They can be categorized based on malicious intent, as described at the beginning of this chapter:

- Suspicious events which could occur during normal user experience with site or browser or as the result of a non-malicious user error
- Attack event which are outside of the normal application flow, or requires special tools or requires special knowledge.

The allocations to these categories are shown below in *Table 31*. This also indicates whether the detection point collects information from each user ("One user") or all users in aggregate ("All users").

Table 31   APPSENSOR DETECTION POINTS CATEGORIZED BY SUSPICIOUS AND ATTACK EVENTS

Source	Category	Suspicious	Attack
One user	Request	RE3 RE5 RE6	RE1 RE2 RE4 RE7 RE8
	Authentication	AE1 AE7 AE13	AE2 AE3 AE4 AE5 AE6 AE8 AE9 AE10 AE11 AE12
	Session	SE3 SE5	SE1 SE2 SE4 SE6
	Access Control	ACE1 ACE3	ACE2 ACE4
	Input Exception	IE1 IE2 IE3	IE4 IE5 IE6 IE7
	Encoding	EE1	EE2
	Command Injec.		CIE1 CIE2 CIE3 CIE4
	File IO	FIO1	FIO2
	Honey Trap		HT1 HT2 HT3
	User Trend	UT1 UT2 UT3 UT4	
	Reputation	RP1 RP2 RP3	
All users	System Trend	STE1 STE2 STE3	
	Reputation	RP4	

Part VI : Reference Materials

Discrete/Aggregating/Modifying

Another categorization has been provided that divides the detection points into three classes:

- Discrete - Detection points that can be activated without any prior knowledge of the user's behavior and thus are related to the scope of the request
- Aggregating - Detection points that require a number of prior identical events to occur before they are activated and thus relate to activities over the duration of a single or multiple sessions (of one or more users)
- Modifying - Detection points that are typically only used to alter the detection thresholds or response actions

The detection points are categorized in this way in *Table 32* below.

Table 32   APPSENSOR DETECTION POINTS CATEGORIZED BY WHETHER THEY ARE DISCRETE, AGGREGATING OR MODIFYING

Source	Detection Points													
	Category	Discrete								Aggregating				Modifying
One user	Request	RE1	RE2	RE3	RE4	RE5	RE6	RE7	RE8					
	Authentication	AE4	AE5	AE6	AE7	AE8	AE9	AE10	AE11 AE12	AE1	AE2	AE3	AE13	
	Session	SE1	SE2	SE3	SE4					SE5	SE6			
	Access Control	ACE1	ACE2	ACE3	ACE4									
	Input Exception	IE1	IE2	IE3	IE4	IE5	IE6	IE7						
	Encoding	EE1	EE2											
	Command Injec.	CIE1	CIE2	CIE3	CIE4									
	File IO	FIO1								FIO2				
	Honey Trap	HT1	HT2	HT3										
	User Trend									UT1	UT2	UT3	UT4	
	Reputation													RP1 RP2 RP3
All users	System Trend									STE1	STE2	STE3		
	Reputation													RP4

Detection Points

Categorization overview

All these categorizations have been summarized in *Figure 36* below. A large color version of this diagram is available from the OWASP website[141].

Figure 36 DIAGRAM SHOWING THE ASSIGNMENT OF DETECTION POINTS TO ALL THE CATEGORIZATIONS

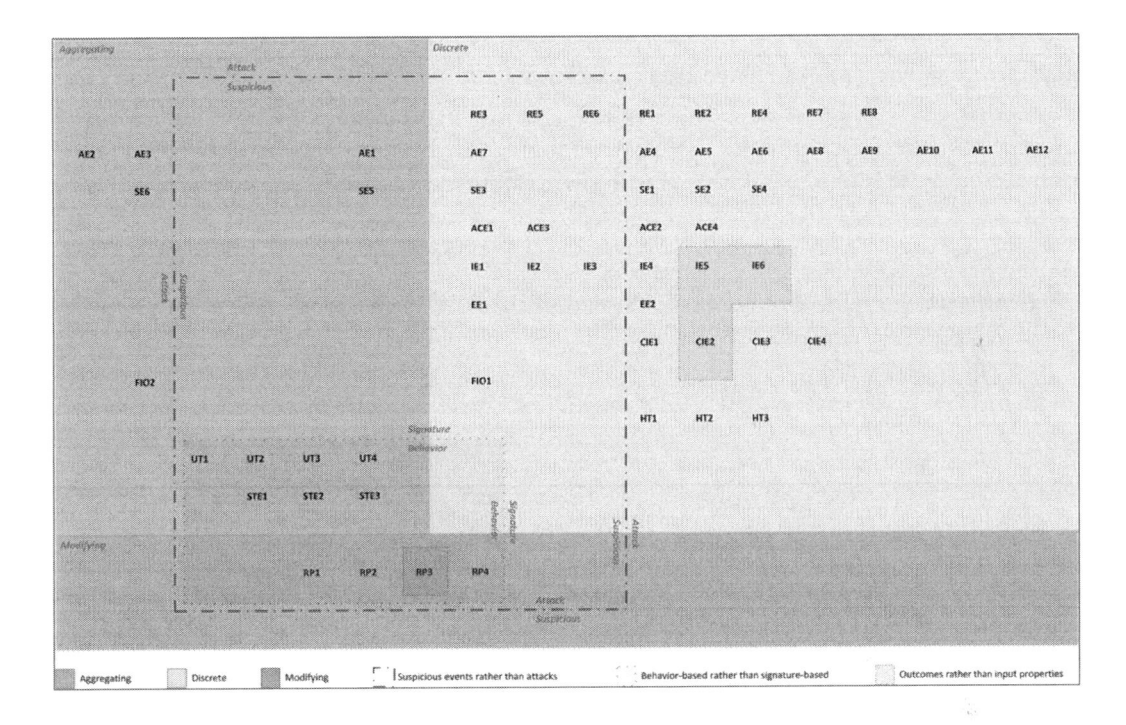

Detection points AE13 and IE7 are not yet included in this diagram.

The diagram illustrates the following properties of the example detection points:

- Detection points within each exception category run across the diagram horizontally, beginning with the Request Exceptions (RE) and finishing with the Reputation ones (RP) at the bottom of the diagram
- Detection point names and exception category can be found by reading the identity codes
- Discrete, aggregating and modifying detection points are separated and indicated by the colored areas
- Suspicious events are bounded by the heavy dashed line
- The four "outcome" detection points are indicated using a hatched background.

Part VI : Reference Materials

This diagram also shows a classification Signature vs. Behavioral used in version 1.1 of the AppSensor book[2]. This classification has been deprecated because the term "signature" can be mistakenly understood to mean a fixed pattern due its use in terminology for anti-malware systems. The use of Discrete/Aggregating/Modifying describes the categorization more accurately.

At a glance, it can be seen that all behavior-based detection points are of the suspicious type, and all are of the aggregating class. The majority of the detection points are in the discrete class, and of those, most detect attack events.

Additionally the detection points italicized and underlined are often used in generic pre-processing or filter modules, rather than deeper within business logic.

Related types

Some detection points can be considered as more specific instances of others. For example Unexpected Type of Characters in Parameter (RE8) could be a sub-type of Violation Of Implemented White Lists (IE2) and/or Violation Of Implemented Black Lists (IE3). These are illustrated in *Figure 37*. A large color version of this diagram is available from the OWASP website[142].

Figure 37 DIAGRAM SHOWING THE RELATED APPSENSOR DETECTION POINTS

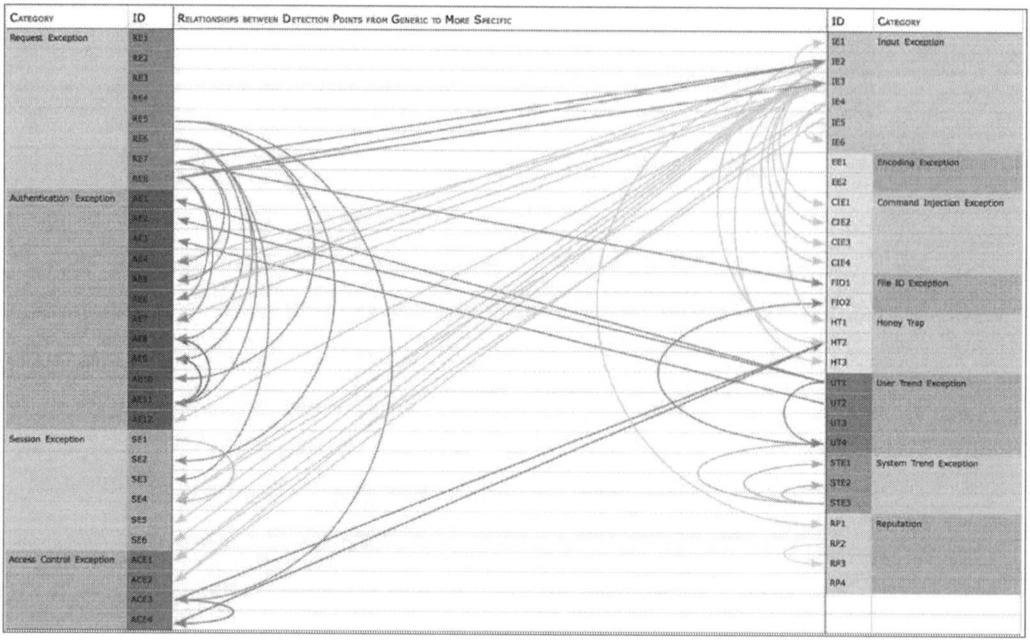

Detection points AE13 and IE7 are not yet included in this diagram.

It should also be noted that a few detection points detect an outcome/result, rather than the input (e.g. user data submission in an HTTP request):

- Violation of Stored Business Data Integrity (IE5)
- Violation of Security Log Integrity (IE6)
- Detect Abnormal Content Output Structure (IE7)
- Detect Abnormal Quantity of Returned Records (CIE2).

In some circumstances RP3 Suspicious Client Side behavior might also be considered an outcome/result–perhaps some XSS occurs on the response page once rendered by the user's web browser. Some outputs are inputs to other processes, so the distinction is not always clear.

Part VI : Reference Materials

Detailed descriptions of detection points

Grouped by detection point category.

Table 33 DESCRIPTIONS OF REQUEST EXCEPTION (RE) DETECTION POINTS

Detection Point Code, Name, Description and Considerations	Examples
RE1 - Unexpected HTTP Command An HTTP request is received which contains unexpected/disallowed commands. A list of accepted commands should be generated (i.e. GET and POST) and all other HTTP commands should generate an event. See HTTP/1.1: Method Definitions[143]. Browsers and proxies using the HEAD method to check whether the content of a file has changed.	• Instead of a GET or POST request, the user sends a TRACE request to the application.
RE2 - Attempt to Invoke Unsupported HTTP Method An HTTP request is received which contains a non-existent HTTP command (does not match anything in this list: HEAD, GET, POST, PUT, DELETE, TRACE, OPTIONS, CONNECT).	• Instead of a GET or POST request, the user sends a TEST request to the application (TEST is not a valid HTTP request method).
RE3 - GET When Expecting POST A page which is expecting only POST requests, is requested by HTTP method GET. Some pages may be designed to receive both GET and POST requests. Some resources may allow both GET and POST methods e.g. an edit form may be hyperlinked using a parameter value defining the record to be edited, but the form is submitted by POST to itself. Users may bookmark a page that is the result of a POST and return to it at a later date.	• The user sends a GET request to a page which has only been used for POSTs.
RE4 - POST When Expecting GET A page which is expecting only GET requests, receives a POST. See also RE3.	• The user utilizes a proxy tool to build a custom POST request and sends it to a page which has been accessed by GET requests.

Table 33 continued…

Detection Point Code, Name, Description and Considerations	Examples
RE5 - Additional/Duplicated Data in Request Additional unexpected parameters or HTTP headers, or duplicates, are received with the request. Additional parameters may be an attempt to override values or to exploit unexposed functionality. Duplicated parameters may be an indication of attempted HTTP parameter pollution. Beware of firing this detector when additional cookies, not used by the application, are found (as opposed to duplicated cookies) since these may relate to third-party code (e.g. advertisements, analytics) or some other application. Note that extra HTTP headers may be added by intermediate proxies, and unless the network configuration is fixed (an internal network perhaps), additional headers cannot be controlled and thus cannot be used to infer existence of a potential attacker. Links from third party sites/services may included additional parameters (e.g. from search engines, from advertisements). Additional cookies headers may be added by other applications or by third parties such as advertisers, and there may be very little control over these. Additional HTTP headers may be added by intermediate network devices (e.g. for traffic management).	• Additional form or URL parameters submitted with request (e.g. debug=1, servervariable=2000). • A parameter is defined more than once in the URL Query String. • An HTTP header is duplicated. • An additional HTTP header is found. • A URL path parameter with the same name as a form parameter is sent with the request.
RE6 - Data Missing from Request Expected parameters or HTTP headers are missing from the request. Bookmarking and use of a browser's "back button" can lead to requests without the expected parameters. A bookmarked page may be missing the required POST parameters (see also RE3). Users may choose to send a blank or different User Agent header value.	• A page is requested without any of the required form parameters. • The HTTP-Accept header is not present in a request.
RE7 - Unexpected Quantity of Characters in Parameter The user provides a parameter value with a large number of characters. If the input field does not have client-side validation and/or MAXLENGTH attributes, a user might inadvertently copy in some text that is longer than expected.	• The user submits a form field with more characters than the form's maxlength attribute and client-side validation would allow • The user submits data in a form's hidden field which is longer than expected.
RE8 - Unexpected Type of Characters in Parameter The user provides a parameter value containing characters outwith the expected range. Text fields may include text from copy and paste operations that contain illegal characters.	• The user sends an HTTP header containing a line break character. • The user sends a URL parameter value that contains ASCII characters below 20 or above 7E.

Part VI : Reference Materials

Table 34   DESCRIPTIONS OF AUTHENTICATION EXCEPTION (AE) DETECTION POINTS

Detection Point Code, Name, Description and Considerations	Examples
AE1 - Use of Multiple Usernames Multiple usernames are attempted when logging into the application. The assignment of login attempts to a user can be based on a sessionID given to the user when they first visit the website. Correlating based on IP address is difficult since multiple users could be using the site from the same IP address (e.g. corporate NAT).	• User first tries username 'bob', then username 'sue', then 'steve', etc.
AE2 - Multiple Failed Passwords For a single username, multiple bad passwords, or other authentication credentials, are entered. See Popularity is Everything[144] section 4 - Attack-Detection Scenarios for ideas about tracking use of unsuccessful passwords and looking whether these are used against multiple accounts. A users providing the same wrong password more than once may be different to different to different wrong passwords. See Account Lockout, Episode 76, OWASP Podcast[145].	• User tries username:password combination of 'user:pass1', 'user:pass2', 'user:pass3', etc. • Multiple failed PINs are attempted for the same customer account. • In an online banking application, several invalid mobile authentication codes, transaction verification codes or transaction authentication numbers are submitted. • A user provides the correct password, but repeatedly fails to provide the required second password correctly.
AE3 - High Rate of Login Attempts The rate of login attempts becomes too high (possibly indicating an automated login attack). The threshold should relate to a limit and period appropriate to the application (e.g. total number in a second or minute or hour).	• User sends the following login attempts within 1 second - 'user1:pass1', 'user1:pass2', 'user2:pass3', 'user2:pass4'.
AE4 - Unexpected Quantity of Characters in Username The user provides a username with a large number of characters (see also RE7).	• The user sends a username that is 200 characters long when 6-8 are expected.
AE5 - Unexpected Quantity of Characters in Password The user provides a password with a large number of characters. Higher limits may be required for sites which allow users to have pass phrases (see also RE7).	• The user sends a password that is 200 characters long, when 5-20 are expected. • The user sends a PIN of 30 characters.

Table 34 continued…

Detection Point Code, Name, Description and Considerations	Examples
AE6 - Unexpected Type of Character in Username The user provides a username which contains characters outwith the expected range. Any characters below hex value 20 or above 7E are often considered illegal (decimal values of below 32 or above 126). Users may be confused between a username, customer identification code and their account number, or even between offline and online identifiers. Mis-typing might add a character like "|" or "#" if these are adjacent to the ENTER/CR key. Whitespace may be appended to values when copied from a spreadsheet cell (e.g. a line feed character when cell values are copied and pasted from Excel). A password may be put in the username field by accident.	• The user sends a username that contains ASCII non-printable characters such as the NULL byte.
AE7 - Unexpected Type of Character in Password The user provides a password containing characters outwith the expected range. Examples include null byte, and characters which need the ALT key to be used.(see also AE6).	• The user sends a password that contains ASCII characters below 20 or above 7E.
AE8 - Providing Only the Username The user submits a POST request which only contains the username variable. The password variable has been removed. This is different from only providing the username in the login form since in that case the password variable would be present and empty.	• The user utilizes a proxy tool to remove the password variable from the submitted POST request.
AE9 - Providing Only the Password The user submits a POST request which only contains the password variable. The username variable has been removed. This is different from only providing the password in the login form since in that case the username variable would be present and empty.	• The user utilizes a proxy tool to remove the username variable from the submitted POST request.
AE10 - Additional POST Variable Additional, unexpected POST variables are received during an authentication request (see also RE5).	• The user utilizes a proxy tool to add the POST variable of 'admin=true' to the request.
AE11 – Missing POST Variables Expected POST variables are not present within the submitted authentication request. (see also RE6).	• The user utilizes a proxy tool to remove an additional POST variable, such as 'guest=true', from the POST request.
AE12 - Utilization of Common Usernames Common dictionary usernames are used to attempt to log into the application. Common usernames might be allowed during self-registration or when editing account details.	• Log in attempted with usernames "administrator", then "admin", then "test"
AE13 - Deviation from Normal GEO Location In some applications, most users log in from one or a just a few geographic locations. If the application learns these GeoIP locations, it can then detect when a user is logging into the application from a different location. This would help to identify possible account hijacking attacks (from phishing, banking trojans).	• A banking customer's IP address has never been seen before when they log in. • A system attempts to authenticate to web services from a different country.

Part VI : Reference Materials

Table 35   DESCRIPTIONS OF SESSION EXCEPTION (SE) DETECTION POINTS

Detection Point Code, Name, Description and Considerations	Examples
SE1 - Modifying Existing Cookie A request is received containing a cookie with a modified value. This could be determined if the cookie is modified to an illegal value. In a poorly designed application, the length of the cookie value, or the combined size of all the cookies, might possibly exceed that which is supported.	• The user utilizes a proxy tool to change the encrypted cookie to an alternative value which does not properly decode within the application. • The user modifies an unencrypted cookie and sets an illegal value for a particular variable.
SE2 - Adding New Cookie A request is received which contains additional cookies that are not expected by the application. A session cookie existing when it should not (e.g. prior to authentication) is probably indicative of an attack. But cookies may also be set by third party sites which get send with the request - these may be harmless. Also consider what other applications exist on sub-domains (e.g. www.example.com, extranet.example.com and sales.example.com) which may also be setting cookies.	• The user utilizes a proxy tool to add cookies to the request.
SE3 - Deleting Existing Cookie A request is received which does not contain the expected cookies. The user may have bookmarked a page they had visited during a previous authenticated session. In a poorly designed application, the number of cookies might exceed the allowed number supported by the user's browser.	• The user utilizes a proxy tool to remove cookies or portions of cookies from a request.
SE4 - Substituting Another User's Valid Session ID or Cookie A request is received which contains cookie data that is clearly from another user or another session. A mis-configured proxy might send the same session ID or cookie for all users.	• The user utilizes a proxy tool to substitute valid data from another user or session into the cookie. An example would be changing some sort of identification number within the cookie.

Table 35 continued…

Detection Point Code, Name, Description and Considerations	Examples
SE5 - Source Location Changes During Session Valid requests, containing valid session credentials, are received from multiple source locations indicating a possible session hijacking attack. A full IP address may not be constant for some users during normal use due to clustered proxies or while mobile. Enforcing single fixed IP addresses for each session in an intranet application may be valid. However, if the application is accessible over public networks, changing IP address cannot be excluded and it may be more useful to consider fixing just part of the IP address, or looking for more significant changes such as when the user's IP address geo-location region or country changes (see Autonomous System Number (ASN) and Detecting Malice with ModSecurity: GeoLocation Data). Note: source port number should not be used in checks since this usually changes very frequently. If the full IP address is used for this, it may change slightly from request to request by the same user.	• User A's session is compromised and User B begins using the account. The requests originating from User B will possibly contain a different source IP address the User A. The source IP addresses could be the same if both users where behind the same NAT. • An application at a fixed server location, which calls web services, changes IP address unexpectedly.
SE6 - Change of User Agent Mid Session The User-Agent value of the header changes during a session. This may indicate a different browser is now being used. Although this value is under the control of the sender, a change in this may indicates that the session has been compromised and is being used another individual. This will likely not be the case that the user has simply copied and pasted the URL from one browser to another on the same system because this action would not copy over the appropriate session identifiers. The User Agent string may change in some browsers when the content type changes (e.g. from HTML to PDF). This detection point may only be useful in environments where a single browser is deployed. Optionally also include other HTTP headers in this check. For example, the Accept-Encoding and Accept-Language headers do not normally change and could be concatenated with the User-Agent and hashed to created an identifier. The ideas[146] described in Panopticlick[147] and Javascript Browser Fingerprinting[148] can also be used to fingerprint a particular client system but require the use of client-side code. Application owners should check the legality of collecting data, and whether it is considered "personal data" which may have additional constraints in some jurisdictions.	• Mid session, the User Agent changes from Firefox to Internet Explorer

Part VI : Reference Materials

Table 36   DESCRIPTIONS OF ACCESS CONTROL EXCEPTION (ACE) DETECTION POINTS

Detection Point Code, Name, Description and Considerations	Examples
ACE1 - Modifying URL Argument Within a GET for Direct Object Access Attempt The application is designed to use an identifier for a particular object, such as using categoryID=4 or user=guest within the URL. A user modifies this value in an attempt to access unauthorized information. This exception should be thrown anytime the identifier received from the user is not authorized due to the identifier being non-existent or the identifier not authorized for that user. Bookmarking, truncation, and mistyping issues could lead to some access control exceptions.	• ? The user modifies the following URL from /viewpage?page=1&user=guest to /viewpage?page=22&user=admin
ACE2 - Modifying Parameter Within A POST for Direct Object Access Attempt The value of a non-free text html form element (i.e. drop down box, radio button) is modified to an illegal value. The value either does not exist or is not authorized for the user. (see also ACE1 regarding bookmarking)	• The user utilizes a proxy tool to intercept a POST request and changes the submitted value to a value that was not available through the normal display. For example, the user encounters a dropdown box containing the numbers 1 through 10. The user selects 5 and then intercepts the request to change the submitted value to 100.
ACE3 - Force Browsing Attempt An authenticated or unauthenticated user sends a request for a non-existent resource (e.g. page, directory listing, image, file, etc), or a resource that is not authorized for that user. Requests for non-existent resources may occur for many reasons such as Benign Unexpected URLs - Part 1 - Missing (404 Not Found Error) Files[149]	• The user is authenticated and requests site.com/PageThatDoesNotExist. • The user is authenticated and requests a video they are not authorized to download/view. • An unauthenticated user (perhaps with a session ID) requests a listing of a directory detailed in the site's robots.txt file.
ACE4 - Evading Presentation Access Control Through Custom POST A POST request is received which is not authorized for the current user and the user could not have performed this action without crafting a custom POST request. This situation is most likely to occur when presentation layer access controls are in place and have removed the user's ability to initiate the action through the presentation of the application. An attacker may be aware of the functionality and attempt to bypass this presentation layer access control by crafting their own custom message and sending this in an attempt to execute the functionality.	• The application contains the ability for an administrator to delete a user. This method is normally invoked by entering the username and submitting to https://oursite/deleteuser Presentation layer access controls ensure the delete user form is not displayed to non-administrator users. A malicious user has access to a non-administrator account and is aware of the delete user functionality. The malicious user sends a custom crafted POST message to https://oursite/deleteuser in an attempt to execute the delete user method.

Table 37 DESCRIPTIONS OF INPUT EXCEPTION (IE) DETECTION POINTS

Detection Point Code, Name, Description and Considerations	Examples
IE1 - Cross Site Scripting Attempt The HTTP request contains common XSS attacks which are often used by attackers probing for XSS vulnerabilities. Detection should be configured to test all GET and POST values as well as all header names and values for the following values. There are many patterns which could be XSS but may also be normal user input to a free text field e.g. "Press the 'drop' button" if a pattern were looking for a single quotation mark followed by SQL commands like DROP, INSERT, UPDATE and DELETE. Applications that are used to discuss or share information about programming, software development and security may want to allow such free text input, provided it is encoded/escaped correctly.	• The user utilizes a proxy tool to add an XSS attack to the header value and the 'displayname' POST variable. The header value could be displayed to an admin viewing log files and the 'displayname' POST variable may be stored in the application and displayed to other users. Note, the following XSS attacks would only be used by an attacker to probe for vulnerability. An actual XSS attack would be customized by the attacker. • A user sends payloads like <script>alert(document.cookie);</script> <script>alert();</script> alert(String.fromCharCode(88,83,83)) <IMG SRC="javascript:alert('XSS');"> <IMG SRC=javascript:alert('XSS')> <IMG SRC=javascript:alert(&quot;XSS&quot;)> <BODY ONLOAD=alert('XSS')>
IE2 - Violation Of Implemented White Lists The application receives user-supplied data that violates an established white list validation. See AC3 (Force Browsing Attempts) about requests for non-existent/unauthorised (i.e. not white listed) URLs. (see also IE1).	• The user submits data that is not correct for the particular field. This may not be attack data necessarily, but repeated violations could be an attempt by the attacker to determine how an application works or to discover a flaw.
IE3 - Violation Of Implemented Black Lists The application receives user-supplied data that violates an established black list validation. This may not be attack data necessarily, but repeated violations could be an attempt by the attacker to determine how an application works or to discover a flaw or to exploit a flaw. This black list approach suffers from the potential for greater false positives than IE2 above, and cannot be used to identify all potential malicious data (see also IE1).	• URL in comment field identified as suspected phishing and malware pages using Google Safe Browsing API[150]. • Parameter value matches a known SQL injection pattern. • Parameter value matches a known XSS pattern.

Table 37 continued...

Detection Point Code, Name, Description and Considerations	Examples
IE4 - Violation of Input Data Integrity The application receives HTTP header or body parameter values which have been tampered with when no change should have occurred. This detection point should only be used with parameters that cannot be altered by accident. Input types text and textarea would not normally be suitable, even if the elements are disabled in the browser. Be wary of assuming JavaScript will prevent modification of form elements in all conditions.	• Hidden form field modified by client. • Select list value submitted in response, not sent by server as an available option value. • Cookie set by server has been manipulated by the client. • Cookie created by client instead of by the server.
IE5 - Violation of Stored Business Data Integrity User's input leads to violation of data integrity.	• A user's action leads to a system integrity error when writing to, or updating, a database. • Business rule checks detect that a user's action is not compatible. • Data accuracy checking detects duplicate records for a user. • User input leads to an unexpected file change (e.g. .htaccess file overwritten, page template changed). • User's request leads to a new, unexpected, outbound network connection being made (e.g. mail sent to an SMTP server, files downloaded from a FTP server).
IE6 - Violation of Security Log Integrity Security or audit log tampering detected. AppSensor may rely on the accuracy of "log" data to make decisions when thresholds are reached. This detector aims to detect the insertion of forged entries, corruption of logs, unauthorised deletion of and changes to records. See also: • NIST SP 800-92 Guide to Security Log Management[151] • Tamper Detection in Audit Logs[152] • Forensic Tamper Detection in SQL Server[153]	• Special characters embedded in logged data about a user's activity cause the data to overwrite a previous log entry. • Log file integrity is broken by modification to an existing log entry.
IE7 - Detect Abnormal Content Output Structure Output data is of an unexpected format, structure or contains unexpected components.	• An abnormal number of inline scripts or iframes are returned in an HTML page indicating a successful XSS injection. • An XML file generated utilizing user input no longer matches the expected structure/schema/document declaration. • Generated JSON data contains does not match expected format.

Detection Points

Table 38　Descriptions of Encoding Exception (EE) Detection Points

Detection Point Code, Name, Description and Considerations	Examples
EE1 - Double Encoded Characters An HTTP request is received which contains one or more double encoded values. Data supplied by other party systems may have encoding issues.	• The user sends encodes the % symbol to %25 and appends 3C. The user is sending %253C which may be interpreted by the application as %3C which is actually <.
EE2 - Unexpected Encoding Used An HTTP request is received which contains values that have encoded in an unexpected format (see also EE1).	• The user encodes an attack such as alert(document.cookie) into the UTF-7 format and sends this data the application. This could bypass validation filters and be rendered to a user in certain situations.

Part VI : Reference Materials

Table 39   DESCRIPTIONS OF COMMAND INJECTION EXCEPTION (CIE) DETECTION POINTS

Detection Point Code, Name, Description and Considerations	Examples
CIE1 - Blacklist Inspection for Common SQL Injection Values A request is received which contains common SQL injection attack attempts. The point of this detection is not to detect all variations of a SQL injection attack, but to detect the common probes which an attacker or tool might use to determine if a SQL injection vulnerability is present. Unless the site contains some sort of message board for discussing SQL injection, there is little reason that the SQL injection examples should ever be received from a user request (see also IE1).	• The user sends a request and modifies a URL parameter from category = 5 to category = 5' OR '1' = '1 in an attempt to perform an SQL injection attack. The user could perform similar attacks by modifying POST variables or even the request headers to contain SQL injection attacks. ' OR '1'='1 ' OR 'a'='a ' OR 1=1-- xp_cmdshell UNION JOIN
CIE2 - Detect Abnormal Quantity of Returned Records A database query is executed which returns more records than expected.	• A query of a non-SQL dataset should only return 1 record but 100 records are returned. • The application is designed to allow a user to maintain 5 profiles. A user makes a request to view all of their profiles. The database SQL query, which is expected to always return 5 or less results, returns 10,000 records. Something in the application, or user's actions, has caused unauthorized data to be returned. • Extraction of data from an XML file should only return one matching node, but more than one is returned.
CIE3 - Null Byte Character in File Request A request is received to download a file from the server. The filename requested contains the null byte the file name. This is an attempted OS injection attack.	• The user modifies the filename of the requested file to download to contain the null byte. The null byte can be added by inserting the hex value %00.
CIE4 - Carriage Return or Line Feed Character in File Request A request is received which contains the carriage return or line feed characters within the POST data or the URL parameters. This is an attempted HTTP split response attack.	• The user includes the hex value %0D or %0A in the HTTP request POST data or URL parameters.

Table 40 DESCRIPTIONS OF FILE INPUT/OUTPUT EXCEPTIONS (FIO) DETECTION POINTS

Detection Point Code, Name, Description and Considerations	Examples
FIO1 - Detect Large Individual File A file upload feature detects that a large file has been submitted for upload which exceeds the maximum upload size.	• The user attempts to upload a large file to occupy resources or fill up disk space.
FIO2 - Detect Large Number of File Uploads A user uploads an excessively large number of files. The limit and period used to determine the threshold rate is application dependent, and may also depend on the user's role.	• A single user attempts to upload multiple small files to occupy resources or fill up disk space.

Part VI : Reference Materials

Table 41 DESCRIPTIONS OF HONEY TRAP (HT) DETECTION POINTS

Detection Point Code, Name, Description and Considerations	Examples
HT1 - Alteration to Honey Trap Data Fake (not otherwise needed by the application) data sent to the user and returned (e.g. as form, URL, cookie values or in the path or HTTP header) is modified[154]. This is usually combined with making the name or value a tempting item for an attacker to try modifying. Similar techniques can also be used for the creation of accessible CAPTCHA.	• Otherwise useless hidden fields, which look like potential vulnerabilities, added to some forms are sent back to the server modified (e.g. `<input type="hidden" name="admin" value="false" />`) • An additional URL parameter, which is not used by the application, is modified by the user (e.g. /account.jsp?debug=0). • An additional fake cookie is added and is modified by the user. • URL rewriting is used and a fake directory name is added; this is modified by the user (e.g. /orders/normaluser/display.php).
HT2 - Honey Trap Resource Requested A purposely leaked resource that has no use in normal application use is requested by a user. Ensure the resource is not linked from normal application content such that a spider or robot might find the resource in any case.	• Page, directory or other resource listed in the application's robots.txt robots exclusion file is requested by the user. • URL identified only in HTML comments is requested by the user. • Unexposed server function call included in Flash file source code is requested by the user.
HT3 - Honey Trap Data Used Special data sent or accessed by a user. For honey trap data that is detected on egress only, use of outbound content monitoring (e.g. a web application firewall or similar technique) may be helpful.	• Fake user name and password only visible in source HTML code used to attempt to log in to the application (e.g. in HTML comments, in server-side code 'accidentally' delivered to the user). • A special code number or account name is left in a discussion forum site; this is then used in the application • An attempt is made to authenticate with the user name listed in the first row (e.g. ID=1) of the application's database table of Users. • Data from a fake account record is sent by the server and detected; this record should not normally be accessible by anyone using the application.

Detection Points

Table 42 DESCRIPTIONS OF USER TREND EXCEPTION (UT) DETECTION POINTS

Detection Point Code, Name, Description and Considerations	Examples
UT1 - Irregular Use of Application The application receives an unusual pattern of requests for the same page or feature from a user. The user may be sending different data combinations or trying to detect errors in the page. Use of bookmarked URLs and the "back" button might generate out-of-sequence requests. See also related frequency of feature use in UT4.	• The user requests a particular page, such as the address update page, numerous times. • The user requests a page out-of-sequence, such as an intermediate step in a multi-stage form, or a series of actions that do not map to a valid business process. • The user only requests dynamic content, and not the associated static files (e.g. images, style sheets). • The user sends a slow request/read in an attempt at application denial of service.
UT2 - Speed of Application Use The speed of requests from a user indicates that an automated tool is being used to access the site. The use of a tool undertaking a high number of requests quickly may indicate unapproved content scraping or data gathering, reconnaissance for an attack, or attempts to identify vulnerabilities in the site. Slow usage (e.g. between account creation and use) might indicate automated account creation that are then used subsequently for attacks. If enforced inappropriately or too rigorously, this detection point could lead to false positives. Time periods need to be set broadly enough to cater for the normal spread in user behavior. Some users may use automated tools that store passwords securely to populate and submit authentication forms.	• The user utilizes an automated tool to request hundreds of pages per minute. • The user does not log in to the site until a long time after their account is created. • New (uncached) static content such as images and style sheets associated with each page are not requested in a similar time period as the page. • A CAPTCHA challenge is responded to more quickly than a human could possibly do. • The user's clickstream data velocity is too high. • The time interval between the applications displaying a page/form and the time for the user to complete the page/form and submit it is too fast. • A web scraping tool is used to obtain content from a website.
UT3 - Frequency of Site Use Change in how often the site is used by a user Some users may correctly change their behavior in the frequency of accessing the application.	• The user normally accesses the site once per week, but this changes to many times per day.
UT4 - Frequency of Feature Use The rate of a user utilizing a particular application feature changes dramatically. It may be valid for some functionality may be requested repeatedly. For example a real customer placing many orders, a press officer publishing a backlog of press releases, or an administrator populating a staff directory.	• The user submits many forum messages in a short period of time. • The user adds many new friends rapidly.

Part VI : Reference Materials

Table 43   DESCRIPTIONS OF SYSTEM TREND EXCEPTION (STE) DETECTION POINTS

Detection Point Code, Name, Description and Considerations	Examples
STE1 - High Number of Logouts Across The Site A sudden spike in logouts across the application could indicate a XSS and CSRF attack placed within the application which is automatically logging off users.	• The hourly usage of the log-off feature of the application suddenly spikes by 500%.
STE2 - High Number of Logins Across The Site A sudden spike in logins across the application could indicate users being redirected to the site from a phishing email looking to exploit a XSS vulnerability in the site.	• The hourly usage of the logon feature of the application suddenly spikes by 1,000%.
STE3 - Significant Change in Usage of Same Transaction Across The Site A sudden spike in similar activity across numerous users of the application may indicate a phishing attack or CSRF attack against the users; a rapid reduction in activity may indicate users are being redirected elsewhere; a significant change in average transaction value or other quantitative measure may indicate suspicious activity. External events (e.g. a news item) may lead to additional unexpected traffic which is not an attack. A special requirement, situation or event may dramatically change the rate of use of certain transactions. (See also UT4)	• The hourly usage of the update email address feature of the application suddenly spikes by 2,000%. • A website is compromised and users are redirected to a malicious site part-way through a process; the number of successful fully completed transactions drops to nil. • A number of slow requests/reads are received in an attempt at application denial of service. • The find contacts functionality is used excessively to identify related friends.

Detection Points

Table 44   DESCRIPTIONS OF REPUTATION (RP) DETECTION POINTS

Detection Point Code, Name, Description and Considerations	Examples
RP1 - Suspicious or Disallowed User Source Location The user is identified as using an IP address associated with a blacklist Considerations Suspicious or invalid geo-location, IP addresses or IP address ranges may be identified using a whitelist, internal blacklist, list of Tor nodes[15], HTTP blacklist[156,157], list of spammers[158] or known botnets[159]. "Suspicious" may also depend upon the type of user e.g. users in the "CMS manager" role should be using an internal network IP address, public users could be from anywhere, customers should only be accessing the application from a particular geographical region, search engine robots should be from a limited range of IP addresses. Take care that "suspicious" does not contribute to greater false positives. The currency and accuracy of needs to be considered when the information is used in AppSensor. The method of challenge and removal of inaccuracies, and the speed of this process, should also be considered.	• A user with an external IP address is accessing an internal application, which should not be occurring. • An authenticated user is accessing the application using a known Tor node, and attack detection thresholds are made stricter. • An authenticated user is accessing the application from a known trustworthy IP address, and thresholds for certain activity (e.g. input data validation errors) are relaxed slightly. • The IP address of the payment authentication server, used by the application for credit card authorization, changes.
RP2 - Suspicious External User Behavior External (to the application) devices and systems (e.g. host and network IDS, file integrity monitoring, disk usage monitoring, anti-malware service, IPS, network firewall, web application firewall, web server logging, XML gateway, database firewall, SIEM) detect anomalous behavior by the user (e.g. session and/or IP address) or suspicious user properties (e.g. fraud score, previously compromised, unusual current/previous behavior). This information can be used by the application to contribute to its knowledge about a potential attacker. In some cases, the information could be detected by the application itself (e.g. XSS pattern black listing), but may be more effectively identified by the external device, or is not known to the application normally (e.g. requests for missing resources that the web server sees, but does not pass onto the application). The greater the knowledge a device or system has about the application, the greater confidence can be given to evidence of suspicious behaviour. Therefore, for example, attempted SQL injection detected by a web application firewall (WAF) might be given greater weight than information from a network firewall about the IP address. The power of AppSensor is its accuracy and low false positive rate, and the usage of external data should be carefully assessed to ensure it does not contribute to a higher false positive rate. The level of trust in information from the external device/system/organization needs to be considered.	• A network IDS has detected suspicious activity by a particular IP address, and this is used to temporarily tighten the attack detection thresholds for requests from all users in the same IP address range. • An application is using the ModSecurity web application firewall with the Core Rule Set, and utilises the anomaly score data passed forward in the X-WAF-Events and X-WAF-Score HTTP headers (optional rules in modsecurity_crs_49_header_tagging.conf) to adjust the level of application logging for each user. • Information from an instance of PHPIDS suggests request data may be malicious. • An adverse score is indicated for the user or IP address by a fraud detection engine, or by an external reputation or fraud rating service (e.g. Open Fraud Detection Project). • The username (email address) is related to an account compromised by a data breach (e.g. http://www.haveibeenpwned.com/).

Table 44 continued…

Part VI : Reference Materials

Detection Point Code, Name, Description and Considerations	Examples
RP3 - Suspicious Client-Side Behavior The application receives a report of client-side security policy exceptions. Take care this information does not contribute to greater false positives.	• An internal corporate intranet application detects use of a non-standard workstation configuration (e.g. using JavaScript font or plugin detection see SE6). An alert is raised for further investigation. • An online banking application receives details of suspicious client-side behaviour that would not be expected in normal application use, via a Content Security Policy[160] violation report. The application increases logging for the user, and decreases the monetary limit at which the user's payments require manual authorization by bank staff. • The HTTP user agent header value does not agree with other indicators (e.g. using JavaScript detection as in the first example above)[161]. • A honey client system monitoring the web application reports unexpected behavior in the generated web pages output. • A third-party monitoring system detects page content that is unauthorised and/or contrary to policy (e.g. structure, included links, HTML validation, inclusion of certain data such as payment card data). • Client-side code is injected that creates a hash of the page content in the receiving client web browser to monitor for manipulated HTML code[162].
RP4 - Change to Environment Threat Level The general threat level (e.g. general risk of attack from the Internet, or specific targeted attacks against an organization) is elevated. This could also be used to change response sensitivity due to short-term effects such as application upgrades/patching. This input could be used to alter thresholds for AppSensor responses. The detection point could receive specially crafted input from an attacker, and therefore the information should be considered as untrusted.	• A machine-readable threat index is read from a third-party and is used to control security logging levels. • Business circumstances (e.g. increased attention by activists) raises the suspicion the application may be at increased risk of mis-use, and response thresholds for attack detection are tightened for non-authenticated users. • The Defense Condition Level (DEFCON)[163] is raised and response thresholds are changed. • Sensor signal missing. • External power source disconnected. • Firmware or software patch signing check failure.

Detection point specification sheets

Figure 38 EXAMPLE DETECTION POINT DEFINITION OVERVIEW SHEET FOR AN INSTANCE OF IE2

DETECTION POINT DEFINITION - OVERVIEW	TYPE	II - Discrete / business layer
CODE/TITLE	IE2	Violation of Implemented White Lists
SERIES/PURPOSE	3000	Detailed parameter validation against white list
DESCRIPTION		Whitelists are defined in XML data associated with the application for each allowed form and URL parameter. This detection point compares the parameter value with two whitelists: 1) valid values: that can be used safely as inputs to subsequent processing 2) invalid values: that should be rejected, but might only be user error (soft rejection) Values that do not match either whitelist are invalid and impermissible (hard rejection).
PRE-REQUISITES		All generic pre-processing detection points
RELATED DPS		None
COMMENTS		The parameters have been previously screened for missing/duplication/extra parameters and values. Some parameters can be defined but have NULL value. Some parameter values may be lists (e.g. comma delimited) of other values.
CHANGE LOG	DATE / BY / ACTION 19 Feb 2013 / CW / Created	

Part VI : Reference Materials

Figure 39 EXAMPLE DETECTION POINT DEFINITION OVERVIEW SHEET FOR AN INSTANCE OF ACE3

DETECTION POINT DEFINITION - OVERVIEW		TYPE	I - Discrete / generic pre-processing
CODE/TITLE	ACE3	Force Browsing Attempts	
SERIES/PURPOSE	1200	Validation of request URL against whitelist of allowable application surface	
DESCRIPTION	All permissible application entry points are defined in the database, together with whether SSL/TLS is mandatory, optional or disallowed. The database also includes URLs of dynamic (e.g. scripts) and static (e.g. style sheets, images, etc) content entry points. This detection point is called for every HTTP request to the application. This detection point checks the path and whether SSL/TLS is being used.		
PRE-REQUISITES	RE1, RE2		
RELATED DPS	RE3, RE4		
COMMENTS	This detection point does not validate user/role permissions for the URL or the presence/absence of parameters.		

CHANGE LOG	DATE	BY	ACTION
	19 Feb 2013	CW	Created
	21 Feb 2013	AK	Note on exclusions added to comments
	21 Feb 2013	MM	Detection point locations added

Figure 40 PART OF EXAMPLE DETECTION POINT SCHEDULE FOR IE2

DETECTION POINT DEFINITION - OVERVIEW TYPE II - Discrete / business layer

CODE/TITLE IE2 Violation of Implemented White Lists

SERIES/PURPOSE 3000 Detailed parameter validation against white list

LOCATIONS

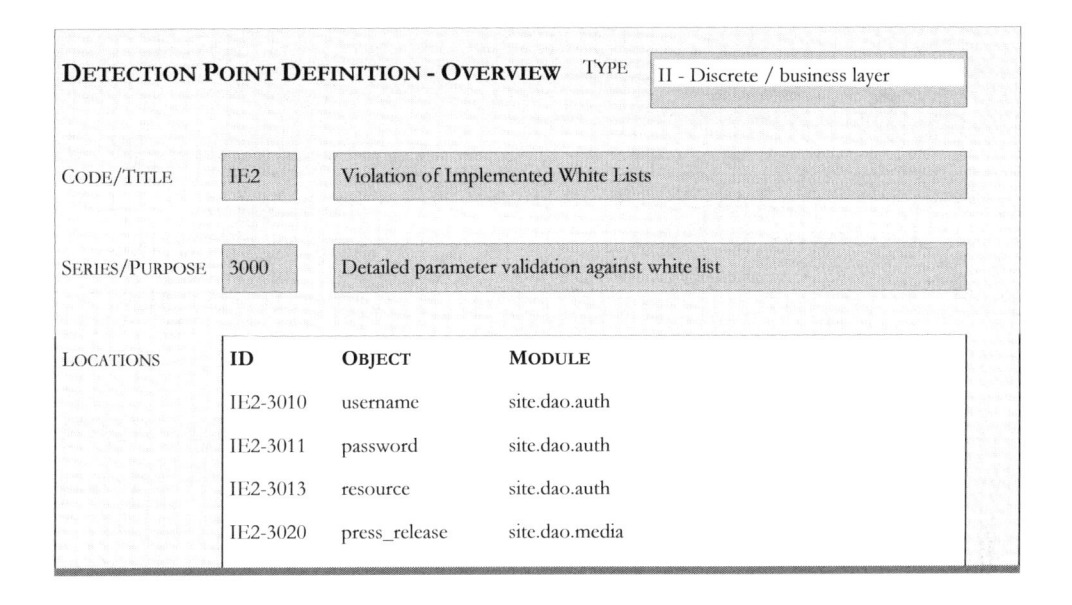

ID	OBJECT	MODULE
IE2-3010	username	site.dao.auth
IE2-3011	password	site.dao.auth
IE2-3013	resource	site.dao.auth
IE2-3020	press_release	site.dao.media

Figure 41 EXAMPLE DETECTION POINT SCHEDULE FOR AE3

DETECTION POINT DEFINITION - OVERVIEW TYPE I - Discrete / generic pre-processing

CODE/TITLE ACE3 Force Browsing Attempts

SERIES/PURPOSE 1200 Validation of request URL against whitelist of allowable application surface

LOCATIONS

ID	OBJECT	MODULE
ACE-1210	URL	site.dao.request

Responses

Listing of responses

Table 45 SUMMARY OF APPSENSOR RESPONSE IDENTIFIERS AND TITLES, GROUPED BY THE EFFECT ON THE USER

Category Type	Description	Response ID	Titles
None	No response	ASR-P	No Response
Silent	User unaware of application's response	ASR-A	Logging Change
		ASR-B	Administrator Notification
		ASR-C	Other Notification
		ASR-N	Proxy
Passive	Changes to user experience but nothing denied	ASR-D	User Status Change
		ASR-E	User Notification
		ASR-F	Timing Change
Active	Application functionality reduced for user(s)	ASR-G	Process Terminated
		ASR-H	Function Amended
		ASR-I	Function Disabled
		ASR-J	Account Logout
		ASR-K	Account Lockout
		ASR-L	Application Disabled
Intrusive	User's environment altered	ASR-M	Collect Data from User

ASR-P for "no response" is usually only output in logs to indicate an event did not initiate an immediate response. For example the event might relate to an aggregating detection point.

This list, and the details in the following tables are maintained on the AppSensor website's list of responses[75]. Always check there for the most recent information.

Detection Points

Categorization of responses

The responses can be categorized by their purpose, whether the response affects one or all users, and whether the response is an instantaneous single event, has a duration or is permanent.

Table 46 ASSIGNMENT OF APPSENSOR RESPONSES TO CATEGORIZATIONS

Response		Classifications				Target User		Response Duration		
		Purpose								
Code	Description	Logging	Notifying	Disrupting	Blocking	One	All	Instantaneous	Period	Permanent
ASR-A	Logging Change	●				●	○	○	○	
ASR-B	Administr'r Notification	●	●			●	●	●		
ASR-C	Other Notification	●	●			●		●		
ASR-D	User Status Change	●				●			●	
ASR-E	User Notification	●	●	●		●		●		
ASR-F	Timing Change	●		●		●	○	○	○	
ASR-G	Process Terminated	●	○	●		●		●		
ASR-H	Function Amended	●	○	●	●	●	○		●	○
ASR-I	Function Disabled	●	○	●	●	●	○		●	○
ASR-J	Account Logout	●	○	●	●	●		●		
ASR-K	Account Lockout	●	○	●	●	●			●	○
ASR-L	Application Disabled	●	○	●	●		●			●
ASR-M	Collect Data from User	●				●			●	
ASR-N	Proxy	●				●	○		●	○
ASP-P	No response									

□□□□ ● always, ○ sometimes

Part VI : Reference Materials

Detailed descriptions of responses

Table 47   DESCRIPTIONS OF APPSENSOR RESPONSES LISTED ALPHABETICALLY BY CODE

Response Code, Name, Description and Considerations	Examples
ASR-A - Logging Change The granularity of logging is changed (typically more logging).	• Capture sanitised request headers and response bodies. • Full stack trace of error messages logged. • Record DNS data on user's IP address. • Security logging level changed to include 'informational' messages.
ASR-B - Administrator Notification A notification message is sent to the application administrator(s).	• Email alert sent to everyone in the administration team. • SMS alert sent to the on-call administrator. • Visual indicator displayed on an application monitoring dashboard. • Audible alarm in the control room.
ASR-C - Other Notification Notification message sent to something or someone other than Administrators (see ASR-B) or the User (see ASR-E). The message recipient (e.g. firewall) could take some action otherwise unavailable to the application (e.g. disruptive - the application makes a silent response, but the firewall actively intervenes and perhaps blocks the user).	• Broadcast event to SIEM. • Signal sent to upstream network firewall, application firewall (e.g. XML, web) or load balancer. • Alert sent to fraud protection department. • Record added to server event log. • Event highlighted in a daily management report. • Email alert to staff member's manager. • Proactive entry added to customer support system (e.g. "Someone had difficulty logging in with this customer's username - request extra validation for telephone enquiries").
ASR-D - User Status Change A parameter related to the user is modified. This may have an impact on functionality or usability of the application, but only for the one user.	• Internal trustworthiness scoring about the user changed. • Reduce payment transfer limit for the customer before additional out-of-band verification is required. • Reduce maximum file size limit for each file upload by the forum user. • Increase data validation strictness for all form submissions by this citizen. • Reduce the number of failed authentication attempts allowed before the user's account is locked (ASR-K).

Table 47 continued...

Detection Points

Response Code, Name, Description and Considerations	Examples
ASR-E - User Notification A visual, audible and/or mechanical (e.g. vibration) signal or message is activated, displayed, or sent by other means, to the user.	• On-screen message about mandatory form fields (e.g. "The 'occupation' must be completed"). • On-screen message about data validation issues (e.g. 'The bank sort code can only contain six digits with optional hyphens'). • Message sent by email to the registered email address to inform them their password has been changed. • On-screen message warning that they have been detected performing malicious activity (e.g. Mr Clippy idea)
ASR-F - Timing Change The usual timescales to perform an operation are altered, usually extended, or delays are added.	• Extend response time for each failed authentication attempt. • File upload process duration extended artificially. • Add fixed time delay into every response. • Order flagged for manual checking. • Goods despatch put on hold (e.g. despatch status changed).
ASR-G - Process Terminated An interruption to the sending, display or process, such that the user has to start again, or start somewhere else. For authenticated users, this would not include termination of their session (see ASR-J). And, they would be free to attempt the process again (e.g. access the resource after logging in, submit a payment transfer, etc).	• Discard data, display message and force user to begin business process from start. • Redirection of an unauthenticated user to the log-in page. • Redirection to home page. • Display other content (i.e. terminate process but display the output of some other page without redirect). • Redirection to a page on another website.

Table 47 continued...

Part VI : Reference Materials

Response Code, Name, Description and Considerations	Examples
ASR-H - Function Amended The usual functionality is amended but not disabled (see ASR-I).	• Limit on feature usage rate imposed. • Reduce number of times/day the user can submit a review. • Additional registration identity validation steps. • Additional anti-automation measures (e.g. out-of-band verification activated, CAPTCHA introduced). • Static rather than dynamic content returned. • Additional validation requirements for delivery address. • Watermarks added to pages, images and other content. • Additional human interactive proof challenges added due to the number of incorrect guesses of CAPTCHAs outnumbering the correct guesses by more than a certain factor (e.g. Token bucket idea). • Fuzz responses to mask real functionality or increase attacker efforts to enumerate the application or its data (e.g. random URL generation using ADHD Spider Trap or Weblabyrinth, realistic but invalid cipher text data using techniques such as honey encryption)
ASR-I - Function Disabled A function or functions are disabled for one, some or all users. Other functionality continues to work as normal. For changes that affect multiple users, be careful the response cannot be used too easily for denial of service.	• 'Add friend' feature inactivated. • 'Recommend to a colleague' feature links removed and disabled. • Document library search disabled. • Prevent new site registrations. • Web service inactivated or cloaked. • Content syndication stopped. • Automated Direct Debit system turned off and manual form offered instead.
ASR-J - Account Logout The current session is terminated on the server, and the user is logged out. Often undertaken in conjunction with process termination (ASR-G) and sometimes lockout (ASR-K).	• Session terminated and user redirected to logged-out message page. • Session terminated only (no redirect).
ASR-K - Account Lockout An account, session or source address is blocked from access and/or authentication. If IP blocking is implemented, it is recommended this is undertaken at the network layer using the operating system (e.g. iptables, Windows firewall) or by a network device (e.g. firewall).	• User account locked for 10 minutes. • User account locked permanently until an Administrator resets it. • One user's IP address range blocked. • Unauthenticated user's session terminated.

Table 47 continued...

Detection Points

Response Code, Name, Description and Considerations	Examples
ASR-L - Application Disabled The whole application is disabled or made unavailable. Be careful the response cannot be used too easily for denial of service.	• Website shut down and replaced with temporary static page. • Application taken offline.
ASR-M - Collect Data from User This response is meant to be non-malicious in intent - it is simply additional information gathering - and not retaliatory or damaging to the user, their systems or data, nor make any permanent change. An alert user might be aware of the action. Be very wary of data collected and perform appropriate validation and sanitization. Ensure any use of this type of response is legally permissible in the relevant jurisdictions, and complies with corporate policies and the application's terms of use, privacy notice and corporate policies. To a certain extent, any additional payload in a response might cause a user's browser or computer to crash, and this might have unforeseen circumstances. The information collection could use techniques such as to gather information on the user's browser and computer configuration[146], inject content into an HTTP response using JavaScript to discover the user's real IP address[164], embed a decloaking engine to discover the real IP address of a web user[16], or use ModSecurity and BeEF to monitor the attacker[166].	• Deploy additional browser fingerprinting using JavaScript in responses. • Deploy a Java applet to collect remote IP address. • Deploy JavaScript to collect information about the user's network. • Record mobile phone fingerprint and IMEI number.
ASR-N - Proxy Send the request to a different back-end location. For redirection that the user will be aware of, see See ASR-G instead.	• Requests from the user invisibly (from the user's perspective) passed through to a hardened system. • Requests are proxied to a special honeypot system which closely mimics or has identical user functionality.
ASR-P - No Response There is no response. This could be used to record in logs that a detection event did not lead to any particular response action.	• A detection point fired, but the threshold for response has not been reached.

Letter "O" is not used for a response code.

Part VI : Reference Materials

Thresholds and responses definition sheets

Figure 42 EXAMPLE THRESHOLD SCHEDULE NO1

RESPONSE ACTIONS - SCHEDULE OF THRESHOLDS

OVERALL NUMBER OF SECURITY EVENTS

CODE	SERIES	THRESHOLD	PERIOD	RESPONSES
(All)	-	3	1 day	ASR-K

Figure 43 EXAMPLE THRESHOLD SCHEDULE NO2

RESPONSE ACTIONS - SCHEDULE OF THRESHOLDS

OVERALL NUMBER OF SECURITY EVENTS

CODE	SERIES	THRESHOLD	PERIOD	RESPONSES
(none)	-	-	-	-

SYSTEM TRENDS (INDIVIDUAL DETECTION POINTS)

CODE	SERIES	THRESHOLD	PERIOD	RESPONSES
STE3	-	+200%	1 hour	ASR-B
STE3	-	+1,000%	1 hour	ASR-I

Figure 44 EXAMPLE THRESHOLD SCHEDULE NO3

RESPONSE ACTIONS - SCHEDULE OF THRESHOLDS

OVERALL NUMBER OF SECURITY EVENTS

CODE	SERIES	THRESHOLD	PERIOD	RESPONSES
(All)	-	5	1 day	ASR-E
(All)	-	45	1 day	ASR-E, ASR-J, ASR-K

SYSTEM TRENDS (INDIVIDUAL DETECTION POINTS)

CODE	SERIES	THRESHOLD	PERIOD	RESPONSES
STE1	1000	+500%	15 minutes	ASR-B
STE2	1000	+1000%	1 hour	ASR-B

USER TRENDS (INDIVIDUAL DETECTION POINTS)

CODE	SERIES	THRESHOLD	PERIOD	RESPONSES
UT1	1000	10	1 hour	ASR-B
UT1	2010	5	15 minutes	ASR-B, ASR-E
UT1	2020	40	1 day	ASR-B, ASR-E, ASR-I
UT3	1000	1	-	ASR-D
UT3	2000	1	-	ASR-B, ASR-I

USER EVENTS (INDIVIDUAL DETECTION POINTS)

CODE	SERIES	THRESHOLD	PERIOD	RESPONSES
RE1	1000	2	1 hour	ASR-G
RE2	1000	2	1 day	ASR-G
RE3	1000	5	1 day	ASR-B, ASR-J
RE4	1000	5	1 day	ASR-B, ASR-J
AE2	1000	1	NA	ASR-K
AE3	1000	1	NA	ASR-K

Part VI : Reference Materials

SE1	1000	1	(session)	ASR-J, ASR-B, ASR-E
SE2	1000	1	1 day	ASR-A
SE5	1010	1	(session)	ASR-A
SE5	1020	1	(session)	ASR-B, ASR-K
ACE1	1000	2	30 days	ASR-B, ASR-K
ACE2	1000	2	30 days	ASR-B, ASR-K
ACE3	1000	5	15 minutes	ASR-A, ASR-F
IE1	1000	2	1 day	ASR-A, ASR-E, ASR-G
IE2	1000	1	1 day	ASR-G, ASR-B
IE2	1010	25	2 hours	ASR-B, ASR-J

Data Signaling Exchange Formats

This AppSensor Guide defines a recommended syntax for event information records between systems. No taxonomy of values is provided. Identity authentication, authorization, integrity, synchronization should be accomplished using the transport protocol utilized. Additionally the particular transportation protocol is not defined since this will be environment-specific.

See also *Part III : Making It Happen - Chapter 15 : Verification, Deployment and Operation - Operation - Logging, signaling, monitoring and reporting*.

Note on detection point identifiers

Sometimes detection points are simply identified as the base inspiration types (e.g. RE4, IE5). However an application may have multiple instances of a particular detection point type (e.g. IE5-001, IE5-002), and it is recommended this is allowed for even in pilot implementations.

Additional information could be appended to these detection IDs, such the application name and version, and hostname, where the information is transmitted to some other system. Alternatively these other identifiers can be transmitted in other fields.

Note on user identifiers

User identification is an important consideration, but not all users will necessarily be identifiable even in authenticated parts of an application. Please see the considerations discussed in *Part I : AppSensor Overview - Chapter 4 : Conceptual Elements - User identification (attribution)*.

Event syntax

Not all the data that is collected for security event logging is necessary for attack identification (see for example *Chapter 18 : AppSensor and Application Event Logging - Application event logs*).

The minimum data to be recorded/signaled when an event occurs is:

- Application/host identity (e.g. application abbreviated name and host code)
- User identity (e.g. username)
- Event identity (e.g. detection point ID)
- Event date/time.

Part VI : Reference Materials

Internally within an application, this may simply be logged to a database or file system, but with an external application or component, the preferred format to use is JSON. Other formats are also discussed below.

AppSensor Event Format in JSON

The JSON Data Interchange Format[167] is used by the demonstration implementation AppSensor WS. Using the minimum information as defined above.

Figure 45 BASIC APPSENSOR EVENT FORMAT FOR JSON DATA

```
{
"user":{
        "username":"USER_USERNAME"
},
"detectionPoint":{
        "id":"DETECTIONPOINT_ID"
},
"timestamp": EVENT_TIMESTAMP
}
```

For a definition of the event data values in AppSensor Event Format (AEF) see *Figure 48 AppSensor Event Format Data Value Definitions*.

Using JSON, the application identity is specified in an HTTP header named "X-AppSensor-Client-Application-Name". A simple example event notification of detection point "RE5-001" activated by the user with username "horacio7" is shown below.

Figure 46 IMPORTANT HTTP HEADERS AND EXAMPLE JSON EVENT DATA

```
Content-Type: text/x-json
X-AppSensor-Client-Application-Name: WebShop-WS05

{"user":{"username":"horacio7"},"detectionPoint":{"id":"RE5-001"},"timestamp":
2014-05-01T11:48:40+01:00 }
```

If additional fields are required from *Table 19* in *Chapter 18 : AppSensor and Application Event Logging - Application event logs*, it is recommended the JSON data could be extended as follows. Note that some of these properties may be inherently defined in the detection point identity already, and thus may be redundant if the receiving event logging system or analysis engine can decode the detection point identity.

Figure 47 EXTENDED APPSENSOR EVENT FORMAT FOR JSON DATA SHOWING OPTIONAL AND CUSTOM FIELDS

```
{
"user":{
        "username":"USER_USERNAME",
        "source":"USER_SOURCE",
        "useragent":"USER_AGENT",
        "fingerprint":"USER_FINGERPRINT"
},
"detectionPoint":{
        "id":"DETECTIONPOINT_ID",
        "process":"DETECTIONPOINT_PROCESS",
        "description":"DETECTIONPOINT_DESCRIPTION",
        "message":"DETECTIONPOINT_MESSAGE"
},
"location":{
        "host":"LOCATION_HOST_ID",
        "application":"LOCATION_APPLICATION_ID",
        "version":"LOCATION_APPLICATION_VERSION",
        "port": "LOCATION_PORT",
        "protocol4": "LOCATION_PROTOCOL_COMMUNICATION",
        "protocol7": "LOCATION_PROTOCOL_APPLICATION",
        "method": "LOCATION_METHOD",
        "entrypoint": "LOCATION_ENTRY_POINT"
        "interaction":"LOCATION_INTERACTION"
},
"classification":{
        "severity": "CLASSIFICATION_SEVERITY",
        "confidence": "CLASSIFICATION_CONFIDENCE",
        "owner": "CLASSIFICATION_OWNER",
        "[CUSTOM_NAME_1]": "[CUSTOM_VALUE_1]",
        "[CUSTOM_NAME_2]": "[CUSTOM_CLASS_VALUE_2]",
        ...
},
"timestamp": EVENT_TIMESTAMP,
"logtimestamp: LOG_TIMESTAMP,
"logid": LOG_ID
}
```

The values for AppSensor Event Format (AEF) are defined in the table below. But see also the references in *Chapter 18 : AppSensor and Application Event Logging - Application event logs*.

Part VI : Reference Materials

Figure 48 AppSensor Event Format Data Value Definitions

[Application] User:
- USER_USERNAME (string)
  An application-specific end user account username, or other user identity such as email address or database key, or sometimes an IP address or physical device identity; never a session identifier or sensitive data; possibly "0" for unauthenticated users
- USER_SOURCE (string)
  User's address e.g. IPv4 or IPv6 address
- USER_AGENT (string)
  User's client software or device identification. e.g. HTTP User Agent string
- USER_FINGERPRINT (string)
  User's client or device fingerprint e.g. SHA1 hash of certain HTTP request headers

[Application] Detection Point:
- DETECTIONPOINT_ID (string)
  The identity assigned to the activated detection point, and could include further detection point details and even host, application, path, code process, logic flow and instance identifiers
- DETECTIPNPOINT_PROCESS (string)
  The code process where the event was detected such as the module, function, subroutine, component or script name (not the URL path – see "entrypoint")
- DETECTIONPOINT_DESCRIPTION (string)
  Human readable description of detection point
- DETECTPOINT_MESSAGE (string)
  Human readable warning message displayed to user

[Detection Point] Location:
- LOCATION_HOST_ID (string)
  Host system identifier e.g. host name, IP address, device identity
- LOCATION_APPLICATION_ID (string)
  Application/service identifier e.g. application name abbreviation
- LOCATION_APPLICATION_VERSION (string)
  Application/service release version
- LOCATION_PORT (integer)
  Network TCP or UDP port number e.g. 443
- LOCATION_PROTOCOL_COMMUNICATION (string)
  Network protocol e.g. TCP, UDP
- LOCATION_PROTOCOL_APPLICATION (string)
  Application protocol or physical event descriptor e.g. FTP, key, HTTP, screen, SIP
- LOCATION_METHOD (string)
  Application protocol method e.g. POST, depress, mouse over, touch
- LOCATION_ENTRYPOINT (string)
  Data submission identifier e.g. URL path, button identifier, form or screen name
- LOCATION_INTERACTION (string)
  A unique identifier used to group all events associated with a single user interaction e.g. when multiple detection points are activated by a single user request

```
continued...

[Event] Classification:
    •   SEVERITY (integer)
        This is the severity level from RFC 5424[168] (The Syslog Protocol) i.e.
        .. 0 (Emergency/Application unavailable for all users)
           1 (Alert/Function unavailable for all users)
           2 (Critical/Function or application unavailable to a single user)
           3 (Error/Other security events not included in codes 0, 1, 2 or 4)
           4 (Warning/A security event but user allowed to continue)
           5 (Notice: normal but significant condition)
           6 (Information/Normal user behavior)
           7 (Debug-level messages)
        Note severity levels 6 and 7 are not normally valid for AppSensor
    •   CONFIDENCE (integer)
        An integer between 0 and 100, where 100 means certain
    •   OWNER (string)
        Event assignment e.g. Operations, Compliance
    •   CUSTOM_NAME and CUSTOM_VALUE
        can be used for additional use but are not necessarily supported by
        other systems

[Event] Chronology:
    •   EVENT_TIMESTAMP
        Timestamp from RFC 3339[169] (Date and Time on the Internet: Timestamps)
        when the event was detected
    •   LOG_TIMESTAMP (signed integer)
        A Unix time (POSIX time) in the GMT time zone designated when the event
        was logged
    •   LOG_ID (string)
    •   Some identifier of the relevant application event log record (there
        should be very many more application events than detection point
        events)
```

This is extended JSON format in not supported by the demonstration web services implementation - see *Part IV : Demonstration Implementations - Chapter 20 : Web Services (AppSensor WS)*.

AppSensor event data using Common Event Format

Common Event Format (CEF) may be more useful in enterprises with existing log aggregation, monitoring and alerting systems. CEF comprises[80] a prefix, message and optional extension requiring a greater number of fields to be sent than for AEF in JSON. Using the minimum AEF information as defined above, CEF may be used for AppSensor event data as follows.

Part VI : Reference Materials

Figure 49   BASIC APPSENSOR EVENT DATA USING CEF

```
"EVENT_TIMESTAMP" "LOCATION_HOST_ID" CEF:0
|"CEF_DEVICE_VENDOR"|"LOCATION_APPLICATION_ID"|"LOCATION_APPLICATION_VERSION"|"
DETECTIONPOINT_ID"|"DETECTIONPOINT_DESCRIPTION"|"SEVERITY"|suser="USER_USERNAME
"
```

IN CEF terminology, the instrumented application is the "device", and the detection point is the "signature". The mappings from the terms for JSON in the previous table to CEF keys are shown in the table below.

Table 48   MAPPING OF APPSENSOR EVENT FORMAT (AEF) TERMS TO COMMON EVENT FORMAT (CEF) KEYS

AEF Term	CEF Key
EVENT_TIMESTAMP	TIMESTAMP
LOCATION_HOST_ID	HOST
LOCATION_APPLICATION_ID	DEVICE PRODUCT
LOCATION_APPLICATION_VERSION	DEVICE VERSION
DETECTIONPOINT_ID	SIGNATURE ID
DETECTIONPOINT_DESCRIPTION	NAME
SEVERITY	SEVERITY (i.e. the same)
USER_USERNAME	SOURCEUSERNAME

The two additional CEF-specific field values are described below.

Figure 50   BASIC ADDITIONAL CEF FIELD VALUES IN THE CONTEXT OF APPSENSOR

```
CEF:
    •   CEF_DEVICE_VENDOR (string)
        The vendor of the application e.g. supplier, organization itself
    •   CEF_SEVERITY (integer)
        0 to 10, lowest to highest; note this is the reverse order to syslog
```

Other CEF extension predefined keys can be used as listed in the CEF standard[80] such as shown in the example below. Custom dictionary extensions could also be used.

Detection Points

Figure 51 EXAMPLE CEF APPSENSOR EVENT DATA USING CEF PREDEFINED KEYS

```
18 04 2014 16:04:53 EST appserver02 CEF:0|widgetco|shoponline|3.7.03|AppSensor|
XSS attempt blocked|7|src=10.25.102.65 suser=W0005 proto=TCP dpt=80 dproc=httpd
request=/catalogue/showProduct/ requestMethod=GET deviceExternalID=AppSensor06
msg=Cross site scripting attempt in parameter prodid cat=detection act=block
cs1Label=requestClientApplication cs1=Mozilla/5.0 (Macintosh; U; Intel Mac OS X
10.8; en-GB; rv:1.9.2.17) Gecko/20110420 cs2Label=AppSensorDetectionPointID
cs2=R03 cs3Label=AppSensorDetectionType cs3=IE1 cs4Label=StatusCode cs4=403
cn1Label=RequestID cn1=000070825566 cn2Label=AppSensorLogID cn2=1650833
cn3Label=Confidence cn3=100
```

When CEF is being used it may be the receiving system has much less knowledge about the application and its workings. In this situation it may be valuable to pass forward other data the application already knows about the user, the detection points and the attack such as CWE[108], CCE[109], CAPEC[68] and SWID[112] identifiers. However, passing forward any type of sensitive data should be assessed and approved first (e.g. privacy impact assessment, information security risk assessment, regulatory compliance check).

Attack syntax

This is expected to be defined in the near future.

Response syntax

Information on responses initiated may need to be transmitted by a discrete Event Analysis Engine, or such data could be broadcast by the application itself to centralized logging and monitoring systems.

This is expected to be defined in the near future.

Part VI : Reference Materials

Awareness and Training Resources

Overview briefing

There is a high-level promotional video about AppSensor at:

    http://www.youtube.com/watch?v=6gxg_t2ybcE

The project's founder Michael Coates was interviewed about the AppSensor Project during AppSec USA in New York during November 2013:

    https://soundcloud.com/owasp-podcast/appsec-usa-2013-michael-coates

Furthermore, the four-page article "Creating Attack-Aware Software Applications with Real-Time Defenses"[10] in the journal CrossTalk provides a high-level summary of the AppSensor concept, benefits and applicability.

    http://www.crosstalkonline.org/storage/issue-archives/2011/201109/201109-Watson.pdf

This article is very suitable for circulation to senior development and information security management.

Detailed documentation

This AppSensor Guide can be downloaded free of charge as an Adobe PDF file, Word document and Google Doc from links on the OWASP AppSensor Project website[1]:

    https://www.owasp.org/index.php/OWASP_AppSensor_Project

It is also available in print at cost from Lulu[170]:

Other electronic formats and language translations may be available in due course. The OWASP AppSensor Project website provides the most up-to-date sources of information, presentation files and links to the latest version of the book.

Video briefings and demonstrations

Overviews:

- Creating Self Defending Applications to Repel Attackers, Michael Coates, 2014
  https://www.youtube.com/watch?v=YOtTPr8r0tI
- OWASP AppSensor - In Theory, In Practice and In Print, Colin Watson, 2013
  https://www.youtube.com/watch?v=QhhG4ty5DdY
- Using the O2 Platform, ZAP and AppSensor, Dinis Cruz, 2013
  http://www.youtube.com/watch?v=dzj3llZ9G6I
- Protección Web Con ESAPI y AppSensor, Manual Lopez Arredondo, 2013
  http://www.youtube.com/watch?v=v2j0oVKCZLw
- Implementing AppSensor in ModSecurity, Ryan Barnett, 2011
  http://www.youtube.com/watch?v=0LJKGNs_rT8
- Real Time Application Defenses: The Reality of AppSensor and ESAPI, 2010
  Part 1 http://www.youtube.com/watch?v=ibQkfkATbVA
  Part 2 http://www.youtube.com/watch?v=du60qMpIQU4
  Part 3 http://www.youtube.com/watch?v=UUEs8CfVWq8

Attack detection and response using a demonstration application:

- OWASP AppSensor: Detecting XSS Probes, Michael Coates, 2009
  http://www.youtube.com/watch?v=CekUMk_VRV8
- OWASP AppSensor: Detecting URL Tampering, Michael Coates, 2009
  http://www.youtube.com/watch?v=LfD4y67qdWE
- OWASP AppSensor: Detecting Verb Tampering, Michael Coates, 2009
  http://www.youtube.com/watch?v=1D6nTlmYjhY
  OWASP AppSensor: Responding to an Attack, Michael Coates, 2009
  http://www.youtube.com/watch?v=8ItfuwvLxRk

Demonstration information dashboards:

- OWASP AppSensor Dashboard Demo No 2 - Ecommerce Application Advanced Configuration
  http://www.youtube.com/watch?v=YZ5zGQ-XLkk
- OWASP AppSensor Dashboard Demo No 1 - Ecommerce Application Base Configuration
  http://www.youtube.com/watch?v=zCaYREAyiRg

Part VI : Reference Materials

Previous guides and workbooks:

- OWASP AppSensor – Detect and Respond to Attacks from Within the Application, v1.1, Michael Coates, 2008-2009
  https://www.owasp.org/images/b/b0/OWASP_AppSensor_Beta_1.1.doc
  https://www.owasp.org/images/2/2f/OWASP_AppSensor_Beta_1.1.pdf
- Attack Detection & Response with OWASP AppSensor - An Implementation Planning Workbook, Colin Watson, 2010-2011
  http://www.owasp.org/index.php/File:Appsensor-planning.zip

Feedback and Testimonials

The volunteers supporting the OWASP AppSensor Project would like to hear about your application-specific real-time attack detection and response:

- Questions
- Suggestions
- Corrections
- Experiences.

Actual production examples and testimonials, anonymous or otherwise, are especially welcome to help the team learn and share knowledge to the wider application development community. The AppSensor project supports OWASP's core values[171] which are:

- OPEN - Everything at OWASP is radically transparent from our finances to our code.
- INNOVATION - OWASP encourages and supports innovation/experiments for solutions to software security challenges.
- GLOBAL - Anyone around the world is encouraged to participate in the OWASP community.
- INTEGRITY - OWASP is an honest and truthful, vendor neutral, global community.

Please also let us know about errors in, improvements to and contributions for this guide.

For open contribution and discussion, please use the PROJECT mailing list:

    https://lists.owasp.org/listinfo/owasp-appsensor-project

To discuss or ask about the reference implementations (AppSensor WS and AppSensor Core), please use the DEVELOPMENT mailing list:

    https://lists.owasp.org/mailman/listinfo/owasp-appsensor-dev

Thank you.

Part VI : Reference Materials

References

[1] OWASP AppSensor Project, OWASP
https://www.owasp.org/index.php/OWASP_AppSensor_Project

[2] Coates M, AppSensor, v1.1, OWASP
https://www.owasp.org/images/2/2f/OWASP_AppSensor_Beta_1.1.pdf

[3] Chiappori PA, Levitt S and Groseclose TG, Testing Mixed-Strategy Equilibria When Players Are Heterogeneous: The Case of Penalty Kicks in Soccer
http://pricetheory.uchicago.edu/levitt/Papers/ChiapporiGrosecloseLevitt2002.pdf

[4] Tossing Coins Experiment
http://gwydir.demon.co.uk/jo/probability/coins.htm

[5] OWASP Security Principles Project, OWASP
https://www.owasp.org/index.php/OWASP_Security_Principles_Project

[6] Coates M, AppSensor: Real Time Defenses, OWASP DC 2009
https://www.owasp.org/images/0/06/Defend_Yourself-Integrating_Real_Time_Defenses_into_Online_Applications-Michael_Coates.pdf

[7] Coates M, Automated Application Defenses to Thwart Advanced Attackers
http://michael-coates.blogspot.com/2010/06/online-presentation-thursday-automated.html

[8] http://michael-coates.blogspot.com/2010/08/mozilla-at-owasp-appsecusa.html

[9] CrossTalk The Journal of Defense Software Engineering
http://www.crosstalkonline.org/

[10] Watson C, Coates M, Melton J and Groves G, Creating Attack-Aware Software Applications with Real-Time Defenses, CrossTalk The Journal of Defense Software Engineering, Vol. 24, No. 5, Sep/Oct 2011
http://www.crosstalkonline.org/storage/issue-archives/2011/201109/201109-Watson.pdf

[11] Resilient Software, Software Assurance, US Department Homeland Security
https://buildsecurityin.us-cert.gov/swa/resilient.html

[12] http://www.bits.org/publications/security/BITSSoftwareAssurance0112.pdf
BITS Software Assurance Framework, Financial Services Roundtable, 2012

[13] Kitten T, New Wave of DDoS Attacks Launched, BankInfoSecurity.com, Information Security Media Group, 6 March 2013
http://www.bankinfosecurity.com/new-wave-ddos-attacks-launched-a-5584/op-1

[14] damontoo, Etsy Has Been One of the Best Companies I've Reported Holes To
http://www.reddit.com/r/netsec/comments/vbrzg/etsy_has_been_one_of_the_best_companies_ive/

[15] Lackey Z, Security at Scale: Effective Approaches to Web Application Security, Etsy
http://www.slideshare.net/zanelackey and http://vimeo.com/54107692

[16] Etsy, Node.js Instrumentation Library
https://github.com/etsy/statsd

[17] Malpas I, Measure Anything, Measure Everything, Code as Craft, Etsy

http://codeascraft.com/2011/02/15/measure-anything-measure-everything/

[18] Ratnam G and King R, Pentagon Seeks $500 Million for Cyber Technologies, Bloomberg
http://www.bloomberg.com/news/2011-02-15/pentagon-seeks-500-million-for-cyber-research-cloud-computing.html

[19] Applegate SD, The Principle of Maneuver in Cyber Operations, Navy Center for Innovation Weblog, Navy Warfare Development Command, 6 June 2012
https://www.nwdc.navy.mil/ncoi/blog/Document%20Library/The%20Principle%20of%20Maneuver%20in%20Cyber%20Operations%20-%20Guest%20Briefing.pdf

[20] McRee R, MORPHINATOR & cyber Maneuver as a Defensive Tactic, HolisticInfoSec blog, 18 July 2012
http://holisticinfosec.blogspot.co.uk/2012/07/morphinator-cyber-maneuver-as-defensive.html

[21] Naraine R, How Google Set a Trap for Pwn2Own Exploit Team, ZDNet, 9 March 2012
http://www.zdnet.com/blog/security/how-google-set-a-trap-for-pwn2own-exploit-team/10641

[22] Google Hack Honeypot
http://ghh.sourceforge.net/

[23] HP Fortify Runtime
https://ssl.www8.hp.com/us/en/software-solutions/software.html?compURI=1337235

[24] Prevoty
https://www.prevoty.com/

[25] Bace R, Intrusion Detection, Sams, 1999
ISBN-10: 1578701856, ISBN-13: 978-1578701858

[26] Bace R and Mell P, NIST Special Publication on Intrusion Detection Systems, NIST
http://www.21cfrpart11.com/files/library/government/intrusion_detection_systems_0201_draft.pdf

[27] Scarfone K and Mell P, SP 800-94 Guide to Intrusion Detection and Prevention Systems (IDPS), NIST, 2007
http://csrc.nist.gov/publications/nistpubs/800-94/SP800-94.pdf

[28] Scarfone K and Mell P, SP 800-94 Revision 1 DRAFT Guide to Intrusion Detection and Prevention Systems (IDPS), NIST, 2012
http://csrc.nist.gov/publications/drafts/800-94-rev1/draft_sp800-94-rev1.pdf

[29] ISO/IEC 7498-2:1989 Information Processing Systems - Open Systems Interconnection - Basic Reference Model - Part 2: Security Architecture
http://www.iso.org/iso/catalogue_detail.htm?csnumber=14256

[30] Recommendation X.800 : Security architecture for Open Systems Interconnection for CCITT applications, ITU, 1991
http://www.itu.int/ITU-T/recommendations/rec.aspx?id=3102

[31] Ferraiolo K, The Systems Security Engineering Capability Maturity Model (SSE-CMM), ISSEA
http://csrc.nist.gov/nissc/2000/proceedings/papers/916slide.pdf

[32] Application Logging Cheat Sheet, OWASP
https://www.owasp.org/index.php/Logging_Cheat_Sheet

[33] Thomassen P, AppSensor: Attack-Aware Applications Compared Against a Web Application

Part VI : Reference Materials

Firewall and an Intrusion Detection System, Norwegian University of Science and Technology, Faculty of Information Technology, Mathematics and Electrical Engineering, Department of Computer and Information Science, 2012
http://ntnu.diva-portal.org/smash/record.jsf?pid=diva2:566091

[34] Snort, Sourcefire
http://www.snort.org/

[35] ModSecurity Open Source Web Application Firewall, Trustwave SpiderLabs
http://www.modsecurity.org/

[36] OWASP ModSecurity Core Rule Set Project, OWASP
https://www.owasp.org/index.php/Category:OWASP_ModSecurity_Core_Rule_Set_Project

[37] OWASP Top Ten Most Critical Web Application Security Risks, 2013, OWASP
http://www.owasp.org/index.php/Category:OWASP_Top_Ten_Project

[38] Transport Layer Security, Wikipedia
http://en.wikipedia.org/wiki/Secure_Sockets_Layer

[39] OSI Model, Wikipedia
http://en.wikipedia.org/wiki/OSI_model

[40] Firesmith D, Common Concepts Underlying Safety, Security, and Survivability Engineering, Software Engineering Institute, Carnegie Mellon University, Technical Note CMU/SEI-2003-TN-033, 2003
http://resources.sei.cmu.edu/library/asset-view.cfm?AssetID=6553

[41] Software Assurance Maturity Model Project (SAMM). OWASP
http://www.owasp.org/index.php/Category:Software_Assurance_Maturity_Model

[42] Software Security Assurance State of the Art Report, DACS/IATAC
http://iac.dtic.mil/iatac/download/security.pdf

[43] Secure Software Engineering Initiatives, ENISA
http://www.enisa.europa.eu/act/application-security/secure-software-engineering/secure-software-engineering-initiatives

[44] Secure SDLC Cheat Sheet, OWASP
https://www.owasp.org/index.php/Secure_SDLC_Cheat_Sheet

[45] BITS Software Assurance Framework, Financial Services Roundtable
http://www.bits.org/publications/security/BITSSoftwareAssurance0112.pdf

[46] Team Software Process for Secure Systems Development (TSP Secure), Software Engineering Institute, Carnegie Mellon University
http://www.cert.org/secure-coding/secure.html

[47] Capability Maturity Model Integration (CMMI), Software Engineering Institute, Carnegie Mellon University
http://www.sei.cmu.edu/cmmi/

[48] CMMI for Acquisition, v1.3, Technical Report CMU/SEI-2010-TR-032, Software Engineering Institute, Carnegie Mellon University
http://www.sei.cmu.edu/reports/10tr032.pdf

[49] Resiliency Management Model, v1.0, CERT

http://www.cert.org/resilience/rmm.html

[50] ISO/IEC 27034 Application Security
http://www.iso.org/iso/iso_catalogue/catalogue_tc/catalogue_detail.htm?csnumber=44378

[51] SP 800-64 Rev2 Security Considerations in the Information System Development Life Cycle, NIST
http://csrc.nist.gov/publications/nistpubs/800-64-Rev2/SP800-64-Revision2.pdf

[52] Software Assurance Forum for Excellence in Code (SAFECode)
http://www.safecode.org/

[53] Software Assurance, Cyber Security Division, Department Homeland Security
https://buildsecurityin.us-cert.gov/swa/

[54] Practical Measurement Framework for Software Assurance and Information Security, v1.0, 2008
http://www.psmsc.com/Downloads/TechnologyPapers/SwA%20Measurement%2010-08-08.pdf

[55] Microsoft Security Development Lifecycle (SDL)
http://www.microsoft.com/security/sdl/

[56] Oracle Software Security Assurance (OSSA)
http://www.oracle.com/us/support/assurance/

[57] Building Security In Maturity Model (BSIMM)
http://bsimm.com/

[58] BSIMM for Vendors (vBSIMM)
http://bsimm.com/related/

[59] Appropriate Software Security Control Types for Third Party Service and Product Providers, Third Party Software Security Working Group, Financial Services Information Sharing and Analysis Center
http://docs.ismgcorp.com/files/external/WP_FSISAC_Third_Party_Software_Security_Working_Group.pdf

[60] Application Security Guide for CISOs, OWASP
https://www.owasp.org/index.php/OWASP_Application_Security_Guide_For_CISOs_Project

[61] CISO Survey and Report, OWASP
https://www.owasp.org/index.php/OWASP_CISO_Survey_Project

[62] DShield.org Web Application Honeypot
http://code.google.com/p/webhoneypot/

[63] Distributed Web Honeypot (DWH) Project
http://projects.webappsec.org/w/page/29606603/Distributed%20Web%20Honeypots

[64] Glastopf Web Application Honeypot
http://glastopf.org/

[65] High Interaction Honeypot Analysis Toolkit (HIHAT)
http://hihat.sourceforge.net/

[66] Riden J, McGeehan R, Engert B and Mueter M, Know your Enemy: Web Application Threats - Using Honeypots to Learn About HTTP-Based Attacks, The Honeynet Project, 2008
http://www.honeynet.org/papers/webapp

Part VI : Reference Materials

[67] Pattern of Life and Temporal Signatures of Hacker Organizations, Analysis Intelligence blog, 9 May 2013
http://analysisintelligence.com/cyber-defense/temporal-signatures-of-hacker-organizations/

[68] Common Attack Pattern Enumeration and Classification (CAPEC), The Mitre Corporation
http://capec.mitre.org/

[69] ModSecurity SQL Injection Challenge: Lessons Learned, Anterior blog, Trustwave SpiderLabs, 26 July 2011
http://blog.spiderlabs.com/2011/07/modsecurity-sql-injection-challenge-lessons-learned.html

[70] SQL Injection Challenge, ModSecurity
http://modsecurity.org/demo/challenge.html

[71] Header Field Definitions, Hypertext Transfer Protocol HTTP/1.1, W3C
http://www.w3.org/Protocols/rfc2616/rfc2616-sec14.html

[72] Panopticlick research project, Electronic Frontier Foundation
https://panopticlick.eff.org/

[73] JavaScript Browser Fingerprinting, Business Info Web Security Applications and Experiments
http://www.businessinfo.co.uk/labs/probe/probe.php

[74] AppSensor Detection Points, AppSensor Project, OWASP
http://www.owasp.org/index.php/AppSensor_DetectionPoints

[75] AppSensor Response Actions, AppSensor Project
https://www.owasp.org/index.php/AppSensor_ResponseActions

[76] Strand J and Asadoorian P, Offensive Countermeasures: The Art of Active Defense, PaulDotCom June 2013

[77] Hacking Banking Websites: Myth or Reality? High-Tech Bridge, 12 Nov 2013
https://www.htbridge.com/news/hacking_banking_websites_myth_or_reality.html

[78] Virtual Patching Best Practices, OWASP
https://www.owasp.org/index.php/Virtual_Patching_Best_Practices

[79] Barnett R, Dynamic DAST/WAF Integration: Realtime Virtual Patching, 5 June 2012
http://blog.spiderlabs.com/2012/06/dynamic-dastwaf-integration-realtime-virtual-patching.html

[80] Common Event Format (CEF), Revision 15, ArcSight, 17 July 2009
http://mita-tac.wikispaces.com/file/view/CEF+White+Paper+071709.pdf

[81] The Incident Object Description Exchange Format, RFC 5070, IETF, December 2007
http://www.ietf.org/rfc/rfc5070.txt

[82] Extended Abuse Reporting Format, x-arf.org
http://www.x-arf.org

[83] Structured Threat Information eXpression, Mitre Corporation
http://stix.mitre.org/

[84] Cyber Observable eXpression, Mitre Corporation
http://cybox.mitre.org/

[85] Protocol Specification For Interfacing to Data Communication Networks, American National Standards Institute Inc, 2008

http://www.nema.org/Standards/ComplimentaryDocuments/ANSI-C1222-2008-Contents-and-Scope.pdf

[86] Automated Copyright Notice System, Motion Picture Association, Inc.
http://www.acns.net/

[87] Vocabulary for Event Recording and Incident Sharing (VERIS), Verizon Inc
http://www.veriscommunity.net/doku.php

[88] AuditConsole, jwall.org
http://www.jwall.org/web/audit/console/index.jsp

[89] WAF-FLE Log and Event Console for ModSecurity
http://www.waf-fle.org/

[90] Watson C, Attack Detection and Response with OWASP AppSensor - An Implementation Planning Workbook, v0.3, August 2011
http://www.owasp.org/index.php/File:Appsensor-planning.zip

[91] Threat Classification, v2.0, Web Application Security Consortium
http://projects.webappsec.org/Threat-Classification

[92] Cornucopia - Ecommerce Website Edition, OWASP
https://www.owasp.org/index.php/OWASP_Cornucopia

[93] Barnett R, Web Application Defender's Cookbook: Battling Hackers and Protecting Users, December 2012, John Wiley & Sons
ISBN: 978-1-118-36218-1

[94] Elevation of Privilege (EoP) Card Game, Microsoft
http://www.microsoft.com/security/sdl/adopt/eop.aspx
http://www.microsoft.com/en-us/download/details.aspx?id=20303

[95] Shostack A, Threat Modeling: Designing for Security, ISBN 1118809998, Wiley, 2014
http://threatmodelingbook.com/

[96] Gallagher B and Eliassi-Rad T, Classification of HTTP Attacks: A Study on the ECML/PKDD 2007 Discovery Challenge, Lawrence Livermore National Laboratory
http://eliassi.org/papers/gallagher-llnltr09.pdf

[97] Hansen R, Detecting Malice
http://www.detectmalice.com/

[98] OWASP Mobile Threat Model Project, OWASP
https://www.owasp.org/index.php/OWASP_Mobile_Security_Project#tab=OWASP_Mobile_Threat_Model_Project

[99] AppSensor Response Actions, OWASP
https://www.owasp.org/index.php/AppSensor_ResponseActions

[100] Logging Cheat Sheet, OWASP
https://www.owasp.org/index.php/Logging_Cheat_Sheet

[101] Chuvakin A and Peterson G, How to Do Application Logging Right,
IEEE Security & Privacy Journal
http://arctecgroup.net/pdf/howtoapplogging.pdf

[102] OWASP ESAPI Logger (Java), OWASP

Part VI : Reference Materials

http://owasp-esapi-java.googlecode.com/svn/trunk_doc/latest/org/owasp/esapi/Logger.html

[103] SP 800-92 Guide to Computer Security Log Management, NIST
http://csrc.nist.gov/publications/nistpubs/800-92/SP800-92.pdf

[104] OWASP Logging Project, OWASP
https://www.owasp.org/index.php/Category:OWASP_Logging_Project#tab=Main

[105] Watson C, Application Security Logging
https://www.clerkendweller.com/2010/8/17/Application-Security-Logging

[106] Watson C, World Summit - AppSensor Results, AppSensor Project Mailing List, OWASP
https://lists.owasp.org/pipermail/owasp-appsensor-project/2011-March/000215.html

[107] The Security Content Automation Protocol (SCAP), NIST
http://scap.nist.gov/

[108] Common Weakness Enumeration, The Mitre Corporation
http://cwe.mitre.org/

[109] Common Configuration Enumeration, NIST
http://nvd.nist.gov/cce/

[110] The Common Misuse Scoring System (CMSS): Metrics for Software Feature Misuse Vulnerabilities, Interagency Report 7864, NIST, July 2012
http://csrc.nist.gov/publications/nistir/ir7864/nistir-7864.pdf

[111] ISO/IEC 19770-2:2009, Software Asset Management -- Part 2: Software Identification Tag
http://www.iso.org/iso/catalogue_detail.htm?csnumber=53670

[112] Software Identification (SWID) Tags, TagVault.org
http://tagvault.org/swid-tags/what-are-swid-tags/

[113] Common Log File Format, July 1995, W3C
http://www.w3.org/Daemon/User/Config/Logging.html#common-logfile-format

[114] Extended Log File Format, March 1996, W3C
http://www.w3.org/TR/WD-logfile.html

[115] Documents Library, PCI SSC
https://www.pcisecuritystandards.org/security_standards/documents.php

[116] Qualified Security Assessor Companies, PCI SSC
https://www.pcisecuritystandards.org/approved_companies_providers/qualified_security_assessors.php

[117] Google Summer of Code 2012, Google
http://www.google-melange.com/gsoc/homepage/google/gsoc2012

[118] SOAP Web Services for AppSensor, Rauf Butt, Google
http://www.google-melange.com/gsoc/project/google/gsoc2012/edil/60002

[119] Google Summer of Code (GSoC), OWASP
https://www.owasp.org/index.php/GSoC

[120] BSD 3-Clause License, Open Source Initiative
http://opensource.org/licenses/BSD-3-Clause

[121] AppSensor – Intrusion Detection, Mária Jurčovičová

http://meri-stuff.blogspot.co.uk/2011/05/appsensor-intrusion-detection.html

[122] phpBB Bulletin Board Software, phpBB Limited
https://www.phpbb.com/

[123] GNU General Public License, version 2 (GPL-2.0)
http://opensource.org/licenses/gpl-2.0.php

[124] How to use the "netsh advfirewall firewall" context instead of the "netsh firewall" context to control Windows Firewall behavior in Windows Server 2008 and in Windows Vista, Microsoft
http://support.microsoft.com/kb/947709

[125] Ensnare for Ruby
https://github.com/ahoernecke/ensnare

[126] Barnett R, Detecting Malice with ModSecurity: Honey Traps, Spider Labs Blog, August 2011
http://blog.spiderlabs.com/2011/08/detecting-malice-with-modsecurity-honeytraps.html

[127] Barnett R, Setting Honey Traps with ModSecurity: Adding Fake robots.txt Disallow Entries, Spider Labs Blog, August 2013
http://blog.spiderlabs.com/2013/08/setting-honeytraps-with-modsecurity-adding-fake-robotstxt-disallow-entries.html

[128] Ensnare Project
https://github.com/ahoernecke/ensnare/wiki

[129] OWASP O2 Platform, OWASP
https://www.owasp.org/index.php/OWASP_O2_Platform

[130] Cruz D, Invoking an OWASP AppSensor Java method from .NET C# REPL (using Jni4Net)
http://blog.diniscruz.com/2013/03/invoking-owasp-appsensor-java-method.html

[131] Owasp-o2-platform Mailing List, OWASP O2 Platform Project
https://lists.owasp.org/listinfo/owasp-o2-platform

[132] Common Event Format, Revision 15, 17 July 2009, ArcSight Inc
http://mita-tac.wikispaces.com/file/detail/CEF+White+Paper+071709.pdf

[133] Shezaf O, ModSecurity Core Rule Set": An Open Source Rule Set for Generic Detection of Attacks against Web Applications
https://www.owasp.org/images/0/07/OWASP6thAppSec_ModSecurityCoreRuleSet_OferShezaf.pdf

[134] Owasp-modsecurity-core-rule-set Mailing List, ModSecurity Core Rule Set Project
https://lists.owasp.org/mailman/listinfo/owasp-modsecurity-core-rule-set

[135] AuditConsole, Christian Bockermann
http://www.jwall.org/web/audit/console/index.jsp

[136] SecViz - Security Visualization
http://secviz.org/

[137] AppSensor Application Logging, Signalling and Dashboards, Clerkendweller Web Security, Usability and Design blog, 14 June 2011
https://www.clerkendweller.com/2011/6/14/AppSensor-Application-Logging-Signalling-and-Dashboards

[138] ThreadFix, Denim Group

Part VI : Reference Materials

http://www.threadfix.org/

[139] National Information Assurance Glossary, CNSS Instruction No. 4009, 26 April 2010, Committee on National Security Systems, National Security Agency
http://www.cnss.gov/Assets/pdf/cnssi_4009.pdf

[140] CWE Glossary, v0.5, 21 February 2013, The MITRE Corporation
http://cwe.mitre.org/documents/glossary/index.html

[141] Overview of AppSensor Detection Point Categorizations, OWASP
https://www.owasp.org/index.php/File:Detection-points-2-venn.png

[142] AppSensor Detection Points Inter-Relationships, OWASP
https://www.owasp.org/index.php/File:Detection-points-interrelationships.png

[143] HTTP/1.1 Method Definitions, W3C
http://www.w3.org/Protocols/rfc2616/rfc2616-sec9.html

[144] Schechter S, Herley C and Mitzenmacher M, Popularity is Everything - A New Approach to Protecting Passwords from Statistical-Guessing Attacks
http://www.eecs.harvard.edu/~michaelm/postscripts/hotsec2010.pdf

[145] Account Lockout, Bill Cheswick, Episode 76, OWASP Podcast, September 22, 2010
http://www.owasp.org/index.php/OWASP_Podcast#tab=Latest_Shows

[146] About Panopticlick, Electronic Frontier Foundation
http://panopticlick.eff.org/about.php

[147] Panopticlick Test, Electronic Frontier Foundation
http://panopticlick.eff.org/

[148] JavaScript Browser Fingerprinting, Labs, Businessinfo
http://www.businessinfo.co.uk/labs/probe/probe.php

[149] Watson C, Benign Unexpected URLs - Part 1 - Missing (404 Not Found Error) Files, Web security, Usability and Design Blog, 26 October 2010
https://www.clerkendweller.com/2010/10/26/Benign-Unexpected-URLs-Part-1-Missing-Files

[150] Safe Browsing API, Google
http://code.google.com/apis/safebrowsing/

[151] SP 800-92 Guide to Security Log Management, NIST
http://csrc.nist.gov/publications/nistpubs/800-92/SP800-92.pdf

[152] Snodgrass RT, Yao SS and Collberg CTamper Detection in Audit Logs, University of Arizona
http://www.cs.toronto.edu/vldb04/protected/eProceedings/contents/pdf/RS13P1.PDF

[153] Forensic Tamper Detection in SQL Server
http://www.sqlsecurity.com/images/tamper/tamperdetection.htm

[154] Ullrich J, My Top 6 Honey Tokens, App Sec Blog, SANS Institute
http://software-security.sans.org/blog/2009/06/04/my-top-6-honeytokens/

[155] Tor nodes
https://torstat.xenobite.eu/

[156] HTTP blacklist
http://www.projecthoneypot.org/httpbl.php

[157] DShield
http://www.dshield.org

[158] Spamhaus
http://www.spamhaus.org/

[159] Shadow Server
http://www.shadowserver.org/wiki/

[160] Content Security Policy 1.0, W3C
http://www.w3.org/TR/CSP/

[161] Browser Detection Autopwn, etc...
http://ha.ckers.org/blog/20100904/browser-detection-autopwn-etc/

[162] ModSecurity Advanced Topic of the Week: Detecting Banking Trojan Page Modifications
http://blog.spiderlabs.com/2013/07/modsecurity-advanced-topic-of-the-week-detecting-banking-trojan-page-modifications.html

[163] Defence Condition Level (DEFCON)
http://www.fas.org/nuke/guide/usa/c3i/defcon.htm

[164] Content Injection, ModSecurity Features, Trustwave SpiderLabs
http://www.modsecurity.org/projects/modsecurity/apache/feature_content_injection.html

[165] Decloaking Engine
http://decloak.net/

[166] Barnett R, Building a Web Attacker Dashboard with ModSecurity and BeEF
https://speakerdeck.com/rcbarnett/building-a-web-attacker-dashboard-with-modsecurity-and-beef

[167] The JSON Data Interchange Format, ECMA-404, ECMA International, October 2013
http://www.ecma-international.org/publications/files/ECMA-ST/ECMA-404.pdf

[168] RFC 5424, The Syslog Protocol, Network Working Group, IETF
https://tools.ietf.org/html/rfc5424

[169] RFC 3339, Date and Time on the Internet Timestamps, Network Working Group, IETF
http://tools.ietf.org/html/rfc3339

[170] OWASP Store, Lulu
http://www.lulu.com/spotlight/owasp

[171] About the Open Web Application Security Project, OWASP
https://www.owasp.org/index.php/About_OWASP